always up to date

The law changes, but Nolo is always on top of it! We offer several ways to make sure you and your Nolo products are always up to date:

1 **Nolo's Legal Updater**
We'll send you an email whenever a new edition of your book is published! Sign up at **www.nolo.com/legalupdater**.

2 **Updates @ Nolo.com**
Check **www.nolo.com/update** to find recent changes in the law that affect the current edition of your book.

3 **Nolo Customer Service**
To make sure that this edition of the book is the most recent one, call us at **800-728-3555** and ask one of our friendly customer service representatives. Or find out at **www.nolo.com**.

please note

We believe accurate and current legal information should help you solve many of your own legal problems on a cost-efficient basis. But this text is not a substitute for personalized advice from a knowledgeable lawyer. If you want the help of a trained professional, consult an attorney licensed to practice in your state.

NOLO

5th edition

Building a Parenting Agreement That Works

How to Put Your Kids First When Your Marriage Doesn't Last

by Mimi E. Lyster

Fifth Edition	SEPTEMBER 2005
Editor	EMILY DOSKOW
Illustrations	MARI STEIN
Cover Design	TONI IHARA
Book Design	TERRI HEARSH
Production	SARAH HINMAN
Index	MICHAEL FERREIRA
Proofreading	MARTIN ARONSON
Printing	CONSOLIDATED PRINTERS, INC.

Lyster, Mimi E.
    Building a parenting agreement that works : how to put your kids first when your marriage
doesn't last / by Mimi E. Lyster. -- 5th ed.
        p.   cm.
Rev. ed. of : child custody/by Mimi E. Lyster. 4th ed. 2003.
    Includes bibliographical references.
    ISBN 1-4133-0359-5 (alk. paper)
    1. Custody of children--United States--Popular works. 2. Divorce settlements--United
States--Popular works.   I. Lyster, Mimi E. child custody. II Title.

KF547.Z9L97 2005
346.7301'73--dc22
                                                2005047763

For information on bulk purchases or corporate premium sales, please contact the Special Sales
Department. For academic sales or textbook adoptions, ask for Academic Sales. Call 800-955-4775
or write to Nolo, 950 Parker Street, Berkeley, CA 94710.

Dedication

To the children who liven up my life and fill our home with joy, Katelyn, Ben, Alysha, and Nichelle. And to my husband, Steve, whose love and support has carried me so far.

Acknowledgments

I continue to owe thanks to:

- Kevin Elkus, John Helie, and Steve Elias for helping me cling to the notion that our virtual team will yet pull a rabbit from some hat
- the editing department at Nolo for helping to bring this edition into being, and
- my mediation mentors, peers, and clients for helping me to learn with increasing clarity the power of facilitated dialogue decision making.

I would also like to thank those that I have come to know and work with in California's court system for their significant contributions to my understanding of this work and the evolving context within which families are helped to find satisfying and child-focused solutions to their parenting disputes.

Table of Contents

I Introduction

Part I   Getting Started

1 Taking Stock of Your Situation

2 An Introduction to Parenting Agreements

Part II   Your Parenting Agreement

7 Finishing Touches

 8 Serious Issues

 9 Special Circumstances

Part III Beyond Your Parenting Agreement

10 Child Support, Alimony, and Jointly Owned Property

11 Making Mediation and Arbitration Work for You

12 Dealing With Changes in Your Agreement

13 Understanding Your Children's Needs

14 Multiracial, Multicultural, and International Families

15 Nontraditional Families

16 State and Federal Laws Affecting Child Custody

17 Help Beyond the Book

A Appendix: Tear-Out Forms

Worksheet 1: Describe Your Child

Worksheet 2: Describe Your Relationship With Your Child

Worksheet 3: Adding the Details

Worksheet 4: Checklist of Issues for Your Parenting Agreement

Parenting Agreement

I Index

Introduction

This is a book for parents who want to reach the best possible agreement about how they will share and divide their parenting responsibilities during or after a separation or divorce.

Whether or not the separation or divorce was your idea, this book will help you consider your current situation and look toward the future with confidence that your children's needs and best interests will stay at the center of your planning process.

This type of agreement can have many names. Most commonly, it's called a "child custody" or "child custody and visitation" agreement. Because these agreements cover much broader issues than custody and visitation, we refer to them as "parenting agreements" and "parenting plans." Whatever label you (or your state's courts) use, parenting plans usually cover:

- who will take care of the children
- how you and your ex-spouse will make necessary decisions about your children
- how children will spend time with each of their parents and any other people who are important to them, and
- how the children's medical, emotional, educational, spiritual, physical, and social needs will be met.

These are important issues. So are the needs, worries, and wishes that you, the other parent, and your children bring to this process. This book will help you think about how you can meet your children's needs in the midst of all the changes. It can also help you draft your first agreement and, later, modify your agreement or court order once things have settled down—or when your lives or your children's needs change.

Parents are not entirely alone in deciding how to parent after they separate or divorce. Ultimately, the state has a duty to pay attention to a child's needs when parents split up. This is especially true when a child's parents cannot agree—or are fighting about—how a child will be raised or cared for.

It's possible to negotiate your own parenting plan and not have it turned into a court order. This is rare, however. Most parenting agreements become a court order. If, for example, you go to court to get a legal separation or divorce or to resolve a dispute about property, assets, or debts that you and the other parent share, you'll almost surely get a court order regarding child custody and visita-

tion as well. You also may end up in court if you and the other parent disagree about where your children should live or how decisions should be made on their behalf. If you go to court to solve the problem, you will probably end up with a court order regarding child custody and visitation. If you and the other parent can work with each other or the court to develop a thoughtful plan, it can become a valued centerpiece of a separation, divorce, or other dispute that will allow you and the other parent to move on with your lives.

A. Make Your Own Custody Decisions If Possible

When parents first think about custody and parenting issues, they are often in the middle of a separation or divorce. It can be difficult for parents to keep their hurt and angry feelings about the other parent from affecting their decisions about their children's future. Often a parent's first instinct is to demand "full custody" of the children. All too often the other parent responds in kind. These instinctive and common responses only add to the cost and pain of child custody litigation. The end result benefits no one and can make the process more painful for everyone involved, particularly the children.

When parents take parenting issues to court rather than resolving them on their own, they are shortchanging themselves. Once these issues go to court, parents are forced to rely on a judge or court-appointed evaluator to understand the family's situation and make good decisions—often after only meeting with the family for a few minutes or hours. It is very difficult for a judge to "get it right" under these conditions.

Each state has guidelines for its judges to follow when making custody decisions. Nonetheless, judges have considerable discretion to interpret these guidelines and impose their own views about what constitutes a good environment for children. The chance that a judge's decision will be ideal for your specific situation is relatively slim.

Most researchers—especially those who study the effects of divorce on children—believe passionately that using the court to resolve custody issues is a mistake in all but a few cases. It is far better for parents to negotiate their own parenting agreement, with the help of outside experts such as mediators, counselors, and lawyers, on an as-needed

authority away—as long as the decisions make sense. In this way, the court can be looked on as a "last resort" to get something decided when the parents can't agree.

Negotiating parenting agreements can be difficult and complicated. Chapters 10 through 16 cover some of the most complex issues in detail. If this is not enough, Chapter 17 provides a list of books, professionals, and other information sources.

⚠ Some of your decisions may have legal consequences. You should consider having an attorney review your agreement to make sure it complies with your state custody and visitation laws. If you are getting a divorce or separation, you must also make sure your agreement complies with any specific court filing or document requirments.

C. Balancing Parenting and Financial Issues

Separation and divorce often require parents to deal with financial issues such as dividing property, paying marital debts, and providing for support. Although this book focuses only on parenting issues, you may find that many of the financial issues are easier to tackle and resolve when you start with an agreement that serves your children's best interests.

For example, if you choose to have one parent take on the majority of the daily parenting responsibilities, you may decide it makes sense for that parent to live in the family home. But if your children will be spending approximately equal amounts of time with each of you, you might choose to sell the family home (especially if it is your primary asset) and use the money to rent or buy a home for each parent that can accommodate the children.

Clearly, decisions about finances affect parenting issues just as decisions about parenting issues can affect finances. This book assumes that, to the greatest possible extent, the "people" issues should come first—your agreement about how to best meet your children's needs should set the stage for deciding the money issues. This is especially true when it comes to child support. Although some parents may stop seeing their children or refuse to pay child support, research shows that the larger the role a parent plays in the lives of his or her children, the more likely that parent is to contribute to the children's support.

basis. Court intervention is appropriate, however, if the children's (or a parent's) safety or well-being is at risk and the parents cannot agree on a way to reduce that risk.

B. What If We Need Outside Help?

Even though it's usually best for a child's parents to be the decision makers, when it comes to developing a parenting plan, this isn't always possible (or wise). Does this mean you're a failure? No! Sometimes it makes *very* good sense to get the help of a counselor, mediator, lawyer, or other expert to understand the issues, or figure out how to resolve a difficult situation. These can be very emotional issues to resolve. Sometimes it's best to involve an expert who can help you identify other ways to solve these problems.

Does involving an expert mean you can't be in the "driver's seat"? No! Sometimes people think if they hire a lawyer, counselor, mediator, or other expert they then have to follow whatever suggestions are made. This isn't true. Though it makes sense to consider what an expert says or recommends, you and the other parent can still make the final decisions about what you will or won't accept. Ultimately, only a judge can override your decisions. Judges, however, seldom want to take a parent's decision-making

D. Why This Book Is Unique

This book has a number of innovative features that address separate parenting and related custody issues, including the following:

1. This Book Builds an Agreement That Can Work and Change Over Time

Parenting agreements almost always change over time. To help parents build an agreement that is done in stages and is likely to change, the parenting agreement in this book is divided into the following four sections:

- Basic Elements
- Finishing Touches
- Serious Issues
- Special Circumstances

These sections prioritize the issues you need to address and are also helpful if you have an existing agreement that you need to modify because of a change in circumstance.

2. This Book Offers Real-World Solutions to Parenting Issues

Parenting encompasses a complex mix of relationships and responsibilities. This book reflects the trials and tribulations of real parents who have encountered and resolved the same issues that you and your children's other parent now face. It presents the research and observations of professionals who help parents resolve separate parenting issues, and it describes the solutions that these parents have fashioned for themselves.

3. This Book Is for Married and Unmarried Parents

Many couples in the United States parent without getting married. If their relationship ends, these parents do not legally separate or divorce, but their needs for parenting plans are just the same as their separated or divorced counterparts. Although most of the examples here are written as though a legal marriage had taken place (and the terms "separation" and "divorce" appear throughout the book), parents who were never married can assume that the terms and examples apply to them as well.

4. This Book Is for Nontraditional Families and Families With Different Cultural Backgrounds

This book is not just for Caucasian, middle-class, and heterosexual-parented families. Incorporated throughout the text, as well as in chapters devoted to multicultural, multiracial, and nontraditional families, is an understanding that all kinds of families need parenting agreements.

5. This Book Is for Families With One Child or Many Children

For convenience, this book is written using the word "children" rather than "child" or "child(ren)." If you have only one child, you can assume that every reference to children includes your child.

6. This Book Can Be Used With or Without Professional Help

This book was written to help you negotiate your own parenting agreement, whether or not you also get help from professionals such as mediators, counselors, attorneys, evaluators, arbitrators, and courts. It includes worksheets you can use for your own negotiations, to record your agreement, or to help any outside professional who might become involved. The book helps you assess whether or not your agreement will work, lists resources for getting outside help if necessary, and explains how you can finalize your agreement if you are involved in a court proceeding.

You may be surprised to find that this book doesn't sound like what your attorney says is important about separation, divorce, and separate parenting. That is because this book is focused on you, your children, and their other parent—not on the law.

Many people who have been through divorce, and the lawyers who represent them, focus on terms like "custody" and "visitation" and ask the one question, "Who gets the kids?" Although these are certainly important issues, this book helps parents understand their children's needs first, then structure their agreement to meet those needs as best they can. After you and the other parent have been able to agree about most aspects of your separate parenting relationship, this book will help you assign the labels that make the most sense.

7. This Book Is a Work in Progress

This book is part of a growing database of real-world solutions to parenting problems. If you come up with an issue or a solution we haven't included, let us know on the Registration Card in the back of the book. If we use your issue or options in future editions, we will acknowledge your contribution (if you wish).

E. A Word to Skeptics

Many parents who go through separation or divorce feel that books like this one and processes like mediation won't work for them. Some parents assume that:

- The only way to handle the emotional conflict between the parties is through all-out legal warfare.
- The other parent will never budge on core issues.
- Nothing will ever be decided because each parent wants the same thing, such as sole or primary custody of the children.

Fortunately, none of these situations is an automatic barrier. Many parents with tough problems like these have negotiated agreements on their own or through mediation.

1. What If the Conflict Is Really Intense?

Conflict is a natural and normal part of separation, divorce, and separate parenting. To presume otherwise would do you, the other parent, and your children a disservice. But conflict—even intense conflict—is not reason enough to assume you cannot negotiate a parenting agreement.

Chapters 4 and 11 contain information on how you and the other parent can handle your own negotiations even if your conflict is bitter or has lasted a long time. Chapter 4 explains how to have an effective meeting and improve your communication style. It also offers specific strategies for managing conflict. Chapter 11 explains mediation and how it can be used to bring parents together for their children's benefit.

If you really think this won't work for you, skim Chapters 4 and 11 before continuing. Hopefully, you will gain some reassurance from what you find there, and you'll be willing to return here and work through the rest of the book. (See Chapter 17 for more resources.)

2. If the Other Parent Won't Budge

Being adamant about a certain position is not necessarily bad. If the less-flexible parent can describe his or her concerns, goals, and perceptions of the situation in some detail, you will often have a good list of issues that must be addressed and resolved to reach a lasting agreement.

Perhaps the most effective way to put your discussions on a positive footing is to shift the focus to your children. The worksheets in Chapter 3 help you identify and describe your concerns, describe your children's needs, and acknowledge the unique situations that your family is facing. Chapter 13 helps you gain insights into what children need and experience at different ages, and how you might structure your agreement to best meet those needs.

By focusing on your children while negotiating parenting arrangements, you'll probably find that you can adjust your positions enough to produce a good parenting agreement.

F. What If You Just Want to Fight?

There are times when a custody fight appears inevitable. You may be willing to be reasonable, but you believe the other parent isn't, and it may seem like there is no choice but to fight it out in court. Or you may be so angry about something the other parent has said or done that you feel the only effective way to deal with it is to "let them have it."

Constant fighting, arguing, and blaming in a marriage generally lead to more of the same in the process of dissolving it. Unfortunately, the consequences of continuing this behavior can be dramatic. Lawsuits often take on a life of their own and can be much harder to stop than to start. This kind of battle can lead to escalating costs, a dramatically reduced standard of living, and significant damage to your children's emotional well-being. Jim Melamed, a family law mediator in Oregon, calls these results "the parade of the horribles"—and appropriately so!

1. Custody Litigation Is Unpredictable

Asking a court to resolve differences over custody and visitation is highly unpredictable. If you doubt this, ask your attorney to guarantee, in writing, what will happen if you choose to litigate your custody and visitation issues.

Part of this unpredictability stems from the fact that most parents believe their cause to be righteous. This means, of course, that at least half of all litigants are unpleasantly surprised by the judge's decision. More important, litigation is unpredictable because judges are human beings who naturally differ in their approach to the kinds of problems that custody and visitation disputes present.

Though it is true that judges are supposed to make decisions that favor the best interests of the children, and the laws of every state list factors that judges should consider when determining what these best interests are, the standards themselves leave considerable room for individual interpretation. (See Chapter 16, Section B for information on how judges determine what is in the best interests of children.) For example, some judges decide that the conflict between the parents is overblown or unnecessary and order joint custody, thereby requiring cooperation between parents who may find the task nearly impossible. Other judges, and some states, consider ongoing contact with both parents to be so important that custody is awarded to the parent who is most likely to foster a healthy relationship with the other parent, thus initiating the battle to be declared "most reasonable and accommodating." Making decisions in this way may or may not be best for the children. In almost every case, some factors favor one parent and others the other parent. This situation can be hardest when two "good" parents face off in court, as both are likely to walk away unhappy with the result.

2. Custody Litigation Is Usually Costly

If you choose to pursue litigation, the next hurdle will be figuring out how to pay for your court battle. If you decide to represent yourself, you will save on attorneys' fees, although the costs and time associated with filing (which includes doing the legal research as well as preparing and serving your court papers) can be significant. If you do hire an attorney, you can expect to pay $5,000 to $15,000 or more in fees for even a "routine" case.

Whether or not you hire an attorney, you may find you have to pay for testimony from a counselor or therapist (which generally requires three to five sessions, at an average rate of $75 to $150 per hour, before he or she will submit any final report) or a custody evaluation (which generally costs between $2,000 and $7,500, depending on

how complicated the issues are and how much conflict exists in the family). (You can read more about custody evaluations in Chapter 6, Issue 9, and in Chapter 17, Section D3.) In addition, you will probably find it necessary to arrange for testimony from friends, relatives, school teachers, clergy members, and neighbors.

Funding a child custody battle can be especially difficult when you consider that, after separation or divorce, the income you shared must now be used to maintain two separate homes. In addition to separate rent or mortgage payments, telephone service, food, and other incidentals, you will have to duplicate the furniture, clothes, and toys that don't travel with the children, and pay whatever costs are associated with the distance between your homes (such as travel and telephone). Many who separate or divorce are stunned by how quickly their money disappears!

3. Custody Litigation Damages the Children Regardless of the Result

As important as money is, the economic consequences of fighting in court can be dwarfed by the impact such a fight will have on your children. Mental health professionals, the court system, attorneys, mediators, and custody evaluators all agree on one thing: Ongoing conflict between parents is often the most damaging stressor for children in the divorce process.

When conflict is obvious and occurs over extended periods of time, children feel torn between loving both parents, hoping someone will magically restore the marriage, and wishing that they could be anywhere but where the battle is raging. This is true even when parents have most of their arguments outside of their children's presence. Because children have spent all of their lives living with and observing their parents, and because children rely on their parents to provide the basic securities of life, they develop an uncanny ability to "read" their parents. Children are exquisitely sensitive to each parent's reactions when the other parent's name is mentioned, the other parent calls, or court papers are served.

4. Avoid Litigating Your Custody Dispute If at All Possible

Hopefully, all that you've read so far has convinced you that litigation should most definitely be a last resort. The purpose of this book is to give you the tools and information that will help you avoid litigation and resolve your differences with the other parent in as friendly a way as possible. Parenting separately is challenging, but it is a job worth doing well. By making the commitment to put your children's interests first, and by taking the time to educate yourself about your options, you, your children, and the other parent may find that you can develop a parenting agreement that each of you feels is essentially fair.

G. Icons Used in This Book

Look for these icons to alert you to certain kinds of information.

 When you see the "fast track" icon, you'll be alerted to a chance to skip some material you may not need to read.

 This icon introduces a family.

 The caution icon warns you of potential problems.

 The briefcase lets you know when you need the advice of an attorney or other expert.

 This icon refers you to other books or resources.

■

Part I

Getting Started

Taking Stock of Your Situation

B efore getting started on your parenting plan, you should understand the context in which your parenting decisions will be made.

A. You Are Not Alone

During the last quarter of a century, the expectation that two people would meet, marry, raise a family, and grow old together has changed. Studies over the past 10 years have confirmed that couples who divorce will be most likely to do so after about seven years of marriage, and that two-thirds of these divorcing families will include at least one child under the age of six. Statistics also show that more than a million children each year for the past 25 years have lived through a divorce.

Other researchers have commented on the changing structure of the family. During the past 35 years, the divorce rate has quadrupled and births outside of marriage have increased by 22%. Many families relocate every few years, which deprives these families of the benefits of living close to extended family. Researchers predict that nearly half of all babies born today will spend some time living in a one-parent family. A family in which biological parents stay together and raise their children to adulthood is now the reality only for about one-third of all couples. The new reality is that most parents will never marry, will marry and later divorce, or will create their families through artificial insemination or adoption.

B. Keep Your Parenting Plan Focused on Your Children

You and your children's other parent are about to undertake a difficult but very important project: making the best possible decisions about your parenting arrangements. Of course, it may be hard to separate the desire to have nothing more to do with your ex from the task of making decisions that are in your children's interest. After all, separation and divorce exist to solve adult problems, not meet children's needs.

Even if your separation or divorce will be better for your children in the long run, for the short term most children feel that things are worse. Divorce or separation can shake a child's confidence that he or she will continue to

be loved, cared for, and safe. This is true even when children understand the reasons behind the decision.

You and the other parent can help your children by using this book to develop an agreement that focuses on meeting your children's individual needs. The more attention you pay to those needs, the more likely you are to build an agreement that works for all of you.

You and the other parent must honestly assess your relationship as parents and your ability to work together. To keep your agreement focused on your children, you must be willing to trust each other and set aside your anger, frustration, and pain, at least for a while. If you've just separated, you may think it will be impossible to trust and cooperate with the other parent. Most find, though, that trustful and cooperative relationships usually evolve over time. (See Section C, below.) One of the most effective strategies for moving toward this kind of relationship is to build on points of agreement until you have crafted a comprehensive parenting plan.

DIVORCE AND SEPARATION AREN'T ONLY ABOUT ENDING AN INTIMATE RELATIONSHIP

Some compare the end of a marriage (or otherwise similarly committed relationship) to a death. If you accept this premise, or find that this describes your inner state, then you should expect to experience the same progression of feelings that Elizabeth Kubler-Ross describes as the pathway to dealing with physical death. These stages are denial, anger, bargaining, and, finally, acceptance.

Others remind us that separation and divorce occur on many levels, including emotional, financial, legal, social, and intimate. Given this complicated series of relationships, you and your ex should think about how you will manage these stages. Your children will benefit most when you can separate the "adult" issues from the parenting issues and keep your children out of the middle.

As you and the other parent gain an understanding of the full scope of your new relationship and the ways in which you will take on new and separate lives, you will find that you are better able to chart your own course, and you will be pleased with the results of your efforts. In fact, the parents who express the greatest levels of satisfaction with their separate parenting arrangements are those who take the time to negotiate comprehensive, child-focused agreements that both parents can accept and support.

C. It Gets Easier Over Time

At the beginning, separation or divorce is often traumatic. Many people behave irrationally or seem unstable. As time passes, however, most parents regain their balance.

Let's look more closely at the typical emotional stages parents go through when they separate, and how these stages might affect each parent's ability to reach an effective, child-focused parenting plan.

1. The First Few Weeks

Just before and/or just after the initial separation, you will probably feel confused. It may seem that there are an end-less number of decisions to make, each of which appears the most important. Like most parents, you will probably ride a roller coaster of emotions. On any given day you may have intense feelings of rage, depression, abandonment, relief, grief, guilt, and excitement. In fact, you may decide that ending a relationship, or having one ended for you, has left you feeling like you are going crazy.

This is not the time to worry about charting a permanent course for your children's future. Instead, try to develop one or more short-term agreements that will allow you, the other parent, and your children to settle in to the new arrangements gradually. By taking it slowly, you will have time to see what makes the most sense in the long run. For most parents, the key to success is to separate the adult relationship issues from the parenting issues and develop a clear, child-centered plan that each parent can easily follow. Your own emotional survival—as well as that of your children—is very much at stake now and must be your first priority.

GET HELP
There are lots of books that can help parents going through separation or divorce cope at the beginning. See Chapter 17 for references.

2. The First Few Months

Several months after the initial separation, your life will probably be a little calmer, but you may find that your relationship with the other parent can still provoke either or both of you in extreme and unexpected ways. Many parents find it hard to distance themselves from each other when they need to stay in contact because they share children. Your children can be a constant reminder of what has gone on (or has gone wrong) and what remains to be done. You may be experimenting with a new partner or a new approach to how you want to live your life. You may feel annoyed if the other parent's presence puts a damper on your newfound freedom.

At the other end of the spectrum, you or the other parent may still feel angry, sad, powerless, or abandoned, as you did when you first separated. If so, either of you may suspect that every action or comment by the other is just another ploy to retaliate or undercut your new stability and confidence.

If you try to negotiate a parenting plan during this phase, you may find it extremely difficult to reach agreement on any but the easiest issues. Many parents, nevertheless, negotiate temporary parenting arrangements early on, especially to resolve a particular issue, such as where the children will attend school. These parents can start with Chapter 6 (Basic Elements) and address only the most pressing issues until they are ready to handle more.

3. One Year Later

A year or more after the initial separation, you may be far more clear-headed about your situation than you were when you first separated. You and the other parent will have firsthand experience with your initial (or temporary) parenting arrangements. You can gauge the effects that these arrangements have had on your life and on your children. At this point, you will probably be ready to negotiate a more comprehensive agreement, and can return to Chapter 7 (Finishing Touches) to add whatever provisions you need.

4. The Second Year and Beyond

Two years or more following a separation, most families have settled into their first stable parenting arrangement. About this time, many realize that their arrangements need at least a few changes to accommodate changes in their own or their children's lives. In fact, many mediators report that significant numbers of families renegotiate their first parenting agreements at this two-year point.

No matter what stage of the separation you are in, remember that one of the few things you can count on is change. Neither you, the other parent, or your children can (or should) expect the first agreement to be your last one. You can never anticipate all the decisions you will have to make about your children. Certain parts of your agreement will work for the long term, while others will need to be revised regularly.

One of the most common reasons parents have to revise their first agreement is the presence of a parent's new partner. Children often have strong opinions about new stepparents, boyfriends, or girlfriends. Additionally, when one parent has a new partner—especially if that is the parent with whom the children primarily live—the other parent may need reassurance that he or she will not be replaced by the new partner.

Other changes that can trigger the need for a modification of an existing arrangement include:

- a parent's desire to move because of a new job
- a parent's desire to move to be closer to relatives
- a child's special needs or a change in schools, or
- a child's desire to live with the other parent.

D. Learn How to Negotiate

Negotiation is the process of reaching an agreement acceptable to the people involved. The more successful the negotiation, the more acceptable the agreement. Negotiation is an integral part of separate parenting because:

- Most parents tend to be involved with their children, at some level, well into their early adulthood. Parents who stay involved in their children's lives must find a way to work together.
- Children usually want to maintain a relationship with both parents—and they suffer when their parents constantly fight. The better the parents are at negotiating satisfactory solutions to their differences, the better their relationships will be with their children.
- When parents are unable to agree on basic or critical decisions about their children's health, education, and welfare, a court will step in and impose decisions. These decisions, though aimed at protecting and preserving the best interests of the children, might be very different from what the parents want or feel is appropriate.

Negotiating your parenting agreement is covered in detail in Chapter 4.

USING MEDIATION TO HELP YOU NEGOTIATE

There are several basic approaches to negotiating a parenting agreement. Some parents resolve the issues on their own. Others ask a counselor to help, work with attorneys, or use mediation. Mediation is a process that uses a trained neutral person (someone who has nothing to gain or lose by what you decide) to help you identify the issues to resolve and reach solutions. It offers many advantages because you control the decision-making process—the mediator doesn't have the power to impose a decision on you.

Mediation is available in all states, either through the court or from private practitioners, and has become very popular—particularly for resolving family conflicts—because it is less adversarial than courtroom litigation. There's more detail about mediation in Chapter 11.

E.   If the Other Parent Is Absent

This book assumes that both parents are at least minimally involved in their children's lives. This, however, might not be true in your case. Some parents leave their families and are never heard from again. Others are around so infrequently that they have abandoned their families in most respects. If this describes your situation, you will probably need the help of an attorney to get a divorce (if you're legally married) and to obtain child support.

If you need help with day-to-day parenting, consider talking to one of the children's grandparents, a favorite aunt or uncle, or a very close friend about having them help out. If it works, you'll have adult help, and your children will have the benefit of another adult's influence.

F.   If There Is Violence or Abuse in the Family

Domestic violence, child abuse, and child neglect are, unfortunately, a fact of life for many in the United States. For some, these events are unique to the period leading up to and during the separation or divorce. For others, a long history of violence, abuse, or neglect convinces one or both parents that the only solution is to separate or divorce.

Physical violence, threats of violence, sexual assault, and child abuse are illegal. Specific definitions of domestic violence vary from state to state. But federal law says it is illegal to injure—or threaten to injure—anyone related by blood or marriage, or with whom you are living and have an intimate relationship. This is true regardless of your cultural or religious heritage, citizenship status, or personal beliefs about discipline or the proper relationship between husbands and wives.

If your divorce, separation, or co-parenting relationship includes acts or threats of domestic violence, emotional abuse, child abuse, child sexual abuse, or child neglect, protecting your and your children's safety must be your first concern. This means getting whatever emotional, legal, or other help you need to understand your options. It also means planning for how you will stay safe while you develop a parenting agreement.

The time when one partner chooses to get help, leave an abusive relationship, or get a restraining order can be the most dangerous of all. This is because one partner might try to hurt or scare the other as a way to stop them from leaving or involving "outsiders" in their "family" or "private" matters.

Although each safety plan will be somewhat different, every one should consider:

- where all family members will live
- whether any family member's whereabouts will be kept secret
- whether legal protection (such as civil protection or restraining orders) is necessary
- whether visits with a violent parent will be supervised, and
- how each affected person will get emotional support.

Situations involving violence or abuse usually call for outside help. (See Chapter 17 for more advice and resources.)

Most of the information in this book assumes that your family situation is conducive to negotiating and reaching a parenting agreement. But what about mediation in violent or potentially violent situations? Some professionals actively discourage victims of domestic violence from getting involved in mediation, family counseling, or other non-court proceedings where batterers and their victims meet face to face. This is because there can be significant power imbalances between people who have been involved in domestic violence. Advocates worry that a victim might be too intimidated by the batterer to effectively represent his or her own interests, or to protect their children's interests.

Many experts worry that any type of negotiations regarding custody and visitation with someone who has committed domestic violence is inappropriate because it implies that somehow the violence is excusable. To address these concerns, some states (especially those that require mediation for custody and visitation disputes) allow victims of domestic violence to either skip mediation or to attend mediation separate from the batterer. Many domestic violence victims feel better if they are accompanied by a domestic violence support person. Several states require a judge to deny custody or unsupervised visitation to a batterer unless the judge can say why doing so is safe and in the child's best interests.

You can find more information on how to understand and handle domestic violence or emotional abuse issues in Chapters 4, 8, and 17. After you have found a way to address these safety issues, you can try to use this book effectively to build a parenting agreement that can help you now and over time as the situation changes or improves. ■

An Introduction to Parenting Agreements

In the broadest sense, a parenting agreement is the sum total of the arrangements parents make about parenting separately during a separation or following a divorce. Common convention and state laws describe these arrangements as "custody" decisions. The term "parenting agreement" better reflects the needs and involvement of all concerned because it implies that the agreement is comprehensive and tailored to meet each family's needs.

A. What Parenting Agreements Cover

Parenting agreements can be vague or detailed, casual or legalistic. But at the very least, you'll need to make sure that your parenting agreement meets your state's minimum legal requirements so it can be enforced by a court or law enforcement agency.

At a minimum, a parenting agreement should describe how the parents plan to meet the children's needs and manage parenting responsibilities regarding:

- taking care of the children
- making necessary decisions on the children's behalf
- making sure the children spend time with both parents, and
- meeting the children's medical, psychological, educational, spiritual, physical, and social needs.

Increasingly, parenting plans address many more issues, such as transporting the children between parents' houses, the roles of parents' new partners, and how parents should communicate when issues arise. Comprehensive agreements offer clarity, anticipate the needs of the parents and children over time, and pave the way for better communication and understanding.

B. Advantages of Parent-Negotiated Agreements

Parents are almost always in the best position to know what arrangements are best for their children. You know your children's interests, hopes, strengths, and weaknesses. You know how your children deal with change and what makes change easier for them to accept. If you can work with the other parent to plan for your children's future, you will provide them the best possible springboard to adjust to your separation or divorce and reassure them that they are loved and cared for.

1. Minimize Court Involvement

Increasingly, state courts are requiring parents to try to resolve custody and visitation issues outside of court. Generally, this means parents are ordered into mediation as a first step. The law, for all its express protections for children, doesn't know your individual children. This is where your experience as a parent is crucial to the process. When you and the other parent focus on understanding and meeting your children's needs and then on finding ways to cooperate to meet those needs, you pave the way for a successful separate parenting relationship.

Cooperation eliminates the need for a judge, a court-appointed evaluator, or some other outside person to make decisions for you. It doesn't mean, however, that parent-negotiated agreements are completely independent of the legal system. Rather, they are created in the "shadow of the law." A court retains the authority to review your agreement and make sure it is in your children's best interests. If the court finds that it is not, the court will reject your plan and impose its own.

All states have their own criteria for determining the best interests of the children. Determining what is or is not in your children's best interests is an inexact process. Some of the factors considered, however, include your children's:

- age
- temperament
- relationships with each parent
- special needs or activities, and
- religious and social values.

WHEN YOU CAN'T AVOID GOING TO COURT

It is unrealistic to think that most parents who are ending their marriage or committed relationship will be able to do so without some conflict. There will always be a court involved—at the very least, to approve your paperwork, and sometimes to resolve an issue or two along the way. Even where conflicts do come up, there are ways to help minimize the impact on you and your children.

Perhaps the most important place to start (and often the most difficult one), is to draw a line between disputes that are about how the other parent has let you down or wronged you, and disputes over how each parent will be involved in helping your children grow up in a healthy and supportive environment. Strategies that can help you strike this balance include:

- Negotiating your parenting agreement in stages (see Chapter 6)
- Going to mediation (see Chapter 11)
- Finding a counselor (see Chapter 17)
- Hiring a "collaborative" lawyer (see Chapter 17).

2. Increase Fairness

Parents, children, and professionals agree that the most successful agreements are those that the parties can describe as fair, meaning that even if each party doesn't "win" everything, they all feel that they have gained something. If your parenting plan is clear and detailed, you will find that day-to-day living is simpler and everyone's responsibilities are understood. Though most children hope for reconciliation, they can probably adapt to almost any plan if they are confident that you believe it is fair.

C. Goals of a Successful Parenting Agreement

Although every parenting agreement is different, the most successful parenting plans emerge out of a commitment by both parents to:

- reduce the conflict between the parents

- encourage good relationships between the children and both parents, and
- make the changes inherent in a separation or divorce easier for the children to accept.

1. Reduce Conflict Between Parents

Many parents initially doubt they can negotiate their own parenting agreement. In addition, parents often question whether any plan can transform the anger, pain, confusion, and disarray of the breakup into a viable parenting plan. Take heart! The experiences of the vast majority of families who separate or divorce show that conflict, legal or otherwise, is far less than the media—or lawyers—would have us believe. In fact, study after study shows that only about 15% of custody agreements are the product of a full court trial. In most cases, parents negotiate their own agreement, often with the help of an outside professional such as an attorney, mediator, or counselor.

Reducing conflict is undoubtedly your most important goal in separate parenting. Despite this, parents sometimes continue to battle long after their separation or divorce. Often, it is because they:

- cannot accept the reality of a separation or divorce
- want to remain involved with the other parent, at any cost
- have unresolved anger
- have incompatible parenting values
- fear for the well-being of their children when they are with the other parent
- have a history of violence between them, or
- blame the other for the failed relationship.

Having these feelings is perfectly normal and quite common. If you let negative feelings linger months and even years after a divorce, however, your ability to cooperate in child rearing will be impaired. Your children will bear the brunt of the anger, blame, and acrimony that you display—and they will carry the scars for a very long time.

HOW CHILDREN REACT TO CONFLICT IN DIVORCE

The American Academy of Child and Adolescent Psychiatry (AACAP) recommends that parents step back and consider how their divorce may impact their children—and find ways to talk to children that will address their special concerns.

In a "Children and Divorce" fact sheet (2004) the AACAP explains:

"Children often believe they have caused the conflict between their mother and father. Many children assume the responsibility for bringing their parents back together, sometimes by sacrificing themselves. Vulnerability to both physical and mental illnesses can originate in the traumatic loss of one or both parents through divorce. With care and attention, however, a family's strengths can be mobilized during a divorce, and children can be helped to deal constructively with the resolution of parental conflict.

Talking to children about a divorce is difficult. The following tips can help both the child and parents deal with the challenge and stress of these conversations:

- Do not keep it a secret or wait until the last minute.
- Tell your child together.
- Keep things simple and straight forward.
- Tell them the divorce is not their fault.
- Admit that this will be sad and upsetting for everyone.
- Reassure your child that you both still love them and will always be their parents.
- Do not discuss each other's faults or problems with the child."

2. Encourage Good Parent-Child Relationships

The fear of losing contact or a relationship with one parent usually looms large in the minds of children whose parents are undergoing a separation or divorce. Even well-intentioned parents can give their children the impression that they will be hurt if their children show open affection and regard for the other parent. This can create intense loyalty conflicts for children, and lead to long-term damage in their relationships with both parents.

There are at least two very compelling reasons why you should *not* undermine your children's relationship with their other parent. First, if you succeed in curtailing or preventing visits with the other parent, your children might lose trust in you, fearful of what other harm you might do. Children have relatively little control over how their lives will be structured under any circumstances, let alone after their parents separate or divorce. Your children will watch you carefully to see if they can trust you to structure their world so that it includes the people they love.

Second, when children are cut off from a parent, they often feel deprived of an important piece of themselves. Many children who are cut off from contact with one parent following a separation or divorce act as adopted children do, searching for their roots by seeking out their biological parents. If you force your children to abandon contact with their other parent, your children may blame you for the lost relationship.

Children will go to great lengths to avoid appearing to "choose" one parent over another. They will often tell you what they think you want to hear—that the other parent is not as good as, not as well liked as, and maybe even more dispensable than you are. Although it is certainly preferable "not to say anything if you can't say something nice," if you are not careful, your children will get the message that the other parent's existence is to be denied in your home if they are to remain in your good graces.

Some parents discourage or prevent children's visits with the other parent because of the environment in that parent's home. Knowing when your concerns are justified is not always easy. If you fear for your children's physical or emotional safety, then you may need to seek supervised, restricted, or no visits with the other parent. If the dangers are less obvious and threatening, you will need to examine your own motives, looking at the situation through your children's eyes whenever possible.

3. Make Changes Easier for Your Children to Accept

The key to helping your children accept the changes that accompany separation and divorce is to work hard to develop a parenting agreement that everyone feels is fair and workable. Children can adapt to their changed circumstances and to the differences in their parents' living arrangements, house rules, and expectations if they see that you are doing your best to be sensitive to their needs. Children can accept that:

- the rules in one household are not necessarily the same as in the other
- each parent is his or her own person and has his or her own style
- each parent has his or her own strengths and weaknesses, and
- their needs can be met even if their parents live in different homes, because there will be an expanding world of people who love and support them.

D. Parenting Agreements and Custody

When parents separate or divorce, the term "custody" often serves as shorthand for "who gets the children." Legally, the term has a much broader meaning because it applies to the total relationship parents have with their children. All parents are obligated to provide for their children's physical and emotional needs, and to protect and preserve what is fundamental to their best interests: medical care, education, food, shelter, and safety. Custody implies all of these responsibilities.

When parents separate, the custody they jointly exercised over their children must change to accommodate the new living arrangements and the new relationship between the parents. The modification may be minor if the parents live near each other and can communicate well, or profound if ongoing conflict prevents cooperation in parenting. For most parents, it's somewhere in between.

In a divorce or legal separation, courts commonly order either sole custody or shared custody. Under a sole custody arrangement, one parent is the primary caregiver and the other parent's visits are defined by a set schedule. Under a shared custody arrangement, both parents enjoy significant amounts of time with their children and make decisions together.

Some states distinguish between legal custody—the authority to make decisions about the children—and

physical custody—the physical care of the children. In these states, courts can make any of the following orders:

- **Sole legal and physical custody.** In this arrangement, one parent assumes the decision-making responsibility, and children spend most of their time with that parent.
- **Shared legal and sole physical custody.** Parents share decision-making authority, but the children spend most of their time with only one parent.
- **Shared legal custody and shared physical custody.** Parents share decision-making authority, and the children divide their time fairly equally between their parents—though it doesn't have to be 50/50 to qualify as shared (or joint) custody.

Chapter 16 contains information on the different forms of custody each state authorizes.

If parents cooperate in drafting and implementing a detailed parenting agreement, the court (if authorized) is likely to issue a shared custody order. On the other hand, if the parents can't reach agreement on important child-rearing issues, the court may issue a sole custody award to one parent, allowing the other "reasonable" visitation. Clearly, a sole custody award heavily favors the "custodial" parent in caring for and making decisions on behalf of the children.

In some states, such as New Hampshire and New Mexico, the court must begin with the premise that it will order shared custody unless it would not be in the children's best interests. In many states, a court may order shared custody even when one of the parents disagrees. (See Chapter 16.) So even if you don't successfully negotiate a parenting plan, you may end up with a shared custody order if you are in court.

In Chapter 6, you will select a specific custody arrangement to include in your parenting plan—assuming you and the other parent are ending a legal marriage. Additional information is in Chapter 13, Understanding Your Children's Needs, and (if applicable) Chapter 15, Nontraditional Families.

MOST OPPOSITE-SEX COUPLES SELECT PRIMARY OR SOLE CUSTODY TO MOTHER

For a variety of reasons, most opposite-sex parenting couples agree that the mother will have primary or sole custody after a separation or divorce and that the father will exercise reasonable visitation. For some, this happens because fathers presume that mothers will be awarded custody. In others, it happens because of the mother's fear that she will be judged poorly if she is not the primary caretaker. In still other situations, the parents agree that the mother has more time, a greater inclination, or a better understanding of the children's daily needs.

■

Getting Organized

As any good builder will tell you, you need the right tools and supplies at hand before you start to build. Your first task when preparing to build your parenting agreement is to review all relevant documents and think carefully about how you and the other parent relate to your children. This chapter includes worksheets that will help you lay the foundatin for creating an effective parenting agreement.

WHEN TO CONSULT AN ATTORNEY

Consult an attorney as soon as possible if you are in any of the following situations:

- Court hearings or deadlines require that you make quick decisions
- You have questions about your legal rights
- You feel you cannot represent your own interests in court
- You have been sued for paternity
- You and the other parent cannot talk at all
- The other parent has hired an attorney
- You or the other parent abuse drugs or alcohol
- There is domestic violence in your relationship
- You are involved in a custody evaluation or "home study"
- The court might terminate your parental rights.

You also might look to an attorney to review your parenting agreement after it is complete, even if none of the circumstances listed above apply to you. An attorney can make sure that the agreement conforms with your state's laws and is worded clearly and effectively. And if you want to turn the agreement into an enforceable court order, a lawyer can help you do that.

Whether or not you choose to hire an attorney, there are many ways to find information that is easy to understand about the legal and parenting issues you face. The Internet is a good resource for finding out about state laws, court forms, and self-help resources in your area. Good keywords to use when searching for information on the Internet are: "divorce," "child custody," "legal information," "self help," and "parenting." You will also find a listing in Chapter 17 of specific websites you can visit.

A. Organize and Review Documents

Before you begin to negotiate with the other parent or work with a professional, collect all the papers that relate to your situation and spend some time thinking about what needs to happen and what you want accomplished. The types of documents you should gather and review include:

- court documents you have filed or received, such as a summons, petition, complaint, response, answer, declaration, or affidavit
- correspondence from an attorney, counselor, mediator, or court official regarding a separation, a divorce, paternity, child support, custody, or visitation
- court orders regarding a legal separation, divorce, paternity declaration, or award of custody
- previously mediated, arbitrated, or negotiated agreements between you and the other parent
- documents dissolving your religious marriage or describing your marital status and your options according to your religious denomination, and
- reports, letters, or evaluations from school officials, counselors, doctors, therapists, or others who have an insight into your children.

Carefully read all the documents. If you need help finding or understanding any of them, consider asking an attorney, court clerk, paralegal, marriage counselor, mediator, member of the clergy, or other professional for assistance. (Chapter 17 offers tips on finding people and resources to help you.)

You won't necessarily need all of these documents to develop a parenting plan. Nevertheless, having them can help, especially if you are going through a legal separation or divorce. For example, if you or the other parent have already started a court proceeding, you may have a deadline for submitting your parenting agreement. If you begin negotiations and they seem to be going well, you will probably want to ask the court for an extension of time (called a "continuance") to let your negotiations continue. Knowing where you stand now will help you take all necessary steps to finalize your agreement, assure your rights, and satisfy all legal requirements.

B. Completing the Worksheets

To prepare to work out a parenting agreement, you'll need to spend time thinking about what will work best for you, your children, and the other parent. The four worksheets in this chapter can help you consider those questions by giving you a process to think about what your child is like, what your relationship with your child is like, the details of what you might want in a parenting agreement, and practical steps you'll take in conjunction with your agreement.

The worksheets are divided up in a way that allows you to complete this process a little at a time. Most parents will want to fill out the first three worksheets separately, so that each parent can do his or her own worksheet. There are no right or wrong answers for the questions on these worksheets. Often, each parent will answer the questions in different ways.

Taking the time to fill out these worksheets will give you a clearer understanding of what you think makes sense for your children and the other parent. The more detail you can develop before you start negotiating with the other parent, the easier it will be for you to build a parenting agreement that everyone can live with later. And you will find the information and help you get in Chapters 6 though 9 will be much more valuable if you have filled out these worksheets. Those chapters include references to the questions from these worksheets.

When parenting agreements work well, it is because the agreement focuses on how to meet your children's needs given the relationship that exists between you and the other parent. Your parenting agreement should describe how you and the other parent will share and divide the time and responsibilities of raising your children and making decisions on their behalf. These worksheets will help you visualize how the world may look through your children's eyes. A school counselor, teacher, trusted adult friend, religious leader, or other adult who knows your children might be able to add insights as well.

TAKE TIME FOR YOURSELF

While thinking about ways each of your children is special can often bring a smile, some of the worksheet questions may bring up feelings of anger or sadness—about the situation, about the impact this may have on your children, or about ways your relationship with the other parent has become difficult. It is important to give yourself time to have these feelings, and to think about ways you can get the support you need to experience them. By acknowledging how sad and difficult this process can be—whether or not you are the one who wants the divorce—you will be better able to maintain a sense of balance at other times so that you can make decisions that are in your children's best interests.

HOW CHILDREN EXPERIENCE DIVORCE

Researchers have studied how children react to divorce for over 30 years. While each researcher seems to focus on slightly different aspects of this question, all agree that children have mixed feelings about their parents' separation or divorce, and they have different ways of coping with all the changes that follow.

Often, a child's feelings or behavior will become more intense if there is significant conflict in their parents' relationship, if their living situation changes abruptly, or if they have no one other than their parents who can be a buffer while these issues are resolved. Some children become overly good, some lash out at anyone and everyone nearby, some withdraw into a shell, and some regress to behavior they had at younger ages. Some children will show many, or even all, of these symptoms at different times. While these changes in your child may be hard to understand, and sometimes hard to tolerate, it is important to notice what your child is experiencing, and to think about how your child handles change. The way he or she adapts to new situations is often a clue about ways you can make the changes following separation or divorce easier to absorb.

To help clarify your feelings and goals for your future relationship with your children, complete the four worksheets. You can use them in your negotiations with the other parent, or to educate people you might work with as you develop your parenting agreement, such as a mediator, counselor, or lawyer.

As we noted above, each parent should complete a separate copy of Worksheets 1, 2, and 3. Working independently lets you each focus on your own feelings and impressions. It also means you don't have to worry about whether you agree on how to answer each question.

You and the other parent can complete Worksheet 4 either separately or together. The answers from the first three worksheets will help you create a checklist in this final worksheet quickly and easily. Because you may have decided not to share your own answers on Worksheets 1–3, this last worksheet may be the first opportunity each of you has to get a sense of what your parenting agreement will need to cover. If you decide to skip filling out the first three worksheets, Worksheet 4 will take a little more time to complete. If you fill out the last worksheet together, make sure that you write down each parent's answers when you disagree.

Parents are likely to find many ways their answers on these questionnaires differ. This is normal and can be viewed as a way to help you see areas where you might need to be creative, or get extra help to find better ways to resolve a problem. If filling out these worksheets leads to arguments, consult Chapter 4 (How to Negotiate a Parenting Agreement), or consider bringing in a mediator or counselor to help. Chapter 11 has information on finding a mediator and making the most of mediation. Chapter 17 has information on finding a counselor.

⚠ GO SLOWLY NOW TO SAVE TIME LATER

Most separating and divorcing parents reach a point when they just want to "be done" so they can get on with their lives. This is normal, and tempting. For parenting agreements to work, however, they must make sense to both parents. Also, the agreement must reflect ways that each parent and each child have different needs or values. Taking some extra time with the worksheets and your discussions about them can save you time later by helping you to organize your thoughts and plan for ways your agreement can help each of you feel comfortable with changes in your family relationships and living arrangements.

C. Sample Worksheets

There are samples of completed worksheets below. The samples are designed to show you what a completed worksheet might look like, though of course your answers will be specific to your family. Blank copies of the worksheets for you to use are in the Appendix. Before filling out the worksheets, make at least two copies of each worksheet for each parent. Set aside the original of each worksheet in case you need to make more copies.

The worksheet questions are designed to help you think in new ways about parenting issues. Go ahead and skip questions that do not make sense in your family situation, and feel free to add extra pages if there are questions that require longer answers, or you think of new ideas to add.

Family profile for sample worksheets:
The fictional family filling out the sample worksheets consists of Cherise (mother), Manny (father), and their three children: Krista (age 7), Carl (age 4), and Justin (age 2). Manny and Cherise have been married for 8 years. Many of those years were difficult, and there were some instances of pushing and shoving between them during their marriage. The most serious incident took place just before they split up six months ago, when Manny hit Cherise hard enough for her to fall and cut her head on a table. Manny has moved into his parents' house while the divorce goes through.

1. Worksheet 1: Describe Your Children

Worksheet 1 asks you to describe your children, and to notice things that make them individuals—including their likes and dislikes; any changes in behavior you've noticed; ways each child can be helped to handle new situations; and who, besides you and the other parent, is important in their world.

Each parent should start with at least two blank copies of this worksheet (separate from the original, in case you need to make more copies later).

This sample worksheet was completed by Cherise (mother).

WORKSHEET 1: DESCRIBE YOUR CHILDREN

1. How would you describe each child?

   All three kids are healthy and normal for their ages. Krista is in second grade, and loves school. Carl and Justin go to the same day care/preschool while I work in the mornings. Carl is getting ready to go to kindergarten, and Justin is experimenting with toilet training.

2. What makes each child special?

   Krista is in Brownies, and really likes earning her badges. She likes to have sleepovers with her friends. Carl is an active four-year old who loves playing with our dog. He seems to get into everything, and is happiest when I take him to the playground a few blocks away. Justin seems a little bit nervous. He sucks his thumb much of the time, but is otherwise a happy child. He is the family clown and loves making noises or faces that will make us laugh.

3. How does each child like the current living and parenting arrangements?

   The children spend alternating weekends with their dad at his parents' house. I bring them over at 6 on Friday evening, and Manny brings them back Sunday mornings at 9 so I can take them to Sunday school. They seem to be handling the arrangements alright, but it sometimes gets in the way when Krista wants to have overnights with her friends. The kids like Manny's parents, but I think they are spoiling them. I also worry that Manny and his parents talk about how they don't like me in front of the kids.

4. Have there been any changes in behavior since the separation or divorce?

   Justin has become much quieter. Even though he still clowns around, he cries for Manny a lot. Both boys seem to miss their dad when they're with me. Krista is sometimes very cold to both of us. All three kids are glad there is less yelling and fighting. They were all there the night Manny hit me, and seem scared of him when he gets mad. Carl has hit a couple of children at preschool, and pulled one girl's hair hard enough that her parents called me that night. Justin is very inconsistent with the toilet training, and I am thinking of putting this off until things settle down more.

5. Have the children expressed preferences for the future?

   Krista and Carl seem to think we will get back together soon, but otherwise the kids are really too young to have many opinions. Krista is getting tired of having to share a room with her brothers when they stay at Manny's folks' house.

6. How does each child react to change?

   As long as the kids are together, they seem to handle things pretty well. They are doing a better job of figuring out what to take when they stay with their dad, although Carl always seems to need just one more toy or game than what he brought. Justin seems to have more temper tantrums when he's tired, so Manny needs to really pay attention to making sure he gets naps when he's there.

7. What strategies help each child to handle change?

   The kids do better when we stick to the schedule we've set up. We change it sometimes for special situations, but they seem to do best when it's the same week after week. They also do better when they can talk to their dad every couple of days on the phone. They seem to fall apart more if I call them when they are with Manny. If we are fighting, though, nothing seems to work well.

8. Who else is important in your children's lives?

   The kids are pretty attached to Manny's parents. They also like visiting my sister and her kids. They see their cousins every few days, and really seem to like that time together.

2. Worksheet 2: Describe Your Relationship With Your Child

Worksheet 2 asks you to describe your relationship with each child. This includes things you like to do together, as well as your plans for their future and your parenting style.

Again, each parent should start with at least two blank copies of this worksheet (separate from the original, in case you need to make more copies later).

Completed by Manny (father).

3. Worksheet 3: Adding the Details

Worksheet 3 will help you remember important documents you might need before working on your parenting plan. It will also help you think of details that you might include in the agreement by listing work schedules, activities, counseling, or medical treatment needs. This worksheet will also help you plan for how to handle substance abuse or domestic violence issues in the future.

As before, each parent should start with at least two blank copies of this worksheet (separate from the original, in case you need to make more copies later).

Completed by Cherise (mother).

4. Worksheet 4: Checklist of Issues for Your Parenting Agreement

Some parents will want to fill this last worksheet out together, others will want to do so separately and then compare their answers when finished. The goal is to get a list of important issues so you can be sure your parenting agreement will make sense for your situation.

Regardless of the approach you take, this worksheet will help you organize the information you've gathered in the first three worksheets. If you fill this worksheet out together, be sure that you write down both parents' answers to questions when you disagree.

If you fill this worksheet out together, make two copies before starting. If you fill this worksheet out separately, make sure each parent has at least two blank copies of this worksheet. Be sure to keep the original worksheet separate, in case you need to make more copies later.

Completed by Manny (father) but reflects comments of both parents.

WORKSHEET 2: DESCRIBE YOUR RELATIONSHIP WITH YOUR CHILD

1. What do you and your children like to do together?

   My children are very important to me, and always have been. I like going to the father-daughter events with Krista, and like to play with Carl and Justin. Carl is starting to learn how to throw a ball pretty well. Justin is a real cutup, so we like to play hide and seek and chasing games.

2. What are your plans and wishes for your children?

   I want my children to grow up feeling that I have been really involved with them. I don't really care what they do as adults, but I expect them to try hard to do it well. I want them to be happy even though Cherise and I have split up.

3. How do you and your children handle and resolve conflict? Discipline?

   I'm pretty clear with them about the rules, but sometimes it's hard to enforce the rules when they spend so little time with me. They fight sometimes, so I pretty much just split them up until they settle down. They stay with my parents if I have to work on Saturdays. My parents love to spoil them when they get the chance.

4. How did you share parenting responsibilities and time when you and the other parent were living together?

   I helped out with taking care of the kids. I gave them baths sometimes, helped with some things around the house, and sometimes put them to bed. I worked 8–5 or 6 though, so I didn't always have a lot of energy left to do things before they went to bed.

5. How do you and the other parent share parenting responsibilities and time with your children now?

   Cherise handles most of the day-to-day things, but I plan to do my share of it as soon as I get my own place and the kids can be with me half the time. I can handle getting them to school or day care in the morning, and deal with the evening stuff just fine. My mother has agreed to help out when they are with me. My mom also takes care of the kids on Wednesday nights when I have classes.

6. Are you happy with the current arrangements? (Please explain)

   I don't have enough time with the kids right now, but it has to be that way until things get sorted out. I like that my kids are getting to see their grandparents so much.

7. Are your children happy with the current arrangements? (Please explain)

   I know it's hard on the kids to all have to share a room when they stay with me, but I think they also like spending time with their grandparents. I know they wish they could spend more time with me, especially Carl and Justin, but that will happen as soon as I can save up some money.

8. If changes are in order, what would you suggest?

   Cherise needs to be more flexible about letting the kids come over during the week or even every weekend sometimes.

WORKSHEET 3: ADDING THE DETAILS

1. List court documents, orders, or agreements that affect your family. (Note that the terms used here might be different in your state. See Chapter 16 for terms used in your state.)

   Papers to file for divorce

   The temporary agreement we worked out when we first separated

2. Each parent's work schedule:

   Cherise works 8:30 to 1:00, Monday through Friday

   Manny works 8:00 to 5:00 or 6:00, Monday through Friday

3. Childrens' schedule of activities, special needs, and interests (such as school, religious training, after-school activities):

   Krista has Brownies every Tuesday after school.

   All three children go to Sunday school at 10:30 each week.

4. Does either parent have plans to move?

   Manny plans to find his own apartment after the divorce is final. He says he will look for a

   two or three bedroom place. Neither of us plans to move out of the area, but Manny has

   said he's concerned that most of the construction jobs seem to be drying up here.

5. Does either parent have a new relationship or plan to remarry?

   Not now

6. Are there any adult relatives or friends with whom the children should or should not have close contact?

   The children should continue to see their grandparents and cousins. They should not be

   around Rosa or George if they have been drinking.

7. Is counseling needed for the children, parents, or the family?

   Right now the kids seem to be OK, but Manny should continue going to the anger

   management classes that the judge ordered.

8. Are there any special medical needs of the children, parents, or the family?

   None of us has any health issues, but I want to be sure that the kids get a checkup at

   least once a year.

9. Do you want your parenting agreement to address domestic violence issues? (Please explain)

   Yes. Even though Manny only hurt me badly once, I'm afraid that he will teach the kids that

   violence is an acceptable way to solve conflicts. I think he needs to finish the anger management

   counseling, and find new ways to handle conflict. He also needs to find ways to explain to

   Carl, especially, why hitting other kids or pulling their hair isn't acceptable behavior.

10. Do you want your parenting agreement to address the use of drugs or alcohol? (Please explain)

    I think Manny should start going to AA meetings again. I'm not sure if he's drinking all the

    time, but he was drinking the night he hit me.

11. Do you have any special concerns about your relationship with the other parent that should be addressed in your agreement? (Please explain)

    I think Manny and his parents bad-mouth me in front of the kids. I want that to stop.

WORKSHEET 4: CHECKLIST OF ISSUES FOR YOUR PARENTING AGREEMENT

1. Existing court documents, orders, or agreements that must be reconsidered or changed to accommodate your new parenting agreement.
   Temporary custody order
   Agreement we worked out 6 months ago

2. Steps you will have to take to resolve legal or religious issues such as divorce, legal separation, etc.
   Finish divorce paperwork, make it final.

3. Any concerns or recommendations made by a counselor, school teacher, therapist, or other interested adult regarding your children's emotional, spiritual, or physical well-being:
   Manny will finish out the anger management classes ordered by the judge. Krista will continue seeing the school counselor every couple of weeks until she can deal with things better.

4. Ways each of you can support your children's relationship with the other parent:
   Both Manny and Cherise agree not to bad-mouth the other parent when talking with family or friends any time the children are present or might overhear the conversation.

5. Ways each parent can help the children address their feelings, reactions, or concerns about the separation or divorce:
   Krista is already seeing the school counselor every couple of weeks. She can continue this until the end of the school year. Manny will try to talk to Carl about not hitting when he is angry.

6. Medical issues that need to be addressed:
   Cherise will take the children for both medical and dental checkups. Manny will keep the kids on his insurance through work. Still need to decide how to handle the cost of any copayments or other medical bills.

7. Ways to reduce conflict between the parents when negotiating agreements, exchanging the children, and addressing the children's needs, interests, and activities:
   We will try to talk on the phone first, so we don't have to talk about it when Cherise drops them off on Fridays.

8. Times when both parents are available to care for the children:
   Some evenings and Saturdays, every Sunday

9. Times when only _____Cherise_____ can care for the children: _____Wednesday and Thursday evenings_____

10. Times when only _____Manny_____ can care for the children: _____none_____

11. Time with other family or friends that should be addressed in the parenting agreement:
    The kids will still spend a lot of time with Manny's parents, even after he gets his own place. They will also spend time with Cherise's sister and her children.

12. Family or friends the children should not spend time (or be alone) with:
    Rosa and George, if they have been drinking.

13. Ways domestic violence issues will be addressed:
    Manny will keep going to the anger management classes ordered by the court.

14. Ways alcohol or other substance-abuse issues will be addressed:
    Both parents will start going to AA again.

15. Other provisions:
    If the children need counseling later, we will try to arrange that through Manny's insurance.

CHAPTER 4

How to Negotiate a Parenting Agreement

Where do you start when you need to negotiate a parenting agreement? Should you cover only the basics or negotiate the whole thing at once? To figure out where to begin, it helps to think about where you are in the process. If this is your first agreement, you could start with the essentials: where the children will live, how they will get medical care, and how decisions will be made. Or you may be further along in the process and ready to tackle more issues or even the entire agreement. Whatever point you are at, read carefully through the entire parenting agreement in the Appendix before you begin your negotiations.

This chapter will show you how to negotiate an effective and lasting agreement, how to handle conflict—even intense conflict—and what to do if parenting issues become too difficult to handle on your own.

A. Knowing What You Need and Want

Although it sounds simple, many parents find it difficult to describe what they want to get out of their negotiations with the other parent. It is important to take your time with each step in this process, because it will help you find workable solutions later. To start this process, write down:

- **what is or is not working well in the current arrangements,** such as the frequency of visits, the need for conversations about parenting styles, or any concerns about child safety issues.
- **problems to be solved,** such as lateness at the exchange, regular arguments over key parenting issues or one parent's concern that a certain activity is unsafe for the child, and
- **what you want to get out of the agreement,** such as a clear statement of how exchanges will happen, a better way to solve conflicts, or a list of the activities that both parents agree the kids will or won't be allowed to do.

As you make this list, pay attention to what your children and the other parent have to say. (The worksheets from Chapter 3 can help you to organize your approach.) Each person's version of "what I need and want" will be somewhat different. Experience shows, however, that the more clearly you describe your needs and wants, and the more carefully you listen to the other parent's needs and wants, the more likely you are to build an agreement that lasts.

1. Good Negotiations

Good negotiations usually lead to good agreements. But unless you are a trained negotiator, you might not know how to direct your efforts, especially when the stakes are high or you have negative feelings about the other parent.

When you first start to talk, make an effort to communicate your needs and wants clearly. Then listen carefully to the other parent's needs and wants. Once you have each had a chance to outline your needs and wants, you can start to work together to:

- understand what fuels your conflict and what obstacles make it difficult for you to negotiate
- focus on the children and on finding ways to solve problems
- develop a realistic parenting plan
- consider more than one approach to solving problems, and
- find win-win solutions that give each of you value.

You will know that your negotiations are going well when you both feel you:

- can safely express your views (especially if there has been a history of domestic violence or verbal or emotional abuse)
- understand what the other person wants and why (even if you don't agree), and
- know what you and the other person each have to gain from a successful agreement.

2. Lasting Agreements

Knowing how you will benefit from having your parenting agreement work well can make it easier to be flexible as you and the other parent negotiate and carry out the agreement. For example, most parents can handle small changes in the schedule or occasional late pick-ups and drop-offs for visits if they think the other parent is considering their needs and the children's needs when making these changes.

There are many ways you can benefit from a successful parenting agreement, including:

- limiting the financial and emotional costs of a court fight
- reducing the tension between you and the other parent
- helping both parents worry less about their children when they are with the other parent

- helping to keep your children out of the middle of their parents' arguments by finding new ways to handle your conflicts, and
- showing your children that you and the other parent can agree on some things.

3. When Parents Don't Trust Each Other

It is possible to create a good parenting agreement even if there is little or no trust between the parents. Most people consider themselves trustworthy. They know, and will tell you, that they will stick to an agreement, even if they doubt that the other person will do the same. When you have two people who feel this way, you are well on your way to building an agreement that can last. Sometimes negotiations succeed because the parties know that failure can mean expensive and exhausting legal battles.

4. Defining Success

Some people think that their negotiations succeed only if they have gotten what they want without spending too much time or money on the process of working out the agreement. These people give little thought to how the other parent feels about the agreement or whether it makes the most sense for their children. Although this strategy might work well for handling some kinds of negotiations (such as buying a used car), it often backfires when people have to cooperate with each other for a long time. Because parenting is a long-term commitment, it pays to lay a strong foundation for the negotiations with the other parent at the outset.

B. When Conflict Gets in the Way

The single biggest barrier to successful negotiations is conflict. Conflict can range from occasional disagreements or shouting matches to persistent arguing, verbal and physical assault, or threats to hurt or kill. Studies have confirmed that children witness domestic violence between their parents in 50%–75% of divorces, and that nearly half of those children are themselves victims of domestic violence, child abuse, or child sexual abuse. Not surprisingly, conflict between parents can feel more like "the clash of the titans" to a child than an example of "Mom and Dad trying to figure out what's best for me."

Some amount of conflict is normal during a divorce or separation. But when arguing, fighting, legal battles, and name-calling are a regular part of your co-parenting landscape, agreements can be very difficult to reach on your own. When do you need help? Ask yourself the following questions:

- Are your court files more than six inches tall when you stack them up on the kitchen table? (Research shows that approximately 5%–10% of all divorces are litigated extensively).
- If someone asked both you and the other parent about how things are going, would one say, "Great!" and the other say, "Awful"?
- When you or the other parent talk about why the arguing continues, do you both say that you are always right and the other parent is always wrong?
- Are your extended families and friends lined up on one side or the other ready to do battle?
- Do one or both of you feel that the other parent has nothing good to offer your children?
- Does one parent feel that the other parent has "cut off" the possibility of having a good relationship with your children?
- Have there been threats of violence, physical violence or verbal or emotional abuse in your relationship (even if it happened only around the time of separation)?

If your answer is "yes" to the last question—or three or more of the other questions—there's a good chance that your conflict may get in the way of negotiating a parenting plan.

Conflict can be very expensive. The most obvious costs can be measured in the dollars it takes to pay attorneys, court fees, child custody evaluators, special masters, visitation supervisors, counselors, and any other professionals you and the other parent must hire to help.

Less obvious, perhaps, are the enormous costs that each of you will pay emotionally. And your children will pay most of all. Children often feel afraid, sad, and confused when their parents argue, blame, threaten each other, or let their anger spiral out of control. Children look to their parents as the people who protect them from the scary parts of the world. Children also need their parents to help them manage the hurt, anger, and other calamities that are part of growing up. When parents are arguing or become violent, children lose confidence that their parents will continue to love them and keep them safe.

Study after study confirms what many parents know from their own experiences: Conflict between the parents takes the greatest toll on children. This conflict—especially when it continues over time—can slow your children's

ability to reach certain milestones in their development, lead to poor performance in school, undermine their ability to relate to friends, and make them feel even more isolated than they already feel because of the separation or divorce.

WHERE DO WE FIT IN?

Sometimes it helps to see where you and the other parent fit along an imagined continuum of low- to high-conflict families. Though no pair of divorcing parents can ever really be "categorized," it is often interesting to consider where you might fit in, and what other models for handling these issues and relationships exist.

Dr. Constance Ahron's list of different family types, discussed in her book *The Good Divorce* (Harper Collins, 1994), still does a good job of capturing different types of relationships between divorced parents—even a decade later. In her book Dr. Ahrons notes that there are lots of divorced pairs that fall into each category, though most divorcing couples cluster near the middle of the list, and these relationships usually shift over time.

"Perfect Pals": These parents are able to remain good friends and communicate regularly with very little conflict. These parents may live next door to, or down the block from, each other. These parents are also more likely to consider "bird nesting" (having the children stay in the family home while the parents switch off living there). When attending the school play or soccer match, they are more likely than not to sit together. These parents are often able to share birthday parties and holiday celebrations, and may keep friendly relationships with their "ex" in-laws.

"Cooperative Colleagues": These parents are generally friendly toward each other, can clearly separate the adult relationship issues from the parenting issues, and are more likely than "perfect pals" to have new partners. Although these parents' homes may still be in the same general area, they are less likely to cross paths on a regular basis. They can communicate easily. When conflicts do come up, these parents are usually able to manage their differences effectively.

"Angry Associates": These parents are frequently angry with each other and have a difficult time separating the adult relationship issues from the parenting issues. Though they can often benefit from working with a mediator, counselor, or attorney to resolve their disputes, they seldom do. These parents frequently involve their children in their conflict, and the children often dread what will happen each time their parents are in the same place at the same time.

"Fiery Foes": These parents seldom have much to do with each other—but when they do, it often turns into a battle. These parents go to court regularly. The issues that end up in court often start as a small matter, such as what time the weekend visit should start or finish. Judges frequently turn to outside professionals (such as a custody evaluator, attorney for the child, counselor, special master, or visitation supervisor) for help in deciding how best to resolve the issue and what court orders might be most effective, and to watch that the court orders are followed. In these situations, children sometimes say they are afraid to be with one of their parents, or they may refuse to visit one parent.

"Dissolved Duos": This situation is different from the other four, because it commonly involves one parent who has nearly, or totally, stopped contact with the ex and his or her child. Parents in this group may consider kidnapping or hiding a child after losing custody because they fear that they have no other option for gaining time with their children.

Although it will be difficult, you and the other parent can find effective ways to reduce the levels of conflict that you experience in your co-parenting relationship. Here are some strategies that both professionals and parents agree are the most effective in reducing conflict.

1.   Separate Relationship Issues From Parenting Issues

Most professionals working with divorced or separated families urge the parents to find ways to keep their adult relationship issues separate from the parenting issues. But what does this really mean? In short, it means that you don't mix up your feelings about why you and the other parent didn't stay together with your children's needs and desires. It also means that you can see your children's needs as separate from your own, or the other parent's, needs.

2.   Deal With Feelings of Revenge

Some parents are so angry or hurt that they feel like they want to "get back" at the other parent. These feelings can be a powerful motivator and a significant roadblock in your negotiations.

When revenge becomes a central theme for one or both parents, its destructive influence makes finding a settlement outside of court less likely.

Some desire for revenge is often a fact of life following a separation or divorce. To help, you can look for ways to bring the feelings out into the open safely and then loosen their hold on your negotiations. As with other intense feelings, you may be able to overcome these destructive feelings by admitting that you have them and acknowledging how much you would like to be able to act on them. Having done this, you might then be able to discard revenge and move forward to negotiate an agreement that nurtures your children.

If you or the other parent still can't shake your desire to get revenge, try thinking about what would actually happen if you got what you think you want. You can start by playing a game of "What if?" Imagine that you are not only successful in getting revenge but that you have succeeded beyond your wildest dreams! For example, if you want to pay the other parent back for taking a new lover, imagine that you've been able to do that and to guarantee that they will not have another happy moment, or date, for the next ten years. If your goal is to force the other parent to admit what a miserable parent he or she is, imagine that they not only know this, but that a court has sentenced them to walk up and down Main Street wearing a sandwich board that proclaims their failings.

Got the idea? Great! Now imagine the consequences. How well will the other parent be able to function as a caregiver? How will your children react to the other parent's fate? How long will your feelings of triumph last? How long might it take and how much might it cost to actually achieve full victory? How motivated will the other parent be to pitch in on miscellaneous expenses for the children or to faithfully pay child support?

Revenge may be sweet for the moment, but it is a poor substitute for confidence in yourself and your value and abilities as a parent. It can so easily backfire and cost you and your children any sense of fulfillment.

THE DIFFERENCE BETWEEN CONFLICT AND HOSTILITY

Though relatively few parents remain locked in high conflict relationships (approximately 10% to 15% of all separated or divorced parents), it is common enough to justify a closer look. By looking closely at what you argue about, or why you can't seem to stop arguing, you can learn important things about the ways that either or both of you need to grow in your communication or problem-solving skills.

Conflict is very complex. For many parents, conflict starts when they cannot communicate over difficult and emotionally charged issues. It continues because they are not successful in getting over what has made those issues difficult or emotionally charged in the first place. It usually takes several months, or years, for people to deal with all of the feelings that come up when a romantic relationship is ending. During that time, it can be especially difficult, but is critically important, to sort out why the conflict exists and what it will take to resolve it. Often this means getting help, at least briefly, from a trained professional such as a mediator, counselor, mental health professional, or attorney.

Some conflict, however, is so intense that it really should be viewed differently. Hostility occurs when arguing goes beyond just disagreeing about what is right or how to resolve a problem. Hostility takes on overtones of "making someone pay" for all of the bad things they have done, and it is not generally the kind of emotion that can be dealt with in a calm negotiation setting between two parents. Hostility is better addressed in counseling or some other controlled setting where a trained professional can help the parents understand what is happening, look for ways to address the underlying issues, and provide emotional and physical safety for everyone involved. You can find more information about different kinds of mental health professionals in Chapter 17.

3. Don't Undermine Your Child's Relationship With the Other Parent

Sometimes, one or both parents try to undermine their children's relationship with the other parent—in a word, they try to "turn" their children away from the other parent. Signs that a parent is engaging in this type of behavior include:

- if one parent regularly discusses his or her concerns about the other parent's ability to care for the child with the children
- a child has decided to resolve his or her feelings about wanting to love both parents by choosing to align with, or be loyal to, one parent, and sees the other parent as dangerous, uncaring, or incapable
- a child refuses to visit, speak on the telephone, or otherwise have any contact with one parent, or
- one parent works hard to make sure the other parent is as absent from the children's lives as possible.

Parents give many reasons for trying to undermine the children's relationship with the other parent. Often this behavior masks a complex range of problems. Sometimes parents actively try to distance children from the other parent because there is a history of emotional, physical, or sexual abuse. In other situations, parents alienate children from the other parent as a way of punishing the other parent for leaving the relationship. More often than not, though, there are many reasons for this behavior. Figuring out the reasons is often difficult, but it is important to do. Generally, parents in this situation need a professional's help to address these situations. (See Chapter 8, Issue 30.)

Note: Though protecting a child from emotional, physical, or sexual abuse is critically important, you must be sure to do so in a way that does not also jeopardize your legal situation. For this reason, it is essential that you meet with an attorney, district attorney, domestic violence counselor, child abuse protection professional, or other similarly qualified person who can help you decide the best way to protect your child without doing something illegal.

4. Stop Arguing!

Constant arguing can become a bad habit. It can be hard, though, to figure out how you got into the habit in the first place. Here are some common reasons why separated parents continue to argue:

Argument for argument's sake. Sometimes one parent keeps arguing because he or she likes to argue, or feels like "there's nothing like a good argument to clear the air." If either you or the other parent argues for these reasons, consider the overall harm this type of behavior can cause—and consider that after awhile constant arguing can feel like abuse. This chapter will give you ideas about other ways to make your point, make decisions, or make yourself heard.

Yelling to make sure you are heard. Sometimes people feel that arguing and yelling are the only ways to get a point across. If this is true for you, consider trying some of the strategies listed later in this chapter or involving a mediator, counselor, or other third party in your discussions with the other parent.

Arguing to stay "connected." Sometimes parents argue as a way to stay "connected." Often, this is because they are unsure about their feelings for the other parent—especially if one parent is not sure about going through with a separation or divorce, or is thinking about getting back together with the other parent. Other times, this type of behavior shows up during a transition in one parent's life, such as starting a new relationship, having a child with a new partner, or making a move out of the area. If you think this might be true in your situation, one or both parents should consider taking this issue to counseling. This way of staying connected can be very destructive and will harm your chances of having a good co-parenting relationship and parent-child relationship.

Verbal fighting instead of hitting. Sometimes people will argue because it feels like a better alternative to pushing, shoving, hitting, throwing things, or resorting to some kind of violence or property damage. In this case, arguing seems to offer the only way to deal with anger that gets out of control. You shouldn't compromise anyone's safety to negotiate your parenting agreement or make important decisions. If arguing is used as an alternative to violence—stop arguing, make sure you are safe, and wait to handle your negotiations through a mediator, counselor, or attorney. For long-term solutions to dealing with intense anger or physical or emotional abuse, most people find that they need counseling or need to participate in an anger management group.

5. Shift Your Perspective

You can start the process of gaining a new perspective on the issues you need to resolve by really listening to the other parent. This will also help you think about how you will present your ideas to him or her. When you're ready to talk, try to think about the issues from the other parent's perspective. This will help you anticipate his or her concerns. The Native American instruction to "walk a mile in another's moccasins" is a good one. Although you may have known the other parent very well at one time, you may not know how the world looks to him or her now.

To see the issues and potential solutions from the other parent's perspective, you must:

- figure out what the other parent cares about (such as making sure the children are supported to do well in school)
- anticipate the other parent's objections to your ideas (for example, he or she might worry that daily tutoring is expensive and gets in the way of a regular Wednesday evening dinner visit)
- develop responses to the other parent's objections (for example, you can say that your child will do better in school or feel better about her- or himself with tutoring, or that program costs can be reduced for low-income parents), and
- suggest alternative solutions that might appeal to the other parent (for example, the other parent might want to take the child to tutoring and keep the child half an hour later for as long as the tutoring is needed).

6. Take Advantage of Each Parent's Strengths

When emotions are running high—as is often the case in parenting disputes—many people find it difficult to be flexible or to try new problem-solving strategies. This is why it is so important for parents to understand what works best for each of them, and to plan for how they will solve problems once they come up.

Each of us has strengths and weaknesses when it comes to how we solve problems. For some, it's best to talk things through from beginning to end before making a decision. For others, it helps to have one person develop a plan that both parents can consider. Many parents find that each of them prefers to solve problems in different ways. If each parent comes to the negotiations prepared to understand the other parent's style, you will have come a long way towards building a parenting agreement that makes sense for both of you and for your children.

C. Using Effective Negotiation and Problem-Solving Strategies

Although you may not yet be an experienced negotiator, you can take advantage of the time-tested strategies and techniques that professional negotiators use. What you will notice running through all of these strategies is an emphasis on looking carefully at a situation to understand why it caused problems in the past and to plan for how you might avoid those problems in the future.

1. Set Ground Rules

Parents can keep control of a conversation and avoid a full-blown battle when they set and follow a few basic ground rules. Ground rules work best when they are simple, easy to remember, and few in number. Some ground rules to use include:

- agreeing that neither parent will interrupt the other (sometimes parents keep a pad of paper handy to make notes so that they don't forget a point they want to make)
- agreeing that neither parent will call the other names or make generalized, negative statements about the other (instead of saying, "You never did care much about how the kids were raised," you might say, "I feel as though you left most of the decisions to me while we were married"), and
- focusing on issues and possible solutions, rather than on who is to blame for having created the problem in the first place.

2. Agree on Common Goals

While many parents disagree about decisions affecting their children, they can often identify a list of common goals. For example, you may agree that you want to reduce the conflict between you, find ways that your children can enjoy the best of their relationships with each of you, and have your children feel confident that they are loved and valued by both parents, regardless of the separation or divorce.

3. Bring in a Neutral Person

Many parents find it easier to focus on making good parenting decisions when a neutral person, such as a counselor or mediator, moderates their discussions. (See Chapter 11, Making Mediation and Arbitration Work for You.)

4. Recall Times When Discussions Were Easier

For some parents, the pain, anger, and confusion of a separation or divorce is so intense they forget those times when they were able to agree. Remembering what made past discussions more successful is often enough to move parents toward an agreement.

5. Tackle the Easier Issues First

Most experienced facilitators or negotiators suggest that when parents begin to negotiate, they should start with the easiest issues first. Once you and the other parent have some experience reaching agreement, you can work your way back to more difficult issues. You will have gained trust and confidence that you can reach agreement.

6. Remove Labels Such as "Good" and "Bad"

Many parents experience a wide range of conflicting emotions and unusual behavior both during and after the separation or divorce. Many are tempted to label those emotions or behaviors as "good" or "bad." If you can remove these labels, however, and just accept the emotions and behavior as a normal part of the experience, you may have fewer problems as you continue your separate parenting relationship.

7. Choose Your Setting for Negotiations

Choosing when and where you will meet to talk with the other parent is very important. You must find a time and place that is convenient and comfortable and allows you to talk without interruptions. This may be a pleasant restaurant or coffee shop with tables that offer privacy. But don't choose a restaurant that you used to frequent as a couple, as the associations with the past might bring up painful emotions best left behind while you are considering your children's future.

Other options for a meeting location include:
- a meeting or conference room at the public library

- a meeting or conference room at a community center, or
- a picnic table in a park (assuming your children are not present).

8.   Set an Agenda

Your discussions will be more productive if you make a list of issues that you want to cover (called an agenda) and then stick to it. You can use the worksheets in Chapter 3 or the parenting agreement to help you set your agenda, or you can develop your agenda based on your needs at the time you meet.

Regardless of how you develop your agenda, start each meeting by agreeing on the issues you will discuss at that time. Part of each agenda should be devoted to reviewing your progress so far, and part should be devoted to deciding what should happen next. A sample agenda is below.

SAMPLE AGENDA

1. Review progress to date.
2. Review each parent's evaluation worksheets.
3. Develop a checklist of parenting issues (complete Worksheet 4 together).
4. Reach agreements about:
   a. medical, dental, and vision care
   b. counseling
   c. education
   d. holidays
   e. religious school
5. Summarize decisions made.
6. Set date, time, and agenda for next meeting.

9.   Give Yourself Enough Time

Negotiations over most parenting issues take time. When you're ready to work on your parenting plan, set aside enough time to carefully consider each decision. Don't schedule your meeting for an hour before one of you needs to leave to catch a plane—give yourself time to be heard and to listen. If any issue on your agenda is likely to involve much discussion, limit the number of issues you will tackle at one time.

10. Know What to Cover and How Much Detail to Provide

It is important to make sure that your parenting agreement covers everything you will need to make the arrangements work smoothly. But there is a delicate balance between covering all of the key items and providing so much detail that you can't handle the real-life variables that are sure to arise.

For some parents, detailed agreements work because they leave little room for misunderstanding or argument. For others, the details just provide that many more issues to fight about. For parents who do best with a lot of detail, the agreement might include a specific list covering each toy and article of clothing, the number of changes of clothes, and the number of disposable diapers that need to be packed for each exchange. Other parents might use that detail to argue over whether the shirts that were packed should have been heavy, medium, or lightweight, or whether you can really count a shirt you provided if it is too dirty to be worn. Often, high-conflict parents do best when they develop very structured agreements that leave little room for interpretation. You will find more discussion on this topic in Section D of this chapter.

11. Choose Your Words Carefully

Language is a very powerful tool. It can make your conversations with the other parent easier, or it can make these talks more difficult, adversarial, and confusing. By choosing your words carefully, you will be better understood and less likely to get into an argument. Here are some specific ideas to improve your communication skills.

a.   Be an Active Listener

Listening involves more than hearing the words spoken—you must also understand them. Simple though it may sound, most people need to practice this skill. This is especially difficult when you negotiate with someone you have known—and argued with—for a long time. Try not to fall into the trap of assuming that you know what the other parent will say or what he or she "really" means.

To be sure that you understand the other parent's comments or concerns, ask questions. For example, you could say: "It sounds as though you are saying '___'; is that right?" Once you truly hear and understand the other, you can be sure that you are reacting to something real and make your decisions accordingly. Who knows? You both might be pleasantly surprised to find that some of your assumptions are mistaken.

b. Say "Yes, … If" Instead of "Yes, … But"

Sometimes the other parent proposes something that you would be willing to go along with, provided certain conditions were met. Instead of starting your response by saying "But," try saying "Yes, . . . if" instead. Responding with "but" can sound like "no" to the other person and lead to unnecessary arguments. Responding with "Yes, . . .if" leads instead to a discussion of what it would take for you to go along with the idea.

Consider the following conversation between two parents:

PARENT A: *"I want the children to live with me during the week, and you can have them on the weekends."*

PARENT B: *"But I want to be able to see them during the week sometimes, too."*

PARENT A: *"There you go again—you always argue. Why can't you just let me have one decision go my way?"*

PARENT B: *"I wasn't arguing! You are as impossible to talk to as always! You can forget it now—the kids will live with me, and you can see them when it's convenient."*

When parents are angry or distrustful, it is easy to jump to the conclusion that "Yes, … but" really means "no." As an alternative, these parents might have approached their discussion like this:

PARENT A: *"I want the children to live with me during the week, and you can have them on the weekends."*

PARENT B: *"That might work, if I can also see them sometimes during the week."*

PARENT A: *"Well, maybe, if I know about it in advance."*

PARENT B: *"I could call at the beginning of the week when I know I will have an afternoon free, and the kids could ride the bus home to my house instead."*

In this second conversation, the parents were careful to phrase their responses positively. Their negotiations are almost certainly going to result in an agreement that is clear and acceptable to both.

c. Use "I" Statements and Give Information

When a parent wants to convey anger, frustration, or some other negative emotion, he or she is often tempted to start sentences with "you," as in, "You are so irresponsible!" By turning these into "I" statements and giving some information about your concerns, you will find that you are much more effective, because the other parent can better understand how you feel and why. Consider how much more effective it would be to say, for example, "I get angry when you are late to pick the children up because I have to deal with their disappointment," rather than, "You don't even care enough about the children to show up on time!"

d. Identify Bothersome Behavior and Suggest Solutions

When registering complaints, you will have greater success if you clearly state the problem and suggest solutions.

> **EXAMPLE:** *I get angry when you are late picking up and returning the kids for two reasons. First, it seems to me that you don't think my time is valuable. Second, it doesn't seem to matter to you whether the children get to bed at a reasonable hour on a school night. If you are going to be late, I need you to call me at least an hour before so the children don't sit around waiting for you. If you can't get them back again at the agreed-upon time, I need you to agree that they will always be home at least half an hour before bedtime.*

12. Look to the Future While Learning From the Past

Examining the past can be valuable, but only if you use it to plan for the future. In fact, getting stuck in the past is a common reason for failing to agree about the future.

When starting in on familiar arguments, many parents say, "Oh no! Not this again!" and stop listening for issues or concerns that can be resolved. Instead of rehashing old issues, shift your focus to making the future work better by asking one or two strategic questions.

> **EXAMPLE:** *I remember that in the past your concerns were "A," "B," and "C." Is this still true? If it is, what should we change so that "A," "B," and "C" are no longer issues?*

A realistic and successful parenting agreement will emphasize the things that work well for your family and will try to compensate for the things that don't. For this to happen, you and the other parent must work just as hard to identify things that you do well together as to point out things that are "wrong." When the situation seems especially dismal, remind yourselves of the things you can take credit for, such as:

- how well your children are doing
- how much of the decision-making process you are handling on your own, or
- how much you really agree on about raising your children.

13. Don't Be Thrown Off Course by "Backsliding"

"Backsliding," or changing your mind about things that you've already agreed on, is very common and is not usually a sign of bad faith in negotiations. Rather, backsliding is often a signal that someone is struggling with a difficult issue. If one of you is retreating from what once seemed to be an acceptable resolution of an issue, take the opportunity to:

- reopen the issue
- discuss what doesn't seem right about the resolution
- try to identify the other parent's real concerns, and
- ask what alternative solutions might work better.

14. Conduct an Effective Meeting

Negotiations between parents generally work better when they are structured. The following list of strategies can help your meetings go more smoothly and make your negotiations more likely to result in lasting agreements:

- Allow each other to speak without interruption.
- Don't criticize each other, even while talking about problems or situations you don't want repeated.
- Describe each problem in terms of your reaction (such as, "When you are late, I get angry because the children are disappointed and it seems you don't value my time").
- Use "I" statements (as opposed to "you" accusations).
- Focus on the issues.

15. Expect Success

While some people are naturally optimistic, others tend to see the gloomy side of things. Looking only for problems and threats can be enough to sour almost every negotiation. With practice and conscious effort, however, many people learn to see that challenges and past conflicts offer opportunities to succeed in the future.

People who succeed more often than they fail tend to expect success and to use past mistakes and conflict as opportunities to learn (unpleasant though the experiences may have been). When you expect to succeed, you will work hard to find solutions to your problems. If you expect to fail, you will usually give up looking for solutions, thereby guaranteeing failure.

When you and the other parent are actually making decisions and developing your parenting agreement, you can set your agreement up to succeed if you:

- develop an action plan and assign responsibilities
- find ways to describe what "success" means for your children
- establish how you will know when a problem is really solved, and
- schedule reviews of your parenting plan and make changes when needed.

D. Breaking Through Impasses

Unsolvable disagreements—or impasses—are common during negotiations. In fact, you should probably expect at least one or two serious disagreements during the creation of your parenting agreement. If you hit a dead end, first review the preparation techniques described in Section B, above. If this doesn't help, consider adopting one of these problem-solving strategies.

1. Set the Issue Aside for a While

One of the easiest ways to deal with an impasse is to set the issue aside for awhile. When setting your agenda, consider resolving the easy issues first—the ones on which you and the other parent generally agree. This lets you rack up some successes and helps build momentum for resolving the more difficult issues. As you confront increasingly difficult topics, remind yourselves of your successful negotiations to date. Use the decision-making strategies that worked on the easy issues to tackle the hard ones.

2. Reestablish Trust

Trust is an essential element to effective communication and decision making, and yet trust is usually eroded or lost during separation or divorce. This can create problems for parents trying to negotiate and implement a parenting agreement. Fortunately, there are ways for parents to recapture trust in each other—at least enough to be convinced that the other will fulfill the agreement.

a. Understand the Problem

Some parents confuse trustworthiness with acceptable behavior. If the other parent's lifestyle or career changes do not meet your expectations, this does not necessarily mean that the person is not worthy of your trust. If you define trustworthiness with words such as "reliable" and "honest," and by characteristics such as a love for your children, common decency, and shared values, you may find you are able to trust the other parent again.

b. Measure Trustworthiness

Once you understand the problem, you may be able to resolve your concerns about trustworthiness by describing how you will demonstrate trustworthiness in the parenting relationship. Forcing yourself to define exactly what the other parent can do to regain your trust will go a long way toward helping you overcome impasses.

> **EXAMPLE:** *I am having trouble trusting my children's father because he keeps changing the visiting schedule. To resolve this problem, at a minimum, he would have to call within 72 hours of any change and limit his changes to once a month.*

> **EXAMPLE:** *My trust in our son's mother is gone because she describes her time with him one way, and he says something else. These inconsistencies worry me because I don't know who to believe. She would relieve my anxieties by letting me speak to my son on most of the days when he is with her.*

c. Agree on Simple Tasks Each Parent Must Carry Out

One way for a parent to believe that the other can be trusted to honor a parenting agreement is to identify simple things that each parent can do in a timely and appropriate manner. One example might be filling out Worksheets 1, 2, and 3 in Chapter 3 so that you can complete Worksheet 4 together. Other examples include:

- maintaining an on-time visitation schedule for a month
- scheduling and keeping appointments with teachers to learn of your children's progress in school, or

- entering and completing a substance-abuse rehabilitation program.

For this strategy to work, the tasks must be clear, achievable, and meaningful. State your goals in positive terms by describing the actions that a parent will take, not those the parent will refrain from. For example, you can say that a parent will be on time, rather than that a parent will not be late.

3. Find your "BATNA" or "WATNA"

Good advice for succeeding in negotiations has been around a long time. *Getting to Yes*, by Fisher and Ury (Penguin Books, 1981) suggests you consider your "BATNA"—or Best Alternative To a Negotiated Agreement. And one of mediation's pioneers, John Haynes, suggests identifying your "WATNA"—or Worst Alternative To a Negotiated Agreement.

An example of a BATNA, or best alternative, might be an evaluation and recommendation by a custody evaluator after observing both parents' homes and relationships with their children. This kind of assessment can be very valuable, assuming it does not polarize you further. One way to avoid increasing the conflict after receiving a professional evaluation is to use it in mediation as a means of breaking the deadlock.

One common WATNA to a negotiated parenting agreement is a full-blown court trial. Considering what a court trial involves often proves to be an effective motivator for parents to negotiate an agreement: Seeking a decision by a judge will cost a lot of money, take a lot of time, and heighten conflict. There is also the risk that the judge will make a decision that neither parent likes.

Considering your BATNA and WATNA can help you feel clear about why you want to reach a negotiated solution—in most circumstances, even your BATNA won't be better than reaching an agreement on your own.

4. Focus on Your Strengths

List ways that your current parenting arrangements work. Your list might include items such as:
- shared love for your children
- agreement about house rules and expected standards of behavior for your children
- agreement about the community in which you want your children to grow up
- agreement about what school your children will attend, and

- agreement about what religious training your children will receive.

Each area of agreement strengthens your chance of finding further areas of agreement, and reduces the chance of future conflict.

5. Expand Your Options

One effective strategy for overcoming an impasse is to think creatively. Most problems have a myriad of possible solutions. If, for example, your homes are not too far apart and your conflict is based on one parent's feeling that he or she is not seeing the children enough, consider adding a regular midweek dinner or having the other parent provide after-school care. If your discussions have broken down because one parent wants to move out of the area, consider having both parents move—assuming they can both find jobs.

6. Balance the Power

For any number of reasons, one parent may be at a disadvantage when trying to negotiate with the other. If domestic violence or emotional abuse has been present, then the threat of force or intimidation might be very real. If one parent is articulate and the other is not, the latter parent may have trouble presenting his or her views and interests, or protecting the interests of the children. Also, some parents think they have few options because they fulfill a stereotyped role of "Mother" or "Father."

If these or similar situations are present, consider one of the options below.

a. Enlist the Help of a Mediator or Counselor

Counselors and mediators have different strengths when it comes to balancing power between two individuals. Counselors can offer parents a safe setting within which they can vent their feelings and deal with emotional as well as practical parenting issues. Mediators can support both parents in their efforts to identify—and communicate more effectively about—practical parenting issues. Because mediators also manage the communication process, they can ensure that each parent has enough time to explain his or her position.

b. Enlist the Help of Attorneys

An attorney can represent a parent's interests in negotiations. This is especially helpful when one parent feels incapable of representing himself or herself. If one parent is represented by counsel, then both should be represented if possible. Be aware, however, that once attorneys get involved, parents can quickly lose control over the kinds of decisions that are made, the kinds of resolutions they can consider, and the costs of reaching an agreement.

While increasing numbers of attorneys support their clients through less adversarial proceedings such as mediation, many still feel more comfortable in a courtroom and may steer their clients that way. Chapter 17 has suggestions on how to find attorneys who are willing to approach separation or divorce cases in the least adversarial way possible.

c. Seek Individual Counseling or Therapy

Some parents have never learned how to stand up for themselves in a discussion or while negotiating an agreement. These parents may have trouble dealing with the emotional content of the discussions or the stress associated with the separation or divorce. If emotional issues make your negotiations particularly difficult, you may need individual counseling before, or during the process of, negotiating your parenting agreement.

d. Negotiate Separately

In some situations, especially when domestic violence or emotional abuse has been present, it is best that the parents choose a neutral facilitator and meet with that person separately. This way, each parent can present his or her views, interests, and objectives separately to the mediator or other facilitator. By going back and forth between the parents, the mediator or other facilitator can help both parents avoid arguments, feel like they can express their views freely, and generate a list of issues and possible resolutions.

e. Consider a Highly Structured Parenting Plan

Some parents find it nearly impossible to manage their parenting arrangements without an argument. Sometimes, the only solution to this problem is to create a highly detailed and structured parenting plan that is almost impossible to misunderstand. These agreements ensure that almost nothing is left to chance. This also means that there is little, if any, room for making changes, unless the parents sit down (preferably with a mediator's, counselor's, or attorney's help) to overhaul the agreement.

A CASE IN POINT

Let's consider a specific example and walk through the process of negotiating an agreement to resolve a particular problem.

Exchanges, or the time your child switches from one home to the other, can be difficult for everyone. The reasons why these times are difficult can be complicated. Let's assume that you and the other parent want to negotiate (or renegotiate) how exchanges happen. In addition to making sure that the exchange is as easy as possible, you might also want to get to the point that your child no longer "falls apart" each time he or she goes back and forth between your two homes.

If you are going to reach agreement about how to manage this issue better, you're going to have to start by figuring out what's right and wrong with the situation now. Each of you can be "experts" on this one. Your first step in the negotiating process, then, is to gather information. You can make a list of what each of you does or doesn't like about the exchange.

For some parents, it might be important to make the time and location of the exchange more convenient, or to avoid having an argument during the exchange.

Depending on your child's age, it might also be a good idea to ask him or her for ideas about what might make the exchange go more smoothly. Although you don't want to put your child in the position of having to make the final decisions, asking his or her opinion can be a good idea.

Some children might need help talking about what they do and don't like during an exchange. You can start this conversation by asking your child what they think about or how they feel just before and just after an exchange. You might also ask what they would change—or what should stay the same.

If you need more information about what makes exchanges difficult, there are a lot of good books, and some videos, about how children deal with divorce and what their parents can do to make things easier. (For some information about good resources, check the Bibliography and Additional Resources sections in Chapter 17). If your child's behavior or "falling apart" seems out of proportion or is alarming, ask a therapist or other counselor about the situation and whether you should consider getting help.

When you have some idea about what problems you want to solve, you are ready to think about what kinds of decisions you will need to make. Consider the time of day, where the exchange takes place, who is present, how well the child has been prepared, and how you handle information exchanges with the other parent.

Some common reasons that a transition might be difficult for a child include:

- regular arguing between the adults
- feeling guilty about leaving one parent alone to be with the other
- wishing that the divorce wasn't real, and
- worrying about what one parent will think if the child shows their affection for the other parent or the other parent's new partner.

Some common strategies to make transitions easier include:

- making the transitions happen at "natural" breaks, such as before or after school, as part of a visit to a grandparent or other relative (if these are stress-free), or before or after an outside activity such as a team sport, youth program, or other event
- using notes, emails, faxes, or separate phone calls about school, activities, health, or special events to avoid an argument
- finding new ways to transfer clothes and toys, such as having parents pick up or drop off suitcases while the child is in school
- addressing each parent's lingering anger, sadness, or other unresolved feelings about the divorce through separate therapy or other counseling services.

Professionals recommend a number of different strategies for helping high-conflict families live with a particular parenting plan.

One way to reduce conflict between parents is to try "parallel parenting." With this approach, the child has two clearly defined (and often completely separate) worlds—each defined by one of the parents. Parents then try to make at least some elements of each world consistent (such as following the same daily routines, using the same child care provider, or having at least two or three of the same house rules), no matter where the child is. Parents can use this strategy to lessen the number and intensity of their arguments by spelling out each item in detail and arranging to almost never be in the same place at the same time. The only purpose for the parents to be together would be to renegotiate an element of the agreement, possibly with the help of a mediator, counselor, or attorney.

The parallel parenting approach can work well in the short term while the level of conflict is high. For the long term, however, this arrangement can cause other problems. In cases where the differences between the homes are great, and the animosity between the parents remains extremely high (or is regularly boiling just under the surface), children can feel that they lead two lives—one to please one parent, and one to please the other. When these arrangements become a way of life, the child may feel as though his or her needs are not being seen, respected, or met by either parent. Sometimes, children in this situation will go so far as to develop a completely different way of living and relating to others in each home.

Carla Garrity and Mitchell Baris (*Caught in the Middle*, Lexington Books, 1994) discuss a similar approach that they call "demarcated joint custody." With this approach, each parent is given decision-making authority for separate issues. For example, one parent may make all of the medical care and education-related decisions, and the other might make the decisions about religious training and summer activities. The advantage of this approach is that each parent feels as though he or she has a direct and important role to play in their child's upbringing—while minimizing the chances that either will feel as though the other has crossed over onto his or her turf. The downside, of course, is that not all issues are as cleanly divided as they might seem. If you consider the example described above, you can see that these parents will find it difficult to figure out who can decide about summer school if their child has a special educational aptitude or need.

E. Knowing Where to Get Help and Support

Regular and intense conflict creates significant problems for everyone. Though the long-term hope is that you and the other parent will come to understand how to minimize—or prevent—regular conflict, that process can take time. In the meantime, it can help to learn more about what causes conflict, find new problem-solving strategies, and get hands-on help from trained professionals.

1. Professional Resources

There are a number of professionals to choose from. All are available in the private sector, but an increasing number of courts around the country will order parents to hire the services of one or more of these professionals to help manage or solve custody and visitation disputes. Although the exact titles these professionals go by will vary somewhat in different parts of the country, a little persistence will generally uncover a few of these professionals in your area.

a. Attorney (Matrimonial or Family Law Specialist)

A lawyer who specializes in family or divorce law. Some lawyers in this category practice "collaborative" law. These lawyers help parents make sure their legal rights are protected without escalating the conflict unnecessarily.

b. Attorney for the Child (Minor's Counsel)

A lawyer who specializes in understanding and representing the legal interests of children, especially when the child's parents are involved in intense conflict or have been charged with child physical, emotional, or sexual abuse or child neglect.

c. Child Custody Evaluator (Investigator)

A trained—and usually licensed—mental health professional who specializes in understanding and making recommendations (usually to a court) about what kinds of parenting, visitation, or other decisions will be in the best interests of a particular child.

d. Child Development Specialist

Generally a medical doctor, nurse, nurse practitioner, or mental health professional who has a detailed understanding of:

- how children grow and develop over time

- the effects of a child's physical or mental health on "normal" development, and
- the effects of "environmental factors" such as how the child is parented, experiences with friends, and the school environment.

e. Clinical Social Worker

A licensed mental health professional who is trained in the assessment and treatment of mental health problems and difficulties with relationships.

f. Court-Appointed Special Advocate (CASA)

A person appointed to accompany and represent the interests of a child through all phases (generally) of juvenile court cases related to dependency (a court considering whether to limit or end a parent's rights to raise their child), adoption, or other planning for placement in the foster care system.

g. Divorce Counselor

A mental health professional who specializes in working with adults and/or children experiencing divorce or the end of a similarly committed relationship.

h. Exchange Supervisor

A person who is appointed by a court to be present when parents exchange their children for visits. Depending on the situation, this can be a friend or relative, a professional, or a service offered by a supervised visitation center. The primary purpose is to make sure that no harm comes to anyone at the time of an exchange. Another reason to have an exchange supervisor is to help a child ease the transition from one parent to the other—especially if the child is reluctant to visit, or if conflict tends to be high at the exchange.

i. Guardian Ad Litem

A person, often a lawyer, appointed by a court to make decisions affecting a child's best interests, health, education, or welfare.

j. Marriage Counselor (Marriage, Family, and Child Counselor)

A mental health professional who specializes in helping couples address individual and relationship issues in a way that might preserve the marriage or otherwise committed relationship.

k. Mediator (Child Custody, Divorce)

A trained professional (often either a mental health professional or lawyer) who helps parents or guardians (and sometimes the entire family) address and reach mutually acceptable agreements resolving some or all of the issues surrounding separation, divorce, or renegotiating parenting agreements. This may or may not include money and property issues and filing court papers to get agreements recorded as legally enforceable court orders.

l. Paralegal

A trained professional who does not give legal advice or represent people in court but is familiar with routine legal matters such as how to prepare certain types of forms or research certain legal issues.

m. Parent Educator

A trained education or mental health professional who teaches classes or provides individual instruction to parents about child development, parenting, conflict resolution, or other matters.

n. Psychiatrist (Child, Adult)

A licensed medical doctor who is trained in diagnosing and treating mental health disorders and can prescribe medication.

o. Psychologist (Child, Adult)

A licensed mental health professional who may provide counseling support for individuals, couples, children, or families, or conduct assessments of adults or children (including conducting and interpreting psychological tests).

p. Social Worker

A mental health professional who provides counseling and practical support to individuals, couples, or families. This might include referrals to other professionals or community resources, or screening to decide whether someone is eligible to receive certain benefits.

q.   Special Master

A trained professional (usually a lawyer, mental health professional, accountant, or other professional) appointed by the court to use special expertise to decide certain types of issues. The special master's decisions are generally binding on the parties as if they were a court order. If one party wants to challenge the decision, a court hearing is required.

r.   Visitation Arbitrator

A trained professional (often a court employee, lawyer, or mediator) who is either appointed by a court or chosen by the parties to decide disputes about how to arrange visits.

s.   Visitation Supervisor

A person appointed by a court to be present any time a particular parent spends time with his or her child. Generally, this type of appointment is made only when there are concerns about a child's safety when he or she visits with that parent. These appointments might also be made, however, if a court wants to find out more about how well a parent and child relate to each other, or if a child is not used to being with one parent who has been absent for a long time.

2.   Community and Other Resources

In addition to professionals available through the private sector, many community organizations offer other helpful resources, such as:

a.   Anger Management/Batterer's Treatment Programs

These programs are focused on helping people who have committed domestic violence. Generally, participants have been convicted of a crime of domestic violence and are ordered to complete the program as part of their probation or other court sentence.

b.   Divorce Support Groups (Parents and/or Children)

These groups can help parents and children deal with issues concerning separation, divorce, or the end of a committed relationship. Some programs have a set curriculum, while others allow participants to decide what they will discuss. The programs can be open-ended (drop-in, voluntary participation, or court-ordered for a certain length of time), or operate for set periods of time (such as three, six, or 12 months) and lead to a "graduation" certificate.

c.   Legal Information Clinics or Help Centers

This is where people can go for access to free or low-cost legal advice or information about their legal rights, how to start or handle a court case, the court process, how to fill out and file court forms, or other similar issues.

d.   Parent Education

These programs give parents detailed information about child development, effective parenting skills, conflict resolution, or other parenting-related subjects.

e.   Parent Orientation

This is a brief class or session (often less than six hours) that lets parents know about the court, mediation, evaluation, supervised visitation, or other process they will be going through as a result of their custody, visitation, dependency, or other dispute.

f.   Twelve-Step or Other Substance-Abuse Programs

These programs help people with alcohol, drug, or other substance-abuse issues understand and find new ways to manage these problems. Attendance might be ordered by the court, drop-in, or voluntarily agreed to as part of a marital settlement, mediation, or other agreement.

g.   Visitation Arbitrators

These are often court employees assigned to make quick decisions about how to handle a particular problem surrounding the visit, such as what time a child will be picked up or returned following a weekend or vacation visit.

h.   Visitation or Visitation Exchange Supervisors

This organization provides trained staff members to supervise visits or provide a safe place for parents to exchange a child for a visit. ■

Part II

Your Parenting Agreement

CHAPTER

5

Building Your Agreement

Parenting agreements have come a long way from the days of "sole custody awarded to the mother with reasonable visitation for the father." These types of agreements frequently resulted in problems because:

- The noncustodial parent in a sole custody/reasonable visitation arrangement often had little or no parental role.
- Vague agreements are frequently disputed and often lead to arguments or court battles over what constitutes "reasonable" visitation.
- Parents denied custody and given only minimum amounts of time with their children have little incentive to maintain contact with their children or to pay child support.

Agreements today are usually more detailed and comprehensive. This means more work for you, particularly at the beginning, as you try to resolve issues you probably never even thought about before. Keep in mind, however, that if you and the other parent can develop a thoughtful plan that works for both of you, it will eventually allow you to move on with your lives. Done properly, with your children's interest as the top priority, it can also be something that will benefit your children and enable them to develop and thrive in their new family arrangements.

A. Where to Begin

To help you approach this task, the sample parenting agreement in this book is divided into four sections:

1. Basic Elements (Chapter 6)
2. Finishing Touches (Chapter 7)
3. Serious Issues (Chapter 8)
4. Special Circumstances (Chappter 9)

These sections prioritize the issues you need to address. You can focus on the most important matters first and then, when you're ready, move on to other areas. The categories are also helpful if you need to go back and change your agreement, or if you already have an existing agreement and simply need to modify it because of a change in circumstance.

If this is your first agreement, you probably want to start with the Basic Elements. This section covers ten issues that most parents need to address immediately in a separation or divorce. Finishing Touches has the next level of detail parents need to round out their agreement, often af-

ter they have lived with their changed circumstances for a while and figured out what works. Serious Issues includes topics that some parents may need to address in their first agreement, like domestic violence and substance abuse. For others, these topics may never be relevant to their situation. The same is true for Special Circumstances. When you negotiate the agreement, you can go through the issues in the order presented, or you can skip around and tackle the easiest issues first. The vast majority of parents who successfully negotiate parenting agreements handle the less-controversial issues first.

In some cases, the agreement may have more detail in a topic area than you are ready to address at the beginning. That's okay. Just complete what you need to start your new separate parenting arrangements. You can always come back and add to the agreement when you are ready. A parenting agreement is usually built over time.

As you fill out the agreement, you can select one or more of the options listed or you can make your own solutions. If you have an issue that is not covered in the agreement, use the same format to describe the issue and your solution. If you have more than one child, you may make different decisions for each child. In that case, use the blank lines to record your different decisions, or attach additional sheets. We suggest you put an "X" in the space to the left of each item on the parenting agreement that you want to address in your agreement. Then put an "X" to identify all options you want to include in that portion of your agreement. When you have finished the entire agreement, go back and number the issues and letter the options you want to include in your agreement.

You will work through the agreement most efficiently if you:

- have Worksheets 1 through 4 from Chapter 3 close at hand (for each issue, refer to the "Worksheet Cross-Reference" chart)
- make at least six copies of the blank parenting agreement
- give the other parent two agreements and keep two for yourself
- complete one copy as you negotiate with the other parent
- write or type your final agreement on one copy, and
- get outside help when you need it.

Keep in mind that how you decide certain issues (such as where the children live, health insurance, and outside activities) may depend in part on how financial matters between you and the other parent are resolved. See Chapter 10, Child Support, Alimony, and Jointly Owned Property, for an overview of some of these topics.

Finally, a word to the wise. Try to pace yourselves in this process. Negotiate your agreement, sit with it for a while (a few days, or even weeks), and then reread it to make sure it's something you can live with.

B. Cooperate! Cooperate! Cooperate!

It is essential that you and the other parent set aside your differences as you plan for your children's future. Ideally, you will find a way to trust each other. For most parents, this is hardest during the first weeks or months following a separation or divorce. Fortunately, feelings of anger and pain usually diminish over time. The more you and the other parent can keep your eyes on the "prize" (to create a workable, child-focused parenting agreement), the better off you will be.

Likewise, keep in mind that the first agreement you negotiate will probably not be your last. As you and your children's needs and interests evolve over time, your agreement will likely need to change as well. This knowledge can make it easier to negotiate your agreement. It may take time and changes to the agreement before it becomes clear what kind of agreement makes the most sense for you, the other parent, and your children

Most parents find that settling into a new life after separation or divorce makes it easier to untangle their "couple" issues from their parenting issues. Regardless of how you

feel right now, keep in mind that many parents, feeling just the way you do, have found solutions that benefit everyone—at least in the long run.

C. Get Outside Help

Negotiating and completing a parenting agreement can be difficult and complicated. Some of the more complex issues that can arise are covered in Chapters 12 through 17. If you need more help, Chapter 17 has information on how to do your own research or get help from other books, professionals, and various information sources.

The parenting agreement in this book does not conform to any specific court's filing requirements. In some jurisdictions, you can attach your completed worksheet to the court's standard form and it will be included in your court order. If you are getting a divorce or legal separation, you must check with your local court, the law library, or a forms service, paralegal, or attorney to find out whether your agreement must be prepared in a special way to be filed with the court.

In addition, because your parenting decisions may have significant legal consequences, consider having a family law or matrimonial attorney review your agreement. The attorney can make sure your agreement conforms to your state's laws regarding child custody and visitation, that it says what you want it to say, and that it accomplishes your objectives.

Your agreement, by itself, will not be enforceable the way a business contract is enforceable. However, an attorney can help you turn the agreement into an enforceable court order.

D. Keep Your Agreement Current

Few parents negotiate a single agreement that stands, unchanged, until their children reach adulthood. In fact, many parents make at least one major change in their parenting arrangements within the first three years after separation or divorce. Changes might also be appropriate if a parent moves, if work schedules change significantly, or if a child wants to live with the other parent.

The agreement in this book covers the broadest spectrum of issues that might be addressed in a parenting agreement. Some of these issues may not be relevant to you now or ever; some may become relevant over time. For example, if you have preschool children, you may not want to spend time now deciding about owning and operating a motor vehicle. Similarly, if neither parent is in a new relationship, planning for how to handle new partners may not make sense. Both of these issues, however, might become important later.

You and the other parent should periodically review your agreement to see if changes are necessary. Issue 25, Making Changes, lets you build a review schedule into your agreement.

Also, keep this book handy for when you want to make changes. Your goal is to create a workable parenting agreement now, and to anticipate the need for changes as time goes on. Agreements that contemplate future changes are better able to respond to your family's changing needs, circumstances, or concerns. The earlier you address a request for a change, the greater chance you have of keeping conflict to a minimum. ■

CHAPTER
6

Basic Elements

In this chapter, we go over the most basic provisions for a parenting agreement. If you are in the beginning stages of a separation or divorce, or if this is your first parenting agreement, you may want to start with an agreement that covers only these ten most basic issues. Figuring out these essentials might provide enough structure to allow you and the other parent to share and divide your responsibilities at first. It probably won't hold you for long, but it could get you through the first stage of your separation or divorce.

Depending on your circumstances, there may be other issues you need to address right away, such as domestic violence or substance abuse. Read through the issues covered in Chapters 7 through 9 (Finishing Touches, Serious Issues, and Special Circumstances). If any of the issues in these other chapters are relevant to your situation, consider including them in this first agreement.

As you work through the issues and options below, you will find references to questions on the worksheets included in Chapter 3. If you haven't yet completed those, you'll need to do it now.

If you need an arrangement to hold you over temporarily, you can start by deciding whether the children will have one primary residence or alternate between the two homes. You can agree to:

- **One primary residence.** With this option, the children spend more time with one parent. For example, you could agree that the children live with one parent during the week, and the other parent on weekends or alternating weekends; or
- **Alternating homes.** With this option, the children spend approximately equal amounts of time with both parents. For example, you could agree that the children alternate weeks, or half-weeks, in each parent's home.

Include as much detail as you are ready to provide at this point. Keep in mind that this first agreement won't be your last. Once you and the other parent are ready to establish a more long-term schedule, you will need to come back to this issue and specify the arrangements in more detail.

A. Issue 1: Where Our Children Will Live

In most cases, deciding where the children will live is the most important issue parents must resolve. It is also one of the most complicated subjects you will have to work out. If you are not ready to figure out the details for your children's living arrangements, you can start with an agreement that addresses only the most basic decisions. Section 1, below, offers a short-term alternative for where the children will live for people who need a temporary arrangement. If you are ready to tackle the issue on a more permanent basis, skip ahead to Section 2, below.

1. Short-Term Provision

#_____ **Where Our Children Will Live**

_____ Our children shall live primarily with _____ [parent] and live with

_____ [other parent] as follows [specify; include days and times of exchanges if possible]:

_____

_____

_____

_____ Our children will alternate between our homes as follows [specify as much detail as possible]:

2. Long-Term Provision

#_____   **Where Our Children Will Live**

_____ Our children will alternate living in each parent's home as follows:

___ They will live primarily with _____ and with _____ on:

___ Alternating weekends from _____ to _____ (give days and times if possible)

___ During the week on _____ (day(s) of the week) from _____ to _____

_____ Overnight

___ They will live primarily with _____ during the school year and with _____ during the summer months.

During the time they are living primarily with one parent, they will live with the other parent on:

___ Alternating weekends from _____ to _____ (give days and times if possible)

___ During the week on _____ (day(s) of the week) from _____ to _____

___ Overnight

_____ The children will live in each parent's home for approximately the same amount of time, and will change homes:

___ Every ___ days

___ Every ___ weeks

___ Every ___ months

___ Other _____ _____

_____ Our children will not live primarily with either parent, but with _____ instead.

Our children will spend time with _____ (parent's name) as follows:

___ Alternating weekends from _____ to _____ (give days and times if possible)

___ During the week on _____ (day(s) of the week) from _____ to _____

___ Overnight

And with _____ (parent's name) as follows:

___ Alternating weekends from _____ to _____ (give days and times if possible)

___ During the week on _____ (day(s) of the week) from _____ to _____

___ Overnight

_____ Our children will live in one home, and each parent will take turns living there:

___ Every ___ days

___ Every ___ weeks

___ Every ___ months

___ Other _____

_____ Our children will live at _____ school

and spend time with each of us as follows [specify; include days and times of exchanges]:

_____

_____

_____ We further agree that [specify]:

_____

_____

_____

Once you and the other parent are ready to establish a long-term schedule for your children's living arrangements, you will need to be specific about how the arrangements will work. Ultimately, your goal should be to have your children spend as much time as possible with each parent, without ignoring their needs for stability, routine, and emotional and physical safety. This can be challenging if domestic violence, emotional abuse, or child abuse have been issues in the past. (See Chapter 8, Serious Issues, for situations involving abuse.) It can also be difficult if a parent and child have little or no relationship, or if the children are old enough to have their own desires and schedules to consider.

In evaluating the options below, consider:
- the ages, needs, wishes, and temperaments of your children
- the distance between your homes
- available transportation
- what you can afford, and
- how well you and the other parent work together.

With a little creativity, you should be able to come up with several possible solutions, each presenting advantages and disadvantages.

AVOID CREATING A "VISITING" PARENT

Sometimes, changing the way you view the parenting agreement and living arrangement is as simple as changing the words you use. In *Mom's House, Dad's House*, by Dr. Isolina Ricci (Macmillan Publishing, 1998), the author recommends that parents and children describe the time spent with each parent as "living" with that parent. Furthermore, she points out that when parents and children describe their arrangements to others, they should acknowledge that they have two families, one with each parent. If at all possible, avoid the notion that children live with one parent and just visit the other. By making one parent the everyday parent and one parent the visiting parent, you run the risk that you and your children will either resent or exploit the lopsided roles and relationships that follow.

"Everyday" parents are sometimes viewed (and often view themselves) as the one responsible for the day-to-day realities of child rearing. As a result, it is easy to assume that the everyday parent is the only real parent. Some everyday parents prefer to control all substantive aspects of their child's life. Others feel overwhelmed and taken advantage of because they miss out on relaxation times with the kids, especially if the children live with their other parent on weekends and holidays.

"Visiting" parents are sometimes accused of becoming the fun or party parent. The reasons some visiting parents adopt this role are as varied as the people who live with these arrangements. Some visiting parents are so starved for time with their children that they try to cram every conceivable activity into short periods of time. Some parents miss the giving that is part of daily caretaking, and compensate with gifts that are more frequent, more expensive, and sometimes problematic.

Although no one can fault parents who seldom see their children for wanting to make every minute count, their relationships with their children will be far more balanced and fulfilling if they can intersperse fun activities with the routines of everyday life. Familiar, daily routines often provide an opening for conversations about thoughts and feelings. If all visits are filled with activities, the parent and children will have few opportunities to "talk," and are apt to drift apart. As a result, visiting parents often become "special," but less significant, influences in their children's lives.

In Issue 9, option e, we discuss the Parent A/Parent B method for resolving impasses about custody issues. If you find that you reach an impasse on where the children will live, jump ahead and look at that discussion. Essentially, the Parent A/Parent B method asks you to first assign parental roles to hypothetical parents and then examine the circumstances to determine which of you would best fit each role.

ISSUE 1 CROSS-REFERENCES

Worksheet	Questions
Worksheet 1	3, 5
Worksheet 2	1, 4, 5, 7, 8
Worksheet 3	2, 3, 4, 6, 8
Worksheet 4	1, 3, 4, 6, 8, 9, 10, 15

a. One Primary Residence

For many children, designating one home as the primary place that children live makes sense. Joan B. Kelly, Ph.D., has developed a comprehensive array of visitation plans for a primary residence arrangement, including variations for school-age children, infants, and toddlers. These plans relate to the routine schedule each week, without regard to holidays or other vacation periods. The discussion includes a description of the amount of time spent with the noncustodial parent (NCP), and the comments parents have made about these plans.

- **Alternating weekends (Friday 6 p.m. to Sunday 6 p.m.).** This arrangement allows four overnights in 28 days; the 12 days between contacts with the NCP can be too long for many children; the NCP-child relationship diminishes in importance to the child; the NCP is not involved in school or academic/achievement activities; in addition, the custodial parent has little time "off duty."
- **Alternating weekends (Friday 6 p.m. to Monday a.m.).** This option allows six overnights in 28 days. It allows the NCP to have a larger weekend block of time with the child, allows the NCP to take the child to school on Monday, necessitates fewer transitions for the child, and provides less opportunity for conflict between parents.

- **Alternating weekends (Friday 6 p.m. to Sunday 6 p.m.), weekly midweek visit (Wednesday 5 p.m. to 8 p.m.).** This arrangement allows four overnights in 28 days but provides NCP-child contact at least every seven days. The three-hour visit on Wednesdays can be "rushed," not allowing enough time for homework; and the transition back into the custodial parent's home each Wednesday can be difficult.
- **Alternating weekends (Friday 6 p.m. to Sunday 6 p.m.), weekly midweek overnight (Wednesday 5 p.m. to Thursday, start of school).** This arrangement allows eight overnights in 28 days, provides no more than six days between visits with the NCP, and allows the NCP to maintain involvement with homework assignments and school activities. The transitions at school times help avoid conflict. The NCP has an opportunity for bedtime and morning rituals on school days, and the custodial parent has midweek evenings off duty.
- **Alternating weekends (Friday 6 p.m. to Monday at school), weekly midweek overnight (Wednesday 5 p.m. to Thursday 7 a.m.).** This arrangement allows ten overnights in 28 days, provides no more than six days between visits with the NCP, and allows longer weekends for the NCP.

For infants and toddlers, where the child has a minimal relationship with the noncustodial parent, the arrangements may be quite different. For example, you might consider:

- **Two to three weekly contacts for two to three hours each; Saturday or Sunday visits gradually expanded to six hours each as the child gains security; overnight visits added approximately six to 12 months after visitation starts as child is secure.**

Other single primary residence options are as follows:

- **Live in home "A" except for alternating weekends, alternating holidays, and a portion of the summer.** This option allows some geographic distance and accommodates parents who don't get along too well, or children who don't want or need more frequent contact.
- **Live in home "A" except for midweek overnights, most weekends, alternating holidays, and a portion of the summer.** This allows for some geographic distance between the homes, but may require both parents to live in the same school district.

- **Live in home "A" and visit other parent for short or day-time visits only.** This accommodates extreme geographic distance or situations where violence, abuse, or neglect require limited and/or supervised visitation.

b.   Dual Residences

Some families prefer to have their children live with each parent for extended periods of time, or to divide their time almost equally between the two homes. Again, there are many possible variations. These living arrangements require extensive coordination between the parents and a willingness to encounter each other and any new partners. Dr. Kelly's examples of this type of arrangement follow, together with other variations on this theme.

- **Monday afternoon to Wednesday a.m. with Parent A, Wednesday p.m. to Friday a.m. with Parent B, alternating weekends, Friday to Monday a.m. with each parent.** This arrangement allows 14 overnights per 28 days with each parent; all transitions can be managed through school or day care; the routine for weekday overnights remains fixed.
- **Monday a.m. to Wednesday a.m. with Parent A, Wednesday a.m. to Friday a.m. with Parent B, each weekend is split (Friday p.m. to Saturday p.m. with one parent, Saturday p.m. to Monday a.m. with other parent).** This arrangement allows 14 overnights per 28 days; the time apart from either parent never exceeds three days; transitions are more frequent.

For infants or toddlers who are attached to both parents:

- **Tuesday and Thursday 4 p.m. to 7 p.m. and Saturday 10 a.m. to Sunday 10 a.m. / or Tuesday 4 p.m. to Wednesday 9 a.m., Thursday 4 p.m. to 7 p.m. and Saturday 5 p.m. to Sunday 5 p.m.** This arrangement allows frequent contact throughout the week; overnights become a regular activity.

Other dual-residence arrangements are as follows:

- **Children alternate living in home "A" and "B" at approximately equal intervals such as every week, two weeks, a month, or six months.** This requires homes in close proximity, especially if children are school age.
- **Children live in home "A" during the week and in home "B" on the weekends.** This option allows somewhat more geographic distance.
- **During the school term, the children live in home "A" during the week and in home "B" on the weekends. In the summer, the children live in home "B" during the week and in home "A" on weekends.** This option will work only if there is a moderate geographic distance between the parents' homes, and it won't work if the children attend school year-round.

c.   Children Live With Someone Other Than a Parent

For some families, it makes sense for the children to live with an adult other than a parent. This third adult may also have custody of the children or may be appointed their guardian.

If you use this option, make sure your parenting agreement specifies the arrangements. The more specific you are, the more everyone will understand their responsibilities to the children and to each other. For example, choosing to have the children live with a grandparent might be a good idea if the parents are struggling to finance separate apartments, looking for jobs, and have substance-abuse problems. Just be sure to specify how each parent will maintain a relationship with the children.

d.   Bird Nesting

Bird nesting means that the children remain in one home and the parents alternate moving in and out. The parents might have separate homes, sleep at a friend's house, or stay with a relative.

Bird nesting is not chosen often, but it can be good for infants or very young children in particular. It requires an unusual degree of coordination and cooperation between the parents and can be expensive if each parent maintains another home. And, you must be clear about who will make decisions about the layout, furnishing, and routines of the household.

THE IMPORTANCE OF THE FATHER-CHILD RELATIONSHIP

It used to be quite common that, after a separation or divorce, fathers were minimally involved in, or absent from, their children's lives. Some reasons given to explain this phenomenon include:

- the bias in the legal system to award the mother custody
- fathers feeling powerless to control how their children are raised when they live with the mother
- fathers resenting being treated as the "cash cow" ("mother stays, father pays")
- vague court orders for "reasonable" visitation, allowing custodial mothers considerable latitude to limit the amount of time fathers spend with their children, therefore eroding the parent-child relationship as contact becomes increasingly limited and sporadic
- men earning more in the workplace, making them less available for full-time parenting arrangements.

Researchers have tried to assess the impact on children when one parent, generally the father, leaves the home and does not maintain significant ongoing relationships. Their findings range from intensified separation anxiety, poor grades or substantially below-ability performance, aggression toward parents, and diminished self-concepts to long-term anger, depression, and juvenile and adult criminal behavior.

Fathers' rights advocates, as well as joint custody advocates, insist that many of these problems would be resolved if both parents had a substantial role in their children's lives—especially after a separation or divorce. Today, more fathers share custody of their children, and there is a growing awareness of the importance of the father's continuing role in a child's life after a separation or divorce.

"A PARENT'S MOVE OUT OF THE AREA CREATES SPECIAL CHALLENGES."

For some parents, staying in the same community, or nearby, is difficult. For example, it may be difficult for parents to encounter each other around town, work may be hard to find, a parent may want to live closer to his or her extended family, a new partner or spouse may need or want to move out of the area, or the parent may choose to attend school elsewhere. Whenever a parent plans to move, your children's living arrangements and need to remain connected with each parent must be considered carefully.

The legal issues can be especially difficult as well. In thinking about these issues, state laws—and sometimes court decisions—take into account the children's current living arrangements, the quality of their relationship with the other parent, and their connections to other family members and the community. Depending on where you live, these issues might be governed by state law, by recent court decisions, or both. Regardless of where the guidelines for making these decisions come from, when the parents cannot agree, these issues are often decided by a court.

Sometimes the law or a court will allow the parent who has the children most of the time to choose where they will live, and how far away from the other parent the children will move. Other states require a parent who wants the children to move someplace that is far away from their other parent to prove that it is in the children's best interests to do so. Alternatively, state laws may require that the children live primarily with the parent who is staying unless the moving parent can show that a change in custody might be harmful.

One way or another, courts can force parents to either stay in their original communities (or that general area), or to leave the children with the parent who will remain.

When these issues become especially contentious, courts often turn to experts to help them gather the information they need to make a decision. This may mean that the family will be required to meet with a social worker, counselor, or another professional who will evaluate the situation and then advise the judge about what he or she feels is best for the children. Sometimes the court will appoint a lawyer to represent just the children. This is often the case when the judge either cannot tell which parent is seeing their children's best interests clearly, or the judge decides that neither parent is effectively representing their children's interests in the legal battle.

As always, if you and the other parent can work out these issues between you, your children will be better able to handle the changes that follow. You will find more information on several important aspects of this question in other sections of this book. For example, you will find information on:

- recording your agreement regarding any moves in Chapter 9, Issue 33
- helping your children to stay in touch with a distant parent in Chapter 9, Issue 37
- resolving your conflict outside of court in Chapter 11
- understanding your children's needs in Chapter 13
- state and federal laws in Chapter 16, and
- working with the various professionals that you choose or that the court appoints in Chapter 17.

B. Issue 2: Medical, Dental, and Vision Care

Most parents want their children to be able to receive competent medical care at a reasonable cost. Making this happen, however, might not always be easy. Use your parenting agreement to specify the details for medical care, including:

- your children's medical providers
- who has authority to make decisions about your children's medical care
- how you will exchange medications your children take
- how much medical information you will share (such as every cold and scrape or only major illnesses and accidents), and
- who will take the children for their regular checkups.

#_____ **Medical, Dental, and Vision Care**

_____ Our children's medical, dental, and vision care providers will be [choose one]:

_____ We will use only the following health care providers:

_____ [medical]
_____ [dental]
_____ [vision]

_____ We will each choose health care providers. We will exchange names, addresses, phone numbers, and releases so that our providers can share records and information.

_____ _____ [parent] will see to it that our children receive their routine care.

_____ Our children's special health care needs will be met as follows [specify]:

_____
_____
_____

_____ In a medical emergency [choose one]:

_____ Either parent may seek medical treatment and must inform the other parent as soon as possible thereafter.

_____ Either parent may seek medical treatment, except for the following procedures or interventions:

_____
_____

_____ _____ [parent] is the only person who may seek medical treatment.

_____ If our children develop an ongoing medical condition or have other special health care concerns, we will assure consistency in their care as follows [choose all that apply]:

_____ We will share all medical records.

_____ We will include the medications with our children as they travel between our homes.

_____ We will each fill all prescriptions and dispense the medications when caring for our children.

_____ We will exchange written instructions on needed care.

_____ We will each keep whatever physical supports or enhancements our children need in our home.

_____ Our children will receive the following dental care [specify]:

_____
_____
_____

_____ Our children will receive the following vision care [specify]:

_____
_____
_____

_____ We further agree that [specify]:

_____
_____
_____

ISSUE 2 CROSS-REFERENCES

Worksheet	Questions
Worksheet 3	4, 8
Worksheet 4	3, 6

1. Choose Health Care Providers

When parents live in the same city or relatively close to each other, they often agree on the primary medical, dental, or mental health care provider for their children. If you and the other parent live further away from each other, however, it makes sense for each of you to find providers for your children so that they can receive care wherever they are. Exchange names, addresses, phone numbers, and releases of the separate providers so they can exchange records and information. Your doctor should be able to provide you with a release.

2. Routine and Special Care

Specify who has the authority to seek routine care for your children, such as immunizations, annual physical exams, and blood tests. Parents often agree to let either parent handle routine care without first discussing it with the other parent. Some circumstances, however, such as immunizations, require coordination to avoid duplication or other problems.

You also need to specify how any special medical, dental, or vision care needs, such as hospitalization, surgery, medication, or experimental treatment, will be met. Most parents who share legal custody (or joint custody in states that do not differentiate between legal and physical custody) require parents to discuss and agree before allowing this level of treatment. (See Chapter 2, Section D for definitions of joint, legal, and physical custody.)

3. Emergency Care

Clearly state how much authority each parent has to seek treatment in a medical emergency. If the children spend a fair amount of time with both of you, you will probably want to allow either parent to obtain emergency treatment without first consulting the other. If you choose to restrict a parent's authority to seek emergency treatment, the parent who must make, or be consulted about, emergency decisions must include a medical release during visits with the other parent, or be available at a moment's notice.

4. Ongoing Medical, Dental, or Vision Care

Some children have medical or physical conditions (such as diabetes, a physical disability, poor vision, or periodontal disease) that require attention for months, years, or even the rest of their lives. In these situations, you must decide whether medications, physical supports, or enhancements (such as crutches or prosthetics) will be kept in each home or will travel with the children.

C. Issue 3: Disparaging Remarks

#_____ **Disparaging Remarks**

_____ We will refrain from making disparaging remarks about the other parent, his/her partner, and his/her chosen life directly to our children or within our children's hearing.

_____ We further agree that [specify]:

_____

_____

_____

You won't help your situation or make things easier for your children if you criticize the other parent, or his or her new partner or lifestyle. However critical children may be of their parents, most children love and revere them and don't want to hear negative remarks.

A parent who makes disparaging remarks about the other in the children's hearing creates two serious problems. First, the critical parent weakens the children's relationship with the other parent. This can make it difficult for the children to live with the other parent and rely on them for care and companionship. Second, the critical parent conveys, quite clearly, that their children cannot express love or admiration for the other parent in that home. Children often grow to resent and distrust the critical parent for interfering in the children's other important relationships.

You can read Chapter 4 for more information on handling high-conflict situations and understanding the negative and alienating effects that these types of behaviors can have on parent-child relationships.

ISSUE 3 CROSS-REFERENCES

Worksheet	Questions
Worksheet 1	4
Worksheet 2	6, 7, 8
Worksheet 3	5, 6, 7, 11
Worksheet 4	3, 4, 5, 7, 12, 15

D. Issue 4: Consistency in Raising Children

#_____ **Consistency in Raising Children**

_____ The standards for discipline in each of our homes will be as follows [choose all that apply]:

    _____ We will abide by the same discipline standards.

    _____ The following behavior rules will apply in both homes:

    _____

    _____

    _____

_____ If either of us has a discipline issue with our children, that parent will explain the issue and response to the other so we can be consistent in our discipline.

_____ If our children complain about discipline in the other parent's home, we will encourage them to talk about it with the other parent.

_____ If we cannot agree on discipline standards that will apply in both homes, we will make an effort to understand and respect the other's right to establish behavior rules for our children.

_____ We further agree that [specify]:

_____

_____

_____

Children need their parents to be as consistent as possible in approving or disapproving their conduct—whether the parents live together or apart. When parents separate or divorce, this is hard to achieve. As a start, you and the other parent might agree on certain daily routines, such as meal times, bedtimes, and finishing homework before playing.

As a rule, children are remarkably flexible. They know their parents are different people, and they can usually handle the variations in each home. Some of the differences between your two homes can be dealt with by saying, "Yes, at the other house you are allowed to do that, but I do things differently." Others cannot be dismissed as easily and require the parents try to reach a common ground. If your parenting styles are vastly different, consider the additional options in Issue 34, discussed in Chapter 9.

ISSUE 4 CROSS-REFERENCES

Worksheet	Questions
Worksheet 1	3, 4, 6, 7
Worksheet 2	3, 4, 5, 6, 7, 8
Worksheet 3	3, 5, 7, 8, 10
Worksheet 4	3, 4, 5, 6, 7

1. Establish a Few Common Rules for Both Homes

Even when parents approach raising children differently, they can maintain a minimum level of consistency by agreeing on a few rules that will be enforced in both homes. Be creative—find issues that matter to both of you and that you agree on. No two people disagree on absolutely everything. For example, you might agree on permitted snack foods, television shows (or the number of hours each day the children can watch television), or requiring the children to show respect for both parents.

2. Exchange Information About Behavior and Discipline

Parents can avoid problems by talking to each other about behavior and disciplinary issues. If you don't, your children will find the chinks in the unified front you may try to maintain and will play one of you off the other.

With this option, each parent lets the other know about any behavior or discipline problems, and what actions the parent took to deal with the situation. In this way, you and the other parent can support each other, even if you might have handled the situation differently.

3. Acknowledge Your Differences

Along the lines of "variety is the spice of life," you can accept that you have different child-rearing styles. These differences can be difficult for your children. Encourage them to describe what bothers them and to talk to the other parent directly to work out a resolution. If you agree to this arrangement, you must also agree to let go—that is, not tell the other person how to handle situations in his or her home.

E. Issue 5: Holidays

#_____ **Holidays**

_____ This agreement covers the following holidays:

_____   _____
_____   _____
_____   _____

_____ Holiday visits will begin at _____ [time] and will end at _____ [time].

_____ We will adopt an odd year/even year plan, as follows:

_____ In odd years, our children will be with _____ [parent] for these holidays:

_____   _____
_____   _____

and with _____ [parent] for these holidays:

_____   _____
_____   _____

In even years, the reverse will be true.

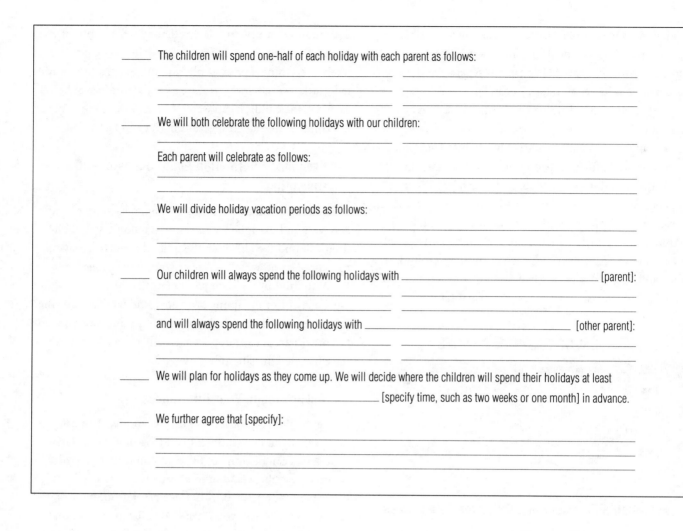

_____ The children will spend one-half of each holiday with each parent as follows:

_____   _____
_____   _____
_____   _____

_____ We will both celebrate the following holidays with our children:

Each parent will celebrate as follows:

_____ We will divide holiday vacation periods as follows:

_____ Our children will always spend the following holidays with _____ [parent]:

and will always spend the following holidays with _____ [other parent]:

_____ We will plan for holidays as they come up. We will decide where the children will spend their holidays at least
_____ [specify time, such as two weeks or one month] in advance.

_____ We further agree that [specify]:

Deciding who your children will spend holidays with can be difficult unless you can think beyond one year. Remember that every holiday comes around every year.

First, make a list of all holidays and other occasions important to your family, including extended school breaks and holidays you celebrate because of your faith, cultural heritage, or family traditions. Then consider the following possible schedules:

- alternate on an odd-year and even-year basis
- split extended holidays in half
- celebrate certain holidays twice
- assign the same holidays to the same parent every year, or
- decide how your children will spend the holidays as each holiday approaches.

ISSUE 5 CROSS-REFERENCES

Worksheet	Questions
Worksheet 1	3, 5, 8
Worksheet 2	1, 4, 5
Worksheet 3	3, 4, 5, 6
Worksheet 4	3, 4, 11, 12, 15

1. Alternate on an Odd-Year/Even-Year Basis

This option assigns certain holidays to each parent in odd years and then reverses the schedule in even years. For example, your children might spend Thanksgiving with you in 2005, and with their other parent in 2006. This plan is comforting because parents know they will never miss spending a holiday with their children more than one year in a row. By contrast, this schedule can be frustrating if a particular holiday is meaningful for only one parent.

2. Divide Holiday Celebrations in Half

Some parents divide the actual holiday celebration (and associated vacation days) in half so that their children can spend part of the time with each parent. This option allows everyone to see each other on the "big day" but requires advance planning so that your children do not miss the main part of the celebration because of travel. Often parents use the odd-year/even-year plan to alternate who spends the first and second halves of the holiday with their children.

3. Celebrate Important Holidays Twice

Some families celebrate holidays twice. For example, one parent might celebrate Christmas with the children a week before the actual date, and the other celebrates it with the children on December 25th. This is certainly easier when one parent's family already celebrates a holiday one week before or one week after the actual date so they can also fit in a "family reunion." Fortunately, few children complain about getting to celebrate twice!

4. Develop a Fixed Holiday Schedule

If you and the other parent differ on which holidays are special, you can assign holiday time so that each of you celebrates the same holidays every year with your children. This option is ideal when, for example, one parent participates in religious celebrations and the other parent chooses nonreligious holiday times for vacations, trips, or other activities.

5. Make Decisions as Each Holiday Approaches

Some parents prefer not to be tied down to a holiday schedule. As long as you are communicating effectively and your ideas about a holiday schedule are similar, this plan works well. It means, however, that you must spend considerable amounts of time arranging every holiday. If you choose this option, decide how far in advance of each holiday you will make your plans.

F. Issue 6: Education

#_____ **Education**

_____ Our children will attend [choose one]:
     _____ public school
     _____ private school
     _____ home school

_____ We will pay for any private or home school as follows [specify]:

_____
_____
_____

_____ Any decision to change schools will be made as follows [choose all that apply]:
     _____ If we agree.
     _____ After consulting our children.
     _____ After consulting with _____ [parent].
     _____ Only _____ [parent] may change our
     children's enrollment in a particular school.

_____ Any decisions to support our children's special educational needs or talents will be made as follows [choose all that apply]:
     _____ If we agree.
     _____ After consulting our children.
     _____ After consulting with _____ [parent].

_____ Only _____ [parent] may decide
how to support our children's special educational needs.

_____ We will participate in parent associations as follows [choose one]:

_____ Either parent may participate.

_____ Only one parent may participate at a time.

_____ _____ [parent] will participate.

_____ We will participate in the classroom as follows [choose one]:

_____ Either parent may participate.

_____ Only one parent may participate at a time.

_____ _____ [parent] will participate.

_____ We will participate in parent-chaperoned events as follows [choose one]:

_____ Either parent may participate.

_____ Only one parent may participate at a time.

_____ _____ [parent] will participate.

_____ We will attend parent-teacher or other school conferences as follows [choose one]:

_____ Both will attend.

_____ Each will schedule a meeting with the teacher or other school official.

_____ _____ [parent] will attend and will inform the other of the matters discussed.

_____ _____ [parent] will attend and will not inform the other of the matters discussed.

_____ Any emergency contact information needed by a school will be completed as follows [choose one]:

_____ We both will be listed in the following order:

_____

_____

_____ Only _____ [parent] will be listed.

_____ Others to be listed will be [list names]:

_____

_____

_____

_____ Good school performance means:

_____

We will encourage good school performance as follows [choose all that apply]:

_____ After discussion and agreement.

_____ After consultation with our children.

_____ With the following rewards:

_____

_____

_____ Poor school performance means:

_____

We will discourage poor school performance by [specify]:

_____

_____

_____

_____ Our children [check one] ☐ may ☐ may not attend sex education classes at school.

_____ _____ [parent] will notify the school of this decision.

_____ Our children's post-secondary education will be paid for as follows [specify]:

_____

_____

_____ Any decisions regarding our children's options for post-secondary education will be made as follows [choose all that apply]:

    _____ By agreement between parents and children.

    _____ Based on the children's interest and ability to be accepted at a particular school.

    _____ Based on what we can afford.

    _____ Other [specify]:

    _____

    _____

    _____

_____ We further agree that [specify]:

_____

_____

School often becomes a dominating influence in children's lives after the age of five. Whether your children attend a public school, private school, or home school, parental involvement in children's education is critical. Making decisions about your children's education is more complicated than simply deciding on the type of school they will attend. You must also consider:

- how you will make decisions about changing your children's school
- how you will address your children's special needs or talents
- who will participate in, and remain informed about, your children's school activities and performance
- whom the school should contact in the event of an emergency
- how you will define and encourage your children's good school performance
- the kind of education you will consider after high school, and
- how you will pay for post–high school education.

ISSUE 6 CROSS-REFERENCES

Worksheet	Questions
Worksheet 1	4, 6, 7
Worksheet 2	2, 7
Worksheet 3	2, 3, 4, 7
Worksheet 4	3, 5, 8, 9, 10

1. Public, Private, or Home Schooling

Most children attend their local public school. If you are not content with the local public school, there may be other options in your public school district worth investigating. Some districts have specialized schools (such as schools that emphasize art, science, or math). Other school districts allow parents and students to choose from more than one school in the district.

If you decide on private school, you will have to decide on what kind of school you want. Private schools come in all sizes and configurations. You can choose from parochial, secular, same-sex, or coed schools. Some private schools allow students to live at home; others require them to live in residence on the campus.

If a parent is willing and able to commit to full-time teaching, then home schooling is also an option. Home schooling requires an enormous commitment by one or both parents, and the curriculum must adhere to state educational standards.

To decide what school is best for your children, you must consider their academic and social needs and preferences. If their schooling will cost money, you must put aside adequate funds. Specify the arrangement in both your parenting agreement and child support agreement, and make sure the decision is the same in both places.

If either parent or the children want a change of schools, you can plan now for how that decision will be made. You can establish criteria (such as the child attaining certain skills or staying within a budget), or specify who will be authorized to make the change.

2. Supporting Special Needs or Talents

Some children need help with certain skills or subjects. Others have special talents that can be cultivated by extra classes or activities. Parents need to be sensitive to these possibilities, as well as to the children's changing needs.

If your children have special needs or talents, consider:

- requesting support from their current school
- supplementing the school resources with private tutors, counselors, or after-school activities, or
- switching schools.

3. Participating in School Activities

You and the other parent must agree on who will:

- participate in any parent-teacher associations
- help in the children's classroom
- attend parent-chaperoned functions, or
- attend other similar activities.

4. Parent-Teacher Conferences

You and the other parent must decide who will attend parent-teacher conferences. Some parents attend together, some designate one to attend and inform the other parent of the matters discussed, and some opt for separate conferences.

5. Emergency Contact Forms

You and the other parent must determine who will be listed on the school's emergency contact forms and in what order these persons will be listed. The school will also need to know who has authority to make medical decisions in the event of an emergency. (See Issue 2 earlier in this chapter.)

6. Encouraging Good Performance

Parents often disagree about how to encourage good school performance or what the consequences should be for poor performance. Some parents give their children money or other rewards for earning good grades. Some parents withhold allowances or other privileges if their children get poor grades. If you and the other parent decide to reward or punish school performance, you will want to define the terms and specify the rewards or punishments you will use.

7. Sex Education

If either you or the other parent does not want your children to participate in sex education classes, specify it here. In addition, you must find out whether you will be asked to give permission for your children to take the class.

8. Post-Secondary Education

Although most children and parents think about post–high school education for their children, such as college or technical training, many families fail to plan until their children reach high school. In fact, there are many planning options available, some of which require more preparation and thought than others.

Consider setting up a special account that you will use to pay for your children's education. If you do this, you will want to indicate how money will be deposited into that account. You can also investigate different loans, grants, or scholarships. If the type of training your children receive is important to you, you can specify what programs you will pay for, such as:

- pay-to-learn apprenticeships
- trade schools, or
- two-year or four-year institutions.

G. Issue 7: Insurance

#_____   **Insurance**

_____ Our children's medical insurance will be provided as follows [choose all that apply]:

_____ We both will obtain coverage if it is available through an employer at low or no cost.

_____ We will share the costs of any uncovered expenses as follows [specify]:

_____

_____

_____ _____ [parent]

will obtain coverage up to $ _____ under the following conditions [choose all that apply]:

_____ Type of coverage: _____

_____ Named beneficiaries: _____

_____ Insurance claims submitted by: _____ [parent]

_____ Our children's dental insurance will be provided as follows [choose all that apply]:

_____ We both will obtain coverage if it is available through an employer at low or no cost.

_____ We will share the costs of any uncovered expenses as follows [specify]:

_____

_____

_____ _____ [parent]

will obtain coverage up to $ _____ under the following conditions [choose all that apply]:

_____ Type of coverage: _____

_____ Named beneficiaries: _____

_____ Insurance claims submitted by: _____ [parent]

_____ Our children's vision care will be provided as follows [choose all that apply]:

_____ We both will obtain coverage if it is available through an employer at low or no cost.

_____ We will share the costs of any uncovered expenses as follows [specify]:

_____

_____

_____ _____ [parent]

will obtain coverage up to $ _____ under the following conditions [choose all that apply]:

_____ Type of coverage: _____

_____ Named beneficiaries: _____

_____ Insurance claims submitted by: _____ [parent]

_____ We will obtain life insurance coverage as follows [choose all that apply]:

_____ We both will obtain coverage if it is available through an employer at low or no cost.

_____ _____ [parent]

will obtain coverage up to $ _____ under the following conditions [choose all that apply]:

_____ Type of coverage: _____

_____ Named beneficiaries: _____

_____ We will obtain _____ insurance as follows [choose all that apply]:

_____ We both will obtain coverage if it is available through an employer at low or no cost.

_____ We will share the costs of any uncovered expenses as follows [specify]:

_____

_____

_____ _____ [parent]
will obtain coverage up to $ _____ under the following conditions [choose all that apply]:
_____ Type of coverage: _____
_____ Named beneficiaries: _____
_____
_____ Insurance claims submitted by: _____ [parent]

Insurance coverage can help with both the predictable and unpredictable expenses of child rearing. Parents can provide insurance for medical, dental, vision, and psychiatric care, and for prescription drugs. Parents can insure their own lives for the benefit of their children and can get life insurance policies for their children that they can later convert to cash to pay for college.

Insurance coverage might be available through a parent's employment, secured as a stand-alone individual policy, or converted from employee coverage to an individual policy if a parent changes jobs. Some parents agree that both will obtain whatever insurance coverage they can as long as it is available at low or no cost through their employer. If you both have insurance, you will have to agree on submitting claims, seeking treatment on the child's behalf, and paying deductibles and other uncovered expenses.

⚠ INSURANCE AND CHILD SUPPORT

Most states require one or both parents to provide health insurance for their children as an obligation of child support. If you are also making a child support agreement, make sure your decisions in this section are consistent with what is in your child support agreement.

Chapter 17 has a list of resources for insurance questions.

ISSUE 7 CROSS-REFERENCES

Worksheet	Questions
Worksheet 3	7, 8
Worksheet 4	6, 15

H. Issue 8: Making Decisions

#_____   **Making Decisions**

_____ Choose all that apply:

  _____ Whenever possible, we will discuss the issues and attempt to reach an agreement.

  _____ We both will make an effort to remain aware of our children's interests, activities, school performance, and overall health.

  _____ _____ [parent] will make an effort to keep _____ [other parent] aware of our children's interests, activities, school performance, and overall health.

  _____ _____ [parent], as the primary caretaker, will be responsible to make [most/all] of the decisions on behalf of our children and will inform _____ [other parent] as soon as possible thereafter.

  _____ _____ [parent], as the primary caretaker, will be responsible to make all of the decisions on behalf of our children and need not inform _____ [other parent] of these decisions.

  _____ _____ [other adult/guardian] will be given authority to make decisions on behalf of our children.

_____ We further agree that [specify]:

_____

_____

_____

When parents are married or living together, they work out their own system for making decisions. Only rarely does a court or other outsider, such as a therapist or physician, get involved in either the process or the actual decision.

When parents separate or divorce, however, they have to figure out how the big and little decisions affecting their children will be made, and who will make them. The question of who makes decisions is especially relevant if either or both parents have new partners. The parents also have to accept that only the larger decisions can be made in advance. Most decisions will be made as the issues arise.

Good decisions are based on your values and needs and should take into consideration your children's values and needs as well. Good decisions stand the test of time because they are the ones that benefit everyone involved. Whenever possible, the advantages of a decision should outweigh the disadvantages for everyone concerned.

You can take some of the guesswork out of the decision-making process by building a sound decision-making framework. To build this kind of framework, ask and answer the following questions for each decision that must be made:

- What will this decision accomplish?
- Who will gain by the decision?
- Who might lose by this decision?
- Whose needs will be met by this decision?
- How will I know that this decision has accomplished my objectives?

Take, for example, the need to choose between two schools for your children. Your answers to the above questions might go something like this:

- What will this decision accomplish? ("The school will provide a good college preparatory education.")
- Who will gain by the decision? ("Our children will gain a good education.")
- Who might lose by this decision? ("We will lose money if we choose an expensive private school. If we select a public school where only one of us lives, the parent who doesn't reside in that district may lose weekday contact with the children.")
- Whose needs will be met by this decision? ("Our children's needs will be met and should come first, but we must be able to afford any private school and have money left over to continue other important activities.")
- How will I know that this decision has accomplished my objectives? ("We will see the children's grades

and test scores improve, and the school counselor will be confident that the children have a good chance of getting into a good college.")

There are basically four models for making decisions, each with its own advantages and disadvantages:

- the parents reach an agreement
- one parent decides and later informs the other
- one parent decides but need not tell the other, or
- another responsible adult (such as a grandparent, aunt, or close family friend) has the authority to make decisions.

ISSUE 8 CROSS-REFERENCES

Worksheet	Questions
Worksheet 1	8
Worksheet 2	5, 6, 8
Worksheet 3	1, 4, 7, 8, 10, 11
Worksheet 4	1, 2, 3, 4, 5, 6, 7, 13, 14, 15

1. The Parents Reach Agreement

Requiring parents to reach agreement on issues can work well when both parents are active in their children's lives, can set aside their conflicts, and have the same or similar child-rearing values. This does not mean you must see things identically, but you generally must be able to reach agreement on your own.

The best way for your parenting agreement to succeed is for you and the other parent to work together to find solutions that are in your children's best interests. Additionally, you both must remain informed about health care, school, and outside activities so you can make decisions with an understanding of how they are likely to play out over time.

You can structure this option in any way that feels comfortable—just be specific. If, for example, you want to let a parent make everyday decisions when the children are with that parent, but want discussion and agreement for significant decisions, you must specify what you mean by "everyday" and "significant" decisions.

Parents usually agree that, in an emergency, the parent caring for the children at the time will handle the situation and inform the other parent as soon as possible. Conversely, parents usually require consultation and agreement on major decisions, such as a change in residence,

surgery, remedial tutoring, support for special talent, or participation in a hazardous activity.

Parents can choose to meet in person, talk by telephone, or start out their discussions in writing. Writing is good if you and the other parent are having trouble communicating in person or by telephone. If you must communicate in writing because of constant arguing, however, reevaluate whether you and the other parent can actually make this decision-making model work.

2. Parent With Primary Care Decides and Informs the Other Parent

This option can work well for parents who argue frequently about child-rearing issues. It ensures that decisions will get made by giving only one parent authority. At the same time, it reduces opportunities for conflict and keeps both parents informed about what is going on in their children's lives. The parent who makes the decisions may have to provide the other parent with a medical release when the children are in the other parent's care. Otherwise, you can handle emergencies as described in Section 1, above.

3. Parent With Primary Care Makes Decisions

This option may be necessary for parents who have a history of harassment, abuse, or violence between them, or when one parent has little involvement in raising the children. The primary caretaker for the children can make the decisions without fear of fighting or interference.

When the parent who does not have the authority to make decisions on the children's behalf spends time with the children, that parent may need a medical release from the other parent to cover emergencies. This decision-making model is consistent with agreements that include supervised, or otherwise very limited, visitation.

4. Parents Choose Another Adult to Make Decisions

If you and the other parent are unable or unwilling to make decisions about your child's welfare, you can appoint a legal guardian for your children who would have complete decision-making authority. You could also consider giving a guardian more limited powers—to make medical or financial decisions, for example—by signing a document called a "power of attorney." Either way, these steps may affect the legal custody label in your parenting plan. (See Issue 10 later in this chapter.)

I. Issue 9: Resolving Disputes

#_____ **Resolving Disputes When Making Decisions Together**

_____ If disagreements arise regarding this Parenting Agreement or our general parenting arrangements, we agree as follows [choose all that apply]:

_____ _____ [parent] has authority to make final decisions when we can't agree.

_____ Before this parent makes a final decision that resolves a disagreement, he/she will consult with _____ [other adult] for advice.

_____ _____ [parent] has authority to make final decisions regarding _____ [specify] and _____ [other parent] has authority to make final decisions regarding _____ [specify].

_____ We will participate in the following, at either parent's request [choose all that apply]:

_____ counseling

_____ mediation

_____ arbitration

_____ meeting with attorney[s]

_____ other: _____ [specify]

_____ We further agree that [specify]:

_____

_____

_____

Even the most experienced negotiators find themselves unable to resolve a particular issue. This is called an impasse. You and the other parent must plan for how you will resolve an impasse; that is, how necessary decisions will be made when you cannot reach agreement on your own.

Part of the problem is understanding the nature of the conflict. In addition to differing views, values, and cultures, people are sometimes driven by jealousy, anger, bitterness, or revenge in these situations. Parents may insist that they have their children's best interests in mind when, in fact, they do not. Often, disagreements between parents are motivated by a desire to improve their own lives rather than to meet the needs of their children. One effective strategy you can use to resolve conflict is to examine your motives for a particular position.

You have several options for resolving disagreements. As you consider these options, make sure that the option you choose allows for decisions to be made in a timely fashion. Your options include:

- giving the primary caretaker authority to decide
- resolving the underlying problems before making decisions
- developing temporary agreements
- using a counselor, therapist, or attorney
- role-playing to see what is best for the children
- mediation, or
- arbitration

For more information on this subject—especially for dealing with high-conflict situations—see Chapter 4.

ISSUE 9 CROSS-REFERENCES

Worksheet	Questions
Worksheet 1	4
Worksheet 2	4, 5, 6, 8
Worksheet 3	4, 7, 9, 10, 11
Worksheet 4	3, 4, 7, 13, 14, 15

When parents cannot resolve their parenting issues, they can take the issue to court. Courts will not decide what clothes your children can wear to school, which friends they can spend time with, or what sports they can play. A court, however, will decide who has authority to make decisions affecting your children, where your children will live, and how they will spend time with both parents.

Most parents and professionals use the court as a last resort for resolving disputes. Going to court can be expensive and time-consuming. More important, the judge making the decision will not know you or your children and will have little time to hear the matter and make a decision. As a result, you risk getting a decision that is less sensitive to your particular needs than if you and the other parent reached an agreement on your own. Furthermore, if you already have a court order, a court will not modify it unless you show that there has been a substantial change in circumstances.

Many states provide their judges with some guidance on how to make custody and visitation decisions. Some judges are urged to avoid contested proceedings whenever possible. These judges usually rely on the recommendations of a custody evaluator when making their decisions. Also, most judges give significant weight to a teen's preference about custody and visitation.

1. The Primary Caretaker Has Authority

If your children will spend significantly more time with one parent than the other, consider giving that parent final authority to make decisions when you otherwise can't agree. Alternatively, you could give one parent final authority on certain issues when you disagree and give the other parent similar authority for different issues.

To put some limits on the parent with decision-making authority, you could require that the parent consult with someone whose opinions both parents value, such as a counselor, religious leader, or family member, before making a final decision. Even when parents cannot agree about

something, they can often agree on whose advice they will trust and follow.

2. Resolve Hidden Conflicts

You can try to "get underneath" a problem by trying to understand why there is a problem in the first place. Mental health professionals are especially skilled at this and can often help parents who regularly battle over certain things to untangle the issues and develop a plan for solving them over the longer term. Regular conflicts over exact pick-up and drop-off times, or whether visits over school holidays should start at the end of school on Friday or some other time, may have to do with larger underlying issues. For example, some parents want to make sure that visitation schedules do not vary more than a few hours one way or the other so that the child support amounts won't change. Other times, parents will refuse to allow a later or earlier pick-up time because they want to "teach" the other parent to be on time (in a way that they were not during the marriage, for example).

3. Use a Counselor, Therapist, or Attorney

You can ask for an evaluation of your situation from a trained professional, such as a psychiatrist, marriage and family counselor, or other mental health professional. You can accept any recommendation that the evaluator makes, use the recommendation to try and reach an agreement on your own, or bring the recommendation into mediation.

Another option is for each of you to consult with an attorney—or meet with one attorney together—to get information. (Be aware that many lawyers refuse to meet with both parties in a divorce dispute.) Many parents want to know "what the law says" before they make a decision. For example, if your state requires that a noncustodial parent be given a certain minimum amount of visitation, consulting an attorney might help you by guiding your decision about where the children will live (Issue 1), holidays (Issue 5), and vacations (Issue 14).

4. Develop Temporary Agreements

Mistrust thwarts most parenting agreements. Sometimes it helps to take baby steps before trying big ones. Parents fighting over big decisions might try making decisions on simple issues for a short time. Hopefully this will improve their ability to communicate, resolve conflicts, and ultimately make decisions on more controversial questions.

For example, you might agree to make decisions about outside activities together for three months before trying to tackle larger decisions. Then you might be ready to tackle larger decisions, like who will provide after-school care, and then even larger decisions, like which schools your children will attend.

5. Parent A/Parent B Plan

This tool for resolving impasses involves assigning roles for a particular issue to two hypothetical parents—Parent A and Parent B. Once these roles are assigned, you then decide, based on the situation, which real parent is best suited to be Parent A and Parent B. For instance, if you decide that your children should spend Christmas with Parent A and three weeks in the summer with Parent B, you then decide which role is most appropriate for you and the other parent—that is, who would be the best Parent A and who the best Parent B. See "Example of How to Use Parent A/Parent B Plan," below.

The Parent A/Parent B approach is most often used when deciding where the children will live a majority of the time (Issue 1). If you have trouble making that decision, you may want to try this decision-making option.

6. Mediate Disagreements

Many parents select mediation to resolve disputes. When the mediator has no authority to make an independent recommendation to the court, the process allows the parents to maintain control over their decisions. As a result, parents can focus on their children and work on communicating with each other.

Mediation is covered in Chapter 11.

7. Arbitrate Disagreements

A few states allow parents to submit parenting decisions to an arbitrator when they cannot reach agreement on their own. Unlike mediators, arbitrators are decision makers. In arbitration, each parent presents his or her views to the arbitrator, who resolves the issues in dispute.

See Chapter 11 for more information on mediation and arbitration, and Chapter 17 for information on working with therapists and counselors.

EXAMPLE OF HOW TO USE PARENT A/PARENT B PLAN

Sometimes parents cannot agree on where their children will live, not because they differ, but because they want the same thing. For example, you and the other parent might decide that "Parent A" will be the primary caretaker for the school year and "Parent B" the primary caretaker for the summer. You agree on how the children will visit each parent when they are with the other parent, and how they will spend holidays, weekends, special occasions, and vacations. The only question remaining is who gets the nine-month chunk of time with the children, and who gets only three.

In deciding who will be Parent A and who will be Parent B, you might consider the following:

- who provided most of the daily child care when you were a couple
- who lives near the better public schools
- whose home is more conducive to studying
- who lives closer to community recreation programs and sports facilities in which your children participate, and
- who lives closer to the children's friends or in a neighborhood with similar-aged children.

WHEN CONSULTING OUTSIDERS

If you turn to an outsider for help in resolving disputes, be sure you maintain control over the process. No matter what type of outsider you use—mediator, counselor, therapist, attorney, or arbitrator—you must decide the following in advance:

- how the outsider will be chosen—will you require any minimum qualifications?
- how the outsider will be paid
- exactly what issues the outsider will be helping you resolve, and
- the scope of the process—will you limit the number of mediation or counseling sessions? Will certain legal rules apply in arbitration? Will attorneys be present in arbitration?

J. Issue 10: Labeling the Custody Arrangement

#_____ **Labeling the Custody Arrangement**

_____ The custody of our children will be as follows [choose one]: *(Note: Read Chapter 16 before completing this option.*
Your state may require you to differentiate between legal and physical custody.)

_____ sole custody

_____ legal

_____ physical

_____ joint custody

_____ legal

_____ physical

_____ joint custody, to mean that we will make decisions and share time with our children as follows [specify]:

_____

_____

_____ split custody

_____ _____ [parent] will have custody of

_____ [children's names].

_____ _____ [other parent] will have custody of

_____ [children's names].

_____ _____ [other adult] will have custody of our children.

_____ We further agree that [specify]:

_____

_____

_____

_____

Living arrangements and custody labels are two different issues. You described your children's actual living arrangement in Issue 1. Here you decide what these arrangements mean in terms of custody—the term used by the court in a divorce or legal separation.

The most common custody labels are:

• sole custody, which gives one parent authority for all decisions

• joint custody, which generally means that parents share child rearing, and

• split custody, which means the children are separated: some of the children go with one parent, and some go with the other parent.

In some states, custody is further defined as "legal" and "physical." Legal custody refers to making decisions about health, education, and the child's best interests. Physical custody means providing the majority of physical care for the children. A common arrangement is for one parent to have sole physical custody while both parents have joint legal custody. (Chapter 16 has a chart with the states that differentiate between legal and physical custody.)

No matter what custody label you use, you have tremendous latitude to spell out whom children will spend their time with. For example, even with a sole custody arrangement, your children may live with the noncustodial parent every other weekend. Similarly, you can agree to joint custody but have your children spend little time with one parent.

COURTS AND CUSTODY

In general, a judge will guarantee a parent's right to spend time with his or her children and a parent's obligation to care for and support his or her children. Furthermore, in most states, custody laws are gender-neutral. This means that neither parent is presumed to be more fit simply because that parent is a mother or a father. A few states retain one exception to this, called the "tender years" doctrine. In these states, a court may assume that very young children should live with their mothers whenever possible.

A parent could be denied contact with his or her children if the judge rules that:

- a parent is legally incompetent (even then, the court may permit supervised visitation)
- a parent is not related to the children by blood or legal adoption—such as a stepparent or same-sex co-parent (you can give that person the status of parent in your agreement, however), or
- the contact would be harmful to the children.

In extreme cases, a court can terminate a person's parental rights—usually after finding that the parent has abandoned the children or engages in behavior highly damaging to the children. If you are named in a hearing to terminate your parental rights, you will have the right to defend yourself—in many states, you will have the right to an appointed attorney if you cannot afford one yourself.

ISSUE 10 CROSS-REFERENCES

Worksheet	Questions
Worksheet 1	3, 4, 5, 8
Worksheet 2	1, 4, 5, 6, 7, 8
Worksheet 3	1, 3, 4, 7, 8, 9, 11
Worksheet 4	1, 2, 3, 4, 6, 7, 8, 9, 10, 13, 14, 15

1. Sole Custody

Parents frequently choose sole custody when distance, acrimony, or other factors make it impossible for parents to collaborate on the decisions that affect their children. If your decision in Issue 8 (Making Decisions) is to have only one parent make decisions, you'll probably want to select sole custody.

A parent with sole custody cannot prevent the other parent from visiting the children. The sole custodian does have considerable discretion in scheduling visitation, however. The more specific you can be about your visitation schedule, the easier your plan will be to live with. The decisions you make here should also be consistent with the decisions you make in Issue 18 (Maintaining Contact).

⚠ SOLE CUSTODY AND CHILD SUPPORT

A sole custody arrangement does not exempt the noncustodial parent from paying child support.

2. Joint Custody

Most parents who choose to make decisions together (Issue 8) choose joint custody or joint legal custody (if their state differentiates between legal and physical custody). Joint legal custody can mean anything from consulting each other on any decision bigger than the clothes to be worn to school, to consulting only on major issues such as whether to allow underage children to marry.

Joint physical custody agreements can also vary widely. The most common joint physical custody awards specify that the children:

- spend equal time with each parent
- spend the school year with one parent and the summer with the other, or
- live primarily with one parent and spend weekly midweek visits or overnights, weekends, and half of the holidays and summer vacation with the other parent.

For joint custody to succeed, you and the other parent must be willing to work together to make decisions, without using your children as either a weapon or an excuse. Your joint custody arrangements will have a greater chance of success if you specify clearly how decisions will be made and how your children will share time with each of you.

All states allow parents to choose joint custody arrangements. A small number of states permit courts to order joint custody, even over the objections of a parent. (Your state's rules on joint custody are spelled out in Chapter 16.)

3. Split Custody

Split custody, where children are separated (some are placed with one parent and some with the other parent), is not recommended except under special circumstances. Such circumstances include:

- a history of irreconcilable conflict between a parent and one or more of the children
- incest or violence between the children, or
- children with different fathers or mothers.

Unfortunately, some parents split custody because it makes each of them feel as though they have "won." If this is your reason for considering it, be careful. Often, the bond between siblings is the only reliable support system children have after their parents separate or divorce. Eliminating it can have very serious consequences, even if the children have only one parent in common.

Consult a mental health professional before splitting custody of your children. If you still decide to opt for it, schedule a lot of time that your children can be together.

4. Third-Party Custody

Some parents are unwilling or unable to care for their children. The parents may be children themselves or may be undergoing psychiatric, substance-abuse, or physical rehabilitation. No matter what the reason, if you are in this situation you will have to choose a third person, such as a grandparent or other relative, to care for your children. You must also specify how you and the other parent will spend time with your children, and how you will regain custody of your children.

You should know that you might find it difficult to re-establish your parenting role with your children if you have created a voluntary guardianship. In some situations, it is hard to prove that there is a good reason to change guardianship back, especially if the guardianship has been in place for some time. For this reason, it is very important that you get legal advice before deciding to give up the guardianship of your children to someone else. ■

CHAPTER

7

Finishing Touches

This chapter covers the next level of issues that need to be addressed in a parenting agreement. These are issues that most parents will want to cover in their parenting agreement to make it a workable plan. Some people may want to include some or all of these topics in their first agreement. Others may prefer to wait and see what works before they try to negotiate and decide these issues. You will have to assess what point you are at and determine when you are ready to tackle these issues.

A. Issue 11: Exchanging Information

#_____ **Exchanging Information**

_____ We will not ask our children to carry messages between us.

_____ We will share information about the children [choose all that apply]:

_____ at least every _____ [specify interval of time]

_____ with each exchange of our children

_____ the day or evening before an exchange

_____ as needed

_____ [Parent/We] will assume the responsibility to establish contact with the appropriate sources of information regarding our children's [choose all that apply]:

_____ health care

_____ school

_____ sports

_____ other: _____ [specify]

_____ We will communicate with each other [choose all that apply]:

_____ in person

_____ by telephone

_____ by letter

_____ by email

_____ other: _____ [specify]

_____ We further agree that [specify]:

_____

_____

Both parents will need and want information about the children from the other parent on an ongoing basis. It may be information about their children's health care, school, outside activities, interests, abilities, or special needs.

Talking with the other parent can be difficult. When parents are angry or hurt over the separation or divorce, or still hope for a reconciliation, they may use information exchanges about the children as an excuse to rehash the adult issues. Though it may be important to discuss adult issues, it should be separated from exchanging information about your children. It's too easy to get sidetracked and forget to discuss your children and their needs if you are trying to work out your adult issues at the same time. Also, some parents use information exchanges about the children as a chance to criticize or pry into the other's new life, partner, or activities. When this happens, the children's interests suffer or are forgotten altogether.

Parents often need to find new ways to communicate effectively. Below are a few options to consider for your parenting agreement. You can choose more than one option. That way, when things are going well you can use one method, and then use a different one when communication is difficult.

For additional help, consider the following:

- review Chapter 4 on negotiations
- evaluate your agreement to see if it addresses everyone's needs
- get help from a mediator or counselor, or
- consult with any other third party whose opinion you respect.

The more ideas you can generate to solve problems, the better.

ISSUE 11 CROSS-REFERENCES

Worksheet	Questions
Worksheet 1	8
Worksheet 2	6, 8
Worksheet 3	3, 4, 5, 7, 9, 10, 11
Worksheet 4	3, 4, 5, 6, 7, 13, 14, 15

1.   Don't Put Your Children in the Middle

One of the worst mistakes you can make—and lots of parents make it—is to put your children in the middle by having them carry messages. You and the other parent must find a way to keep each other informed without passing messages through your children.

Children are apt to forget, distort, or misunderstand your message. Children also soon resent the role and cringe when they deliver a message that the other parent doesn't want to hear. Some children may temporarily like the power of being the "information highway," but that soon fades. If you need to change plans, collect child support, find out about the other parent's activities, or understand what discipline is being used in the other parent's home, communicate with the other parent directly.

2.   Establish a Businesslike Relationship

Many therapists, mediators, counselors, and attorneys know that the relationship between parents has to change from intimate partners to business partners to let hostilities cool. Parents who have been through this can tell you how difficult that change can be. Nevertheless, the strategies for bringing this new relationship about are fairly simple.

You and the other parent must learn to make your conversations brief, focused only on the children, and courteous. You must make an effort to inform each other about the little things, such as what your children have been doing for fun or have accomplished recently, as well as the significant information about illnesses, behavior, special events, and report cards.

If things don't go well when you talk in person, consider scheduling telephone calls. If that doesn't work, exchange notes through the mail, via email, at a convenient drop-off location or, as a last resort (and only if your children can't read yet), in your children's suitcase.

3.   Establish Separate Relationships With Activities and Care Providers

For some parents, exchanging information about health care, school, counseling, or outside activities doesn't work. These parents must establish separate contacts with the children's health care providers, school officials, and event and activity coordinators.

Be sure that both parents are legally entitled to information if your plan is to have each parent get information separately from schools, doctors, or others. In this situation, you often need a joint legal custody agreement. If you are not sure whether you are entitled to this information, or you do not have a joint legal custody agreement, you will need to check with an attorney to find out what the law allows in your state.

Many schools, doctors, counselors, club leaders, and coaches do not like to communicate with parents separately. You may need to be persistent. Keep in mind, however, that scout leaders, coaches, doctors, and others dread getting between parents battling over control of their children. You will have an easier time dealing with these people if you make your contacts brief, friendly, and to the point. Don't rely on these people to give you information about the other parent or to relay messages. If children resent being made into message carriers, outsiders resent it even more.

B. Issue 12: Child Care

#_____   **Child Care**

_____ In securing child care, we will proceed as follows [choose all that apply]:

_____ Any child care provider will [choose all that apply]:

_____ be a licensed child care provider

_____ be over the age of _____

_____ be a relative or close friend

_____ not care for more than _____ children at any time when our children are there

_____ come into the home

_____ other: _____ [specify]

_____ Each parent has the discretion to select the child care provider, but may not use [list names or traits unacceptable]:

_____

_____ Each parent will call the other first to care for the children in that parent's absence.

_____ We will try to share child care responsibilities with neighbors and friends.

_____ Our children can care for themselves, but _____ [other adult] will check in with them.

_____ Our children can care for themselves as long as they follow these rules:

_____

_____

_____

_____ We further agree that [specify]:

_____

_____

_____

Child care is an important issue for many parents as they go their separate ways. Assessing the need for adult-supervised childcare can be difficult. There is no magic age at which all children are ready to care for themselves. While many teens can care for themselves for limited periods of time, those same teens may not be able to resist inviting friends over, spending unlimited amounts of time on the telephone, or accessing "adult" materials on cable TV or the Internet. Younger children may be very compliant about following your rules but may not be as well equipped to handle a medical or other emergency, know how to respond to strangers who call or come to the door, or observe basic safety precautions when preparing or heating up food for themselves. Similarly, children who are skilled babysitters for others may not be as responsible, or may have more difficulty getting cooperation, when caring for siblings.

Although parents may feel that they have few childcare options, there are usually quite a few different possibilities. You must consider your child's age, where you live, how well you know your neighbors, how far away you will be, how long you will be gone, and whether you can easily be reached in an emergency. Some different ways to handle this include:

- children care for themselves
- older children care for younger children
- family member or friend cares for children
- parents participate in a "baby-sitting co-op" (parents trade caring for each other's children)
- occasional babysitters from neighborhood
- after-school care
- community recreation programs/child care centers
- licensed day care
- agency-provided sitters (usually licensed or bonded).

As you consider whether your children need some form of adult-supervised childcare, you should create guidelines for their time alone, and then assess whether each of your children can realistically fulfill your expectations. For example, do you trust the children to:

- follow basic safety rules regarding strangers who call or come to the door
- respond in an appropriate manner to medical or other emergencies
- provide responsible care for siblings
- follow your rules for when friends may visit, and
- follow your rules for using the telephone, watching television, using the Internet, and so on.

If you decide that at least some adult-supervised child care will be necessary, you should deal with this issue in your parenting agreement, although you may have difficulty finding such care. In some families, a grandparent or other relative or friend may have already been a frequent care provider. Sometimes this person can continue to provide care after the separation or divorce. In other families, finding child care providers that are acceptable to both parents is more difficult.

ISSUE 12 CROSS-REFERENCES

Worksheet	Questions
Worksheet 1	3, 6, 7, 8
Worksheet 2	4, 5, 6, 8
Worksheet 3	2, 3, 4, 5, 6, 9, 10
Worksheet 4	3, 4, 8, 9, 10, 11, 12, 13, 14, 15

1. Agree on Care Provider's Minimum Qualifications

Parents may not have a clear idea of who will provide child care but may be able to agree on certain minimum qualifications. Parents often consider the care provider's age, physical location, and licensure. Depending upon the distance between your homes, you can use the same provider (offering more continuity in your children's care), or you can each find a provider with the minimum qualifications you agree upon.

2. Agree on Ineligible Care Providers

You may be more anxious about preventing certain people from caring for your children than deciding who can provide care. If this is the case, name these individuals in your parenting agreement or describe the characteristics you find unacceptable, such as being under the age of 17, using drugs or alcohol, or operating a child care facility more than 10 miles from your home.

3. Address the Role of a Parent's New Partner

Sometimes the care provider that a parent wants to exclude is the other parent's new partner. This can fuel an intense battle, so approach the situation with caution.

First, ask yourself your motive for not wanting the new partner to care for your children. If your concerns are motivated by jealousy, rivalry, or a fear of being "replaced" as a parent, consider more direct and productive ways to express and resolve your fears than to exclude that person as a care provider. Feeling jealous of the other parent's new partner is common, even if you don't want to have the other parent back as a partner. Similarly, a fear of being displaced is natural, and can be handled by:

- agreeing that your children will never be told that you are anything other than their parent
- finding special names for the new partner other than "Mom" or "Dad," and
- talking directly to your children about your fears.

Additional decisions about new partners are in Issue 36 (When Parents Have New Partners), discussed in Chapter 9. If you find yourself unable to manage your feelings about the other parent's new partner, a counselor might be able to help.

4. Agree to Call Each Other for Child Care

When parents' homes are close by, they can consider providing child care for each other. For some parents, this means that one parent provides all after-school care until the other returns from work. For others, it means that one parent "covers" for the other for business or vacation trips.

This option offers several advantages:

- It allows parents to extend the time they spend with their children.
- It provides for greater continuity in care, which is especially important for young children.
- It keeps child care costs down.
- It shows children that their parents can still cooperate—at least about them.

There are disadvantages to this arrangement, however. First, some parents use the chance to be called whenever child care is needed as "proof" that the other parent leaves the children too often. Second, you may find it difficult to maintain a separate life if the other parent is constantly around and able to keep track of your activities.

⚠ If one parent increases the amount of time he or she cares for the children over a long period of time, it could affect child support payments. Make sure you know your child support guidelines if you decide on this type of child care arrangement.

5. Find an Adult Neighbor Who Can Check on Your Child

Some children are old enough to stay home by themselves for short periods. Others can take care of themselves with a neighbor's help. If your children need only minimal supervision, consider asking an adult in the neighborhood to call or stop by to see how things are going, or to be available by telephone in the event of an emergency.

⚠ Do not leave your children home without adult supervision unless they are fully capable of caring for themselves and know whom to call in the event of an emergency. Although you may have difficulty finding child care, unless your children can care for themselves or your oldest child is truly capable of caring for younger siblings, you could be taking a dangerous risk by leaving them unattended. (Chapter 17 contains referrals to books to help you assess your children's readiness to stay home alone.)

C. Issue 13: Special Occasions and Family Events

#_____ **Special Occasions and Family Events**

_____ Special occasions and family events are defined as follows:

_____

_____

_____

_____ We will attend special occasions and family events together whenever possible.

_____ We will attend special occasions and family events as our children wish.

_____ We will attend special occasions and family events as we decide.

_____ _____ [parent] will attend the following special occasions and family events:

_____

_____

_____ _____ [parent] will attend the following special occasions and family events:

_____

_____

_____ We further agree that [specify]:

_____

_____

_____

Although you and the other parent have gone your separate ways, your children may want either or both of you to attend special events or ceremonies. By planning ahead, these decisions are considerably easier to make. With very little imagination, you can expect this issue to come up over back-to-school night, a football game, a family picnic for your children's scout troop, graduation, or a school play.

Although these events are meant to be fun and special for the participating families, they can also become frustrating and confusing. You, your children, and the other parent need to develop a strategy for dealing with these invitations so that the events remain fun and are as simple to plan as possible.

Some parents alternate who attends each event ("You go to back-to-school night and I'll go to the open house"), others attend together, and still others attend the events that have the most meaning in their relationship with their child ("I'll do scouts if you do baseball").

ISSUE 13 CROSS-REFERENCES

Worksheet	Questions
Worksheet 1	6, 8
Worksheet 2	4, 5, 8
Worksheet 3	4, 5, 6, 9, 10, 11
Worksheet 4	3, 4, 7, 11, 12, 13, 14, 15

D. Issue 14: Vacations

#_____ **Vacations**

_____ We will inform each other at least _____ [period of time] in advance of any planned vacation.

_____ We will provide each other with an itinerary of any trip, and contact information.

_____ Our children may accompany one of us on a vacation under the following conditions:

    _____ Any time missed from a regularly scheduled visit with the other parent will be made up as follows:

    _____

    _____

    _____ Travel will be restricted to:

       _____ local area

       _____ in state

       _____ in the United States

       _____ the following countries: _____

    _____ Activities will be limited to _____.

    _____ Activities will not include _____.

    _____ Our children will not be away for longer than _____.

_____ We further agree that [specify]:

_____

_____

Vacationing can raise a multitude of questions. Among other things, you and the other parent should discuss:

- travel out of the area, out of the state, or out of the country
- whether each parent must provide the other with an itinerary and contact information
- whether certain activities (such as hang gliding) will be permitted
- how long the children can be away, and
- whether you will schedule "makeup" visits.

Informing the other parent well in advance of your intentions allows everyone to deal with schedule changes more easily. If you know how much vacation time you will have in a given year and how you'd like to spend it, you and the other parent can start early to figure out how the children will fit in.

ISSUE 14 CROSS-REFERENCES

Worksheet	Questions
Worksheet 1	6, 7, 8
Worksheet 2	1
Worksheet 3	1, 3, 4, 6, 9, 10, 11
Worksheet 4	1, 3, 4, 7, 11, 12, 13, 14

E. Issue 15: Outside Activities

#_____ **Outside Activities**

_____ Our children may participate in [list all appropriate activities]:

_____
_____
_____

_____ Our children may *not* participate in [list all appropriate activities]:

_____
_____
_____

_____ We will make decisions about which activities our children may participate in as follows:

_____ By consensus agreement.

_____ _____ [parent's name] may make decisions about

[fill in the blank] _____ activities.

_____ _____ [parent's name] may make decisions about

[fill in the blank] _____ activities.

_____ We will use the decision-making process outlined in issue #_____ [fill in the right number from your completed

agreement. This section refers to Issue 8 in Chapter 6 called "Making Decisions"].

_____ We further agree that [specify]:

_____
_____
_____

Scheduling a child's outside activities can become more complicated during a separation or divorce. Participating in team sports may conflict with visitation schedules or other scheduled family time. It is also possible that one parent might not approve of a child's interests—like possibly dangerous contact sports—or insist on certain activities such as Bible study, bar mitzvah preparation, or extra academic classes. For these reasons, it may make sense to decide in advance what types of activities you will encourage, discourage, insist on, or prohibit altogether.

ISSUE 15 CROSS-REFERENCES

Worksheet	Questions
Worksheet 1	2, 3, 5
Worksheet 2	1, 4, 5, 7
Worksheet 3	3, 4
Worksheet 4	3, 4, 8, 9, 10

F. Issue 16: Transporting the Children

#_____ **Transporting the Children**

_____ Transporting our children between our homes will be as follows [choose all that apply]:

_____ We will meet for exchanges at _____ [specify time and location].

_____ We will alternate transporting our children back and forth.

_____ [parent] will actually transport our children

and _____ [other parent] will share in costs as follows:

_____

_____

_____ _____ [parent] will travel to our children for visits.

_____ _____ [parent] will bring our children for visits to the other parent.

_____ Our children may travel on their own by train, bus, or airplane when they reach age _____.

_____ We further agree that [specify]:

_____

_____

_____

_____

Transporting children for their time with each parent can be simple if you live near each other. Some children walk, ride their bicycles, or take the city bus back and forth. For most parents, however, this subject is more troublesome. One way to ease your frustration is to agree on as many details as possible: how you will make exchanges, the time for pick-ups and drop-offs, how each parent will notify the other of last-minute changes, and who will pay for transportation costs.

Your options will depend on several factors, including how far apart you live, how often your children will see each parent, who has access to a car, and the costs of transportation. If there has been violence between the parents, you may want to choose a busy public location for your exchanges. If weather is an issue in your area, you will want to choose a location that allows you, the other parent, and your children to wait indoors—such as a shopping mall or museum—in the event of bad weather. If you or the other parent must use public transportation to make the exchanges, you will need to know the schedules and plan accordingly.

ISSUE 16 CROSS-REFERENCES

Worksheet	Questions
Worksheet 2	4, 5
Worksheet 3	2, 3, 4, 6, 10
Worksheet 4	8, 9, 10, 14

1. Meet at a Midpoint

This option lets the parents share the travel time by choosing a neutral location for exchanges. It requires that each parent has access to a vehicle and arrives at the exchange point at approximately the same time.

2. Alternate Travel Responsibilities

In an effort to share the responsibility fairly equally, some parents alternate transporting the children over the entire distance. This option requires that each parent can obtain reliable transportation when it is his or her turn to drive, but allows more flexibility in setting a time for the exchange.

3. One Parent Transports

This option is ideal for parents who cannot absorb equally the time and vehicle maintenance necessary for transporting children. If one parent is without a vehicle, or cannot take the time to provide transportation, perhaps that parent can compensate by reimbursing the cost of gas or other expenses.

4. Parent Travels to Children

When parents don't live near each other, some parents travel to the children and either rent an apartment or motel room, stay with a friend nearby, or live with the children for the visit. This option allows parents to visit without otherwise disrupting their children's normal activities.

Parents often consider this option when the distant parent has more travel time available than the children. Usually this happens during the school year when the recess is too short to allow the children to visit at their other parent's home. If you choose this arrangement, you will need to decide where the parent will stay, how travel expenses will be allocated, and which parent will participate in the children's activities.

5. Parent Brings Children to Other Parent and Leaves

With this option, one parent takes the children to the other parent's home, and then vacations or visits friends before picking up the children at the end of the visit. This option probably won't work for other than occasional visits, but it can add variety or help one parent out if he or she has vehicle problems.

6. Children Travel by Themselves

Some parents let their children travel alone between homes —by train, bus, or airplane—once they reach a certain age. Of course, the parents must still get the children to and from the stations, but this option can save a lot in time, money, and aggravation.

G. Issue 17: Improving Transition Times

#_____ **Improving Transition Times**

_____ We will make the transitions between our homes easier for our children by doing as follows [choose all that apply]:

_____ Our children will start visits with _____ [parent] at _____ [specify time or event, such as after school or after work]. The visits will end at _____ [specify time or event].

_____ When our children are changing homes, we will minimize the contact between us.

_____ We will exchange information regarding our children the night before they change homes.

_____ When our children are changing homes, the parent starting the visit will take time to give each child some undivided attention.

_____ The parent starting a visit will let our children have some quiet time before any scheduled activities or trips.

_____ _____ [parent] will try to establish and maintain a simple ritual to start and end his/her visits with our children.

_____ We will try to be patient regarding any questions that the children wish to ask about the custody and visitation arrangements.

_____ We further agree that [specify]:

_____

_____

_____

Many parents have difficulty handling the inevitable ups and downs that come when children travel between homes. This is especially true just after the separation or for a parent who hasn't seen the children in quite some time. Many parents have high expectations when their children are about to arrive, and get depressed when their children leave.

For children, the ups and downs are worse. Young children, especially, gear up when anticipating a visit with one parent and simultaneously crash because of the separation from the other. A child may be afraid of forgetting the schedule, particularly if it is new or irregular. Some children worry a good deal about going to the right home after school or getting in trouble for making a mistake.

Difficult transitions should not persist, however. If they continue for more than a couple of months after you set your parenting agreement in motion, you should look for a deeper cause. Often, persistently difficult transitions indicate that there are larger, more troubling issues that deserve some time and attention. Allowing the difficulties to go on for long periods of time will only make things worse—possibly damaging your children's relationships with one or both parents for a long time to come.

ISSUE 17 CROSS-REFERENCES

Worksheet	Questions
Worksheet 1	4, 6, 7
Worksheet 2	4, 5
Worksheet 3	3, 4, 7, 11
Worksheet 4	3, 4, 5, 7, 13, 14

1. Time the Exchange With Other Regular Transitions

By timing your exchange with a drop-off or pick-up at school, after a sporting event, or before or after some other regular activity, the exchange won't feel artificial or forced.

2. Make Exchanges Simple and Quick

Children generally have an easier time saying good-bye to one parent and taking up with the other if the actual exchange is quick and casual. One strategy is to carry out the exchange at a busy public place, such as a park, restaurant, or shopping mall.

Another way to expedite the exchange is for parents to minimize their communication. Speak the day or evening before to discuss necessary information about the children's health, school, and activities. Not only does this allow the exchange of the children to be brief but it also helps parents exchange vital information without making the children sit around and wait. This is especially useful when tension is high.

3. Give Children Your Undivided Attention at the Start of the Visit

The start of any time with your children can be easier and more relaxing if you delay other activities, at least briefly, to give your children some time during which they have your undivided attention. This may be as simple as giving them uninterrupted time to tell you about their activities while with the other parent. If you have more than one child, taking them to a park or the zoo can give each child a chance to talk while the others play. This might be especially helpful if your children have half-siblings or stepsiblings from your new relationship.

4. Give Your Children Some "Breathing Room"

Some children need quiet time at the start of a visit to get reacquainted with you and your household. For these children, jumping right into a frenzy of activity will often backfire. You might give this child some pictures to look through, a book to read or some paper to color on, take this child on a short walk, or find some other low-key activity to do together.

5. Be Patient When Your Children Ask Questions

Children have many questions after their parents go separate ways. Depending on their age and temperament, they may ask why you are no longer together, how decisions are being made, how they will be cared for, whether they will be able to form lasting intimate relationships as an adult, or any number of other questions. You can best help your children by hearing and answering their questions patiently. Eventually, your children's questions will decrease and their comfort with the situation will increase.

Most mental health professionals agree that children don't really need, or necessarily want, to know the intimate details of your relationship. Be careful that in answering your children's questions you don't burden them with your frustration, anger, or disappointment over your partner's sexual performance or compatibility. If they ask, don't ignore them, but redirect the conversation to a more appropriate topic.

6. Establish New Rituals

Children thrive on routines and love rituals. It's important to make sure children have some personal belongings—such as a favorite toy, outfit, or book—with each exchange. You can also set aside a small amount of time at the begin-

ning and end of each visit for a special activity or small ritual. Keep the exchanges predictable, setting them for approximately the same time of day, and at fairly regular intervals. Some children do better making exchanges in the morning or afternoon. Other children handle exchanges better if they are dropped off at the other parent's home. These are some ways to ease the awkwardness of coming together and the discomfort of separation for both you and your children.

H. Issue 18: Maintaining Contact

#_____ **Maintaining Contact When the Children Are With the Other Parent**

_____ Our children and _____ [parent] will make an

effort to talk at least every _____ [specify frequency] as follows:

_____ _____ [parent or children] will initiate each call.

  _____ Calls will be made between _____ and _____.

  _____ If either _____ [parent] or children

  will be unavailable at the usual time, the unavailable person will arrange a new time by:

   _____ calling the other parent

   _____ sending a note

   _____ email message

   _____ other: _____ [specify]

_____ Our children and _____ [parent] will not call back and forth more than every

_____ [specify] unless something unusual happens or it is a special occasion.

_____ Our children will be given their own telephone line.

  _____ _____ [parent] will be responsible to teach telephone rules.

  _____ _____ [parent or children] will be responsible for telephone bills.

_____ _____ [parent] and the children can also communicate by:

  _____ letter

  _____ audio- or videotapes

  _____ email or electronic conferencing

  _____ other: _____ [specify]

_____ Visits with _____ [parent] will include

a midweek dinner on _____ [day of week] as follows [specify time for exchange]:

_____

_____

_____

_____ We will arrange for our children to communicate with _____ [parent]

while our children are away on vacation.

_____ We further agree that [specify]:

_____

_____

_____

Neither children nor adults can be in two places at one time. Keeping up with your children and their interests and activities is important. By planning now for how to stay in touch, you ensure that you will maintain, and even deepen, your relationships with your children.

Maintaining contact with your children demonstrates your love and support, keeps communication channels open, and offers new ways to have fun together—especially if you are creative. Your contact with your children can be both scheduled and spontaneous. Ideally, you will find a mix that works best for everyone.

Scheduled contact should occur at regular times and be convenient for everyone involved. Spontaneous contact is, by definition, unscheduled, but it should not be disruptive. Parents can consider the following options to create a happy medium of both scheduled and spur-of-the-moment contact that can make for rich, well-balanced relationships, regardless of the distance between you and your children.

ISSUE 18 CROSS-REFERENCES

Worksheet	Questions
Worksheet 1	4, 7, 8
Worksheet 2	1, 4, 5
Worksheet 3	4, 5, 6
Worksheet 4	3, 4, 5

1. Set Up a Contact Schedule

Many parents agree to a minimum number of calls between the children and the other parent. For example, you might agree that the parent who doesn't have the children can initiate at least one call per week to the children. Many parents allow their children to initiate additional calls whenever they like.

In some families, the problem isn't too little communication but too much. Calling a child too frequently may cause problems. If you call as often as once or twice a day, you may be communicating that you fear for your children's safety while in the other parent's care, or that you are desperately lonely. By pacing your calls, you can stay in touch without introducing unnecessary worry or anxiety. If, in fact, you are extremely lonely or anxious, discuss the situation with a trusted advisor or mental health professional.

2. Set a Regular Contact Time

Some parents forget that calling their children when they are eating dinner, doing homework, doing chores, or getting ready for school can be disruptive. To avoid this, many parents schedule regular times each week when they can be reasonably sure that their children will be free to talk. Telephone time is set up to be as convenient as possible for both parents and their children. It may take some planning to find this time, but it usually pays off in enjoyable conversations and a minimum amount of disruption in daily routines.

3. Give Children Their Own Telephone Line

It is common for many parents to have less-than-friendly feelings for the other parent after separation or divorce. Therefore, receiving calls from the other parent, even for the brief moment of calling your children to the telephone, can be distasteful. To avoid this, consider getting your children a separate telephone line, or a line with a different ring, so that when it rings only the children answer.

If you choose this option, be prepared to establish ground rules on acceptable telephone use. Your telephone company may have ideas for regulating telephone use and blocking certain types of calls (such as 900 numbers).

4. Schedule a Midweek Dinner

When the parents' homes are in the same general area, scheduling a regular midweek dinner might be a great way to shorten the time between visits and create a special occasion for everyone. If you set up regular midweek dinners, you must specify who will transport your children, as well as the pick-up and drop-off times. (See Issue 16 earlier in this chapter.)

5. Plan for Contact During Trips

Parents need to plan with the other parent for how they can stay in touch with their children when the children are away on a trip. The simplest solution is to leave an itinerary and include telephone numbers for where and when the children can be reached.

6. Be Spontaneous—and Creative!

Letters, care packages, and the like are all inexpensive, nonintrusive ways to stay in touch with your children. Care packages can include books, toys, interesting shells, dried flowers, games, cookies, or almost anything else you and your child might enjoy. Pictures can be mounted on construction paper and assembled into quick "memory" books and sent along to fill your child in on your activities, share your vacation vicariously, or learn about places or things that interest you. Computers and fax machines expand the possibilities even further. Consider faxing cartoons, interesting or funny stories, or your favorite jokes. Email offers instant communication, and the Internet offers the possibility for private "chats" in real time, or even a treasure hunt through the World Wide Web.

7. Extend a "Personal Touch" Into Your Child's Daily Life

Another way for parents to stay in touch is to buy or make small, personalized things that your child can wear, use, or see on a daily basis. While these things need not be expensive or fancy, they can provide a regular reminder that you care. For example, consider personalized pencils, barrettes, a sticker for the bathroom mirror, notepaper, a box for small treasures, or a bookmark.

I. Issue 19: Grandparents, Relatives, and Important Friends

#_____ **Grandparents, Relatives, and Important Friends**

_____ Our children will maintain their relationships with grandparents, other relatives, and important friends as follows:

_____

_____

_____

After your separation or divorce, it is important that you find ways for your children to maintain relationships with other adults who are important to them—namely, grandparents, aunts, uncles, neighbors, and family friends. Children need the security of familiar friends and relationships. These familiar people can help ease the transition for children when their parents no longer live together.

You should consider the following options in your parenting agreement:

- Each parent ensures that the children maintain relationships with the parent's own extended family.
- The parents agree on specific holidays or times when the children will be with particular extended family members.

- One parent arranges for all visits with extended family members. (This option is especially appropriate if one parent has moved out of state while all of the extended family lives near the parent who remains).

Once you have agreed on these issues, be sure to explain them to the relatives and friends involved.

ISSUE 19 CROSS-REFERENCES

Worksheet	Questions
Worksheet 1	4, 8
Worksheet 2	7, 8
Worksheet 3	4, 5
Worksheet 4	5, 11, 12, 15

J. Issue 20: Psychiatric and Other Mental Health Care

#_____   Psychiatric and Other Mental Health Care

_____ Our children may undergo psychiatric or other mental health care as follows [choose all that apply]:

     _____ if either parent feels it is necessary

     _____ if it is recommended by a school counselor or other health care provider

     _____ only if we agree

     _____ only if it is made available through the school

     _____ only if it is available at low or no cost to us

_____ Either of us may undergo psychiatric or other mental health care as follows [choose all that apply]:

     _____ if either parent feels it is necessary

     _____ if it is recommended by a school counselor or other health care provider

     _____ only if we agree

     _____ only if it is made available through the school

     _____ only if it is available at low or no cost to us

_____ Our children's other mental health issues, such as _____ [specify], will be addressed as follows [specify]:

_____

_____

_____

Although many parents are willing to consider providing some mental health or emotional support for their children, few know what signs to look for in the child's behavior. Perhaps the most obvious indicator of emotional or other mental health care needs is a dramatic change in your child's behavior that persists over some period of time. Some of the warning signs include:

- unusual stress, clinging, and/or nervous tics
- regression to previous behavioral stages (for example, bedwetting or thumb-sucking)
- loss of motivation for school, making friends, or having fun
- sleeping too much or too little
- becoming unusually rebellious or argumentative, and
- becoming unusually cooperative and compliant.

Children with a serious medical illness or condition are more at risk for developing psychological problems.

Deciding on psychiatric or other mental health care can be difficult. If you and the other parent discuss this issue, keep in mind that you need to decide the following:

- whether you will permit or require psychiatric or other counseling for your children
- whether you will require psychiatric or other counseling for either parent
- who may provide the care, and
- how you will determine when the need for counseling has ended.

If mental illness is already part of your family's situation, you should pay close attention to your children's needs in this area. Although hereditary links to mental illness are not always clearly defined, professionals note that when parents suffer from manic-depression (bipolar disease), schizophrenia, alcoholism, or other drug abuse, their children are more prone to mental illness.

Counseling for parents is included here because a parent's state of mind and mental health can have a significant impact on children. Whether the parents attend counseling together or define goals to work towards in separate counseling sessions, time spent in counseling usually results in better parenting plans.

Specific provisions in your parenting plan might:

- identify the issues to be addressed (such as anger, frustration, jealousy, or violence)
- allow the counselor and patient to agree when these issues are resolved, and
- provide for a letter from the counselor to the other parent stating that the counselor and the patient agree that the counseling has accomplished its objectives.

ISSUE 20 CROSS-REFERENCES

Worksheet	Questions
Worksheet 1	4, 6
Worksheet 2	7
Worksheet 3	7, 8, 9, 10
Worksheet 4	3, 5, 6, 7, 13, 14

K. Issue 21: Religious Training

#_____ **Religious Training**

_____ Our children's religious training will be as follows [choose all that apply]:

_____ Our children will be raised _____ [specify].

_____ Our children will be taught about both of our religions: _____

and _____ .

_____ Our children may choose their religious training as long as it generally conforms to the principles of the

_____ religion.

_____ Our children may choose their religious training. _____ [parent]
will supervise such training.

_____ We further agree that [specify]:

_____

_____

_____

After separation or divorce, parents may need to plan for their children's religious training. For some parents, this is easy; for others, it presents difficult choices. In many families, parents have different religions. Whether you will expose your children to one religion, agree to disagree, teach two religions, give your children no formal religious training, or let your children choose for themselves, religion can be an important aspect of a child's development. It can also have a big influence on how you decide other elements of the agreement, such as medical care (Issue 2), mental health care (Issue 20), education (Issue 6), child care (Issue 12), and outside activities (Issue 15), among others. (Additional information on multicultural families is in Chapter 14.)

ISSUE 21 CROSS-REFERENCES

Worksheet	Questions
Worksheet 1	9
Worksheet 2	1, 2, 3
Worksheet 3	3, 4
Worksheet 4	3, 5

1. Teach One Religion

This is probably the approach you will take if both parents have the same religion. But even if your religions differ, you may choose one religion for the sake of simplicity or because one parent has stronger religious ties. This is especially common when children have two Christian parents who belong to different denominations, or have one parent who strongly identifies with being Jewish while the other parent has nominal ties with a Christian denomination.

2. Teach Both Religions

Some parents agree that they want their children to grow up understanding both parents' religious beliefs. If this is your choice, consider whether either parent will be allowed to confirm, convert, or otherwise formally indoctrinate the children in a particular faith.

3. Agree on Basic Tenets and Allow Children to Choose Denomination

Some parents don't have a strong preference about which denomination their children are raised in, as long as the principal values follow a general religious belief, such as

Christian, Moslem, Jewish, Hindu, or Buddhist. In this situation, consider who will expose the children to the faith and take them to services. Also consider what you will do if your children express an interest in a particular denomination.

4. Let Children Choose Religious Participation

Some parents do not subscribe to any particular faith, are not active in any congregation, or have no interest in providing religious training for their children. In this situation, decide how you will respond if your children some day express an interest in religion. You might decide to take them to religious services of their choice, expose them to several different religions, or refuse to let them participate. Also, if you and the other parent do participate religiously but you want to let your children choose for themselves, consider what you will do if your children select no religious training.

L. Issue 22: Surname

#_____ **Surname**

_____ Our children's surname is _____.

Any decision to change that surname will be made as follows [choose all that apply]:

_____ Our children will keep this surname until they become legal adults.

_____ Our children may choose their surname.

_____ Our children may choose their surname after age _____.

_____ We will discuss and agree on any change of surname.

_____ _____ [parent] has the authority to change our children's surname.

_____ We further agree that [specify]:

_____

_____

_____

Many parents never question what last name their children will use after divorce or separation; however, the issue does come up. In general, courts require that a child's surname be chosen with the child's best interests in mind.

In some families, everyone has the same last name. In other families, they are all different. Some of the options you can consider include:

- give the children one parent's surname
- create a new name from both parents' surnames (such as a hyphenated name), or
- have the children use one parent's last name from a new relationship or marriage.

After separation or divorce—especially if one or both parents changed names when the couple married or began living together—either or both parents might choose to return to a previous name. Additionally, a parent who begins a new relationship after divorce or separation might change his or her last name to match the new mate's surname.

Your children will need to know what their last name is and who has the authority to change that name. Some parents let their children choose their name; others allow the children that choice only after they reach a certain age.

Some parents attempt to change their children's last name without the other parent's consent. They might even register the children in school, with the doctor, or elsewhere under the new name. Asking children to assume a new last name without the other parent's consent can be confusing for the children and often provokes an argument with the other parent. It also means that your children's school, medical, and other records might be difficult to piece together. Finally, a court may require you to change the child's name back.

In most states, when you change a minor's last name, you must obtain court approval.

ISSUE 22 CROSS-REFERENCES

Worksheet	Questions
Worksheet 3	1,5
Worksheet 4	1, 2

M. Issue 23: Treating Each Child as an Individual

#_____   **Treating Each Child as an Individual**

_____ Each of our children will sometimes need separate or special time with each of us. Therefore, we will set up short separate visits as follows [specify]:

_____

_____

_____ Each of our children will sometimes need separate or special time with each of us. Therefore, we will set up separate time for each child while visiting together as follows [specify]:

_____

_____

_____ Each of our children will sometimes need separate or special time with each of us. Therefore, we further agree that [specify]:

_____

_____

_____

Many parents assume that visits should always be the same for each child, and that children should always visit their parents together. Parents, however, can do their children a great service by tailoring some visits to meet the needs, personalities, and interests of only one child at a time.

In the book *Divorce and Your Child* (Yale University Press, 1984), authors Sonja Goldstein and Albert Solnit observed that:

> *While it is generally preferable for brothers and sisters not to be separated by their parent's divorce, it does not follow that in a smoothly working joint custody situation … all the children must spend the same day or parts of days with the same parent in the same manner. This is not the way it is for children whose parents live together; older and younger brothers and sisters do not have the same activities, and it would place an unwarranted burden on children of divorced parents if joint custody were to hamper them.*

This is not to say that all visits should be separate, but only to suggest that parents consider occasional arrangements to allow each child time alone with each parent.

ISSUE 23 CROSS-REFERENCES

Worksheet	Questions
Worksheet 1	1, 2, 3, 4, 5, 6, 7
Worksheet 2	1, 4, 5, 7
Worksheet 3	3, 6, 7, 8
Worksheet 4	3, 4, 5, 6, 11

1. Schedule Short, Separate Visits With Each Child

Scheduling a separate visit with each child allows you and each child to plan a special activity for just the two of you. It is a good strategy for smoothing over rough spots in the relationship, as well as providing a fun time that only the two of you have shared. To make the most of this kind of visit, have your child help plan the activities, and take pictures or collect mementos of your "adventure" for your child to keep.

2. Children Take Turns Being the Center of Your Attention

You may not be able to schedule separate visits for your children. You can still carve out special time for each child by:

- setting aside a small amount of time for each child during each visit
- having the children take turns deciding which activities everyone will engage in during your visits, or
- staggering the arrival or departure times for each child (school or other activity schedules may facilitate this) to allow special time for each child.

N. Issue 24: Separating Adult and Parenting Issues

#_____   **Separating Adult Relationship Issues From Parenting Issues**

_____   We agree that we will separate our adult relationship issues from the parenting issues as follows [choose all that apply]:

_____   agree to resolve all parenting decisions first

_____   schedule separate telephone calls

_____   arrange to discuss adult relationship issues when away from our children

_____   discuss adult relationship issues during joint counseling sessions

_____   We further agree that [specify]:

_____

_____

_____

It is essential to remember how important it is to keep your children out of the middle of your issues with the other parent. You must learn to separate your adult relationship issues from the parenting decisions you must make. Parents face two common problems when they begin to parent separately: First, they often get so wrapped up in adult relationship issues that they either forget to discuss the children or get so angry that further discussion and agreement becomes impossible. Second, their adult relationship issues become entangled with parenting issues, making it increasingly difficult to focus on the children's best interests.

While most parents see the value in separating their adult relationship issues from the parenting issues, many wonder just how they will be able to do it. Here are some concrete ideas you can incorporate into your agreement to help you keep the two issues as separate from each other as possible.

1. Agree to Resolve Parenting Decisions First

Perhaps the simplest way to ensure that adult relationship issues do not cloud your parenting decisions is to agree that you will always resolve the "kid issues" before discussing any adult issues you have.

2. Schedule Separate Telephone Calls

Some parents have a difficult time following the ground rule described above—that is, to resolve parenting decisions first. For them, it often helps if they can at least agree to set up a separate telephone call or meeting time when they will discuss whatever adult relationship issues need to be resolved. This often works best when parents have already agreed to have regular telephone calls to discuss the children. If either parent wishes to raise non-child-related issues for discussion, they can let the other know during the regularly scheduled "kid update" call, and set another time for that conversation to take place.

3. Discuss Adult Relationship Issues Away From Your Children

Some parents can resolve the parenting issues first, but then proceed to take up adult issues within their children's earshot. For these parents, incorporating a provision of this kind helps to remind each of them that they must handle their adult business elsewhere.

4. Discuss Adult Relationship Issues During Joint Counseling Sessions

Many parents still have substantial and reoccurring adult issues to resolve long after the divorce is final. If this is true for you and the other parent, it may be more productive—and better for your children—if you save your conversations for a joint mediation or counseling session when someone can facilitate your discussions. It can also help you to find ways to resolve those issues on a more permanent basis.

ISSUE 24 CROSS-REFERENCES

Worksheet	Questions
Worksheet 1	4, 8
Worksheet 2	6, 7, 8, 10
Worksheet 3	7, 9, 10, 11
Worksheet 4	2, 3, 7, 13, 14

O. Issue 25: Making Changes

#_____ **Making Changes**

_____ We will regularly review this agreement as follows: _____ [list dates or frequency, as appropriate]

_____ We will review this agreement when problems arise.

_____ Reviews will be:

    _____ by telephone

    _____ in person

    _____ through:

        _____ counseling

        _____ mediation

        _____ arbitration

        _____ other: _____ [specify]

_____ Our children may participate in the discussions.

_____ Our children may participate in the decisions.

Most parents would like their parenting agreement to last for the entire course of their separate parenting relationship. The reality, however, is that changes are pretty much unavoidable. Parents generally need to renegotiate substantial portions of their parenting agreement approximately every two and a half to three years.

Any number of things might require you to make changes to your parenting plan, including your children's changing needs, interests, and activities as they get older. Some of the other events that commonly trigger the need for a change to your existing arrangements include:

- one or both parents "settle down" with a new partner or spouse
- one parent plans to move a substantial distance away from the other parent
- your preteen or teen wants to change their primary residence, or develop a primary residence, rather than splitting the time equally between both homes
- one or more children develop a serious discipline problem in one home
- the schools in one parent's area no longer meet the children's needs
- the primary caretaking parent needs to devote more time to school or a career, or
- the primary caretaking parent is making it difficult for the children to spend time with their other parent, in violation of existing court orders.

All parents need to respond to the inevitable changes in their children's, or their own, lives. By anticipating the need to modify your agreement in the future, you can minimize much of the conflict parents normally experience when troublesome issues arise, or if your children ask for modifications. (For more information on this particular issue, see Chapter 12, Dealing With Changes in Your Agreement.)

ISSUE 25 CROSS-REFERENCES

Worksheet	Questions
Worksheet 1	6, 7
Worksheet 2	2, 3, 8, 9, 10
Worksheet 3	1, 4, 5, 7, 9, 10
Worksheet 4	1, 2, 3, 4, 5, 7, 13, 14

1. Set Up Regular Reviews

Consider reviewing your parenting agreement:

- once a year
- when your children change schools, or
- as your children reach certain ages.

In the first few years after you separate or divorce, you might consider more frequent reviews (such as every six months) until you are sure you have settled upon a final agreement.

Give yourselves enough time to negotiate whatever changes are necessary. Scheduling the review approximately one month before the school year begins or about one month before the start of the summer break should give you plenty of time.

When you review your agreement, you may discover that you have already informally negotiated changes, or that certain aspects of the agreement no longer work. If you negotiate changes to the agreement, modify it in writing to reflect the changes.

2. Allow Your Children to Share in Decisions

You may want to give your children a role in deciding where they will live and how they will spend time with both parents. Some parents solicit their children's opinions no matter what their ages; others wait until the children are teenagers.

Though it is often a good idea to ask your children for their thoughts on what they would like the most—or what kinds of arrangement they think would work best—you and the other parent need to be careful that you are not putting too much pressure on your children. It is a very difficult, but critically important, balancing act. The balancing act can become even more challenging if a child wants to be involved. Often, this will happen with later elementary school–aged children or adolescents. The key is to hear what they have to say, ask questions to see if you can understand why they want what they are asking for, and then tell the child that their views will be taken into

account as you and the other parent go through your decision-making process. Some of the ways that parents put too much pressure on their children when they involve them in the discussion about making changes to the parenting agreement are by:

- making the child feel that he or she has to "choose" between one parent or the other
- making the child demonstrate which parent he or she loves more by making the choices that parent wants, or show who he or she wants to be with more by choosing to be with that parent more of the time
- treating them as if they have the same authority as an adult to decide what is in their best interests (almost setting them up as a co-parent, or allowing them to make the decisions as if they were the parent).

3. Consider Mediation

You may be willing to evaluate or renegotiate your parenting agreement only if a third party is present. In this situation, include an automatic mediation schedule for reviewing your agreement, or allow either parent to schedule mediation as necessary. (More information on mediation is in Chapter 11.)

4. Get an Expert Opinion

There are many services and professionals that can help separating or divorcing parents handle almost any problem they might encounter in their separate parenting relationship.

P. Issue 26: Making Substantive Changes to the Agreement

#_____ **Making Substantive Changes to This Agreement**

_____ If we negotiate a substantive modification of this agreement, _____ [parent] will prepare (or make sure that someone else prepares) a summary of the agreement so that we may obtain a court order incorporating our changes. Each parent will be responsible to review the agreement prior to its submission to the court, and to seek independent advice on the agreement to ensure that it says what we intend it to say, accomplishes our objectives, and is within the general parameters of what a court is likely to approve.

_____ We further agree that [specify]:

_____

_____

If you make a substantive change to your parenting agreement, you will want to modify existing court orders so that your agreement is enforceable. This may seem unnecessary if your relationship with the other parent is working well; if it deteriorates, however, you may not be able to enforce your agreement.

ISSUE 26 CROSS-REFERENCES

Worksheet	Questions
Worksheet 1	6, 7
Worksheet 2	7, 8
Worksheet 3	1, 4, 5, 7
Worksheet 4	1, 2, 4, 5, 7

Q. Issue 27: Explaining the Agreement to Your Children

#_____ **Explaining the Agreement to Our Children**

_____ _____ [parent] will explain this agreement to our children. _____ [other parent] will be available to answer any questions the children might have.

_____ We further agree that [specify]:

_____

_____

_____

You and the other parent must consider how to tell your children about your parenting agreement. If possible, tell them together. If that won't work, decide who will tell them and what that person will say. You must also decide how your children's questions will be answered. You can agree that either parent will answer any questions that the children have. Alternatively, you can select one parent to field some, or all, of the questions.

Some children, especially younger children, have difficulty understanding that they will continue to be loved even though their parents no longer love each other. Many children fear they were the cause of the separation or divorce, especially if you and the other parent argued frequently about child-rearing issues. To help your children, stress that the decision to separate or divorce was made because of the relationship between the parents, not because of anything that the children did or did not do. No matter what you say, find a way to make sure that your children know they are loved.

Calendars and dates don't mean much to preschoolers. They do understand, however, the sequence of familiar events. Try to explain when they will see you or the other parent again in relation to other events that they enjoy. For example, if your children attend swimming lessons on Tuesdays and Thursdays, explain that you will see them after two more swimming lessons.

You can also talk briefly (under five minutes), and often, about how the new arrangements will work. Give children age-appropriate books, videos, or workbooks that explain what it's like to live in two homes, or to live primarily with one parent and visit with the other parent on weekends or holidays. Ideally, you should tell the children about the parenting plan and how it will work before any changes are made. Although some children can handle this kind of information fairly well on their own, other children need help (perhaps from a counselor) to deal with all of the feelings that come up when they see how their lives will change. Some of the ways that parents choose to tell

their children about the parenting plan for the first time include:

- telling the children together
- having only one parent tell the children
- having one or both parents explain the plan during a counseling session (especially if they are already seeing a counselor), or
- inviting the children to attend the last part of a mediation session to learn about the new agreement.

Regardless of which option you choose, your children should not find out about the parenting plan by reading any of the court documents, especially if they include evaluations or declarations about a parent's weaknesses or why they should or should not have primary custody of the children.

ISSUE 27 CROSS-REFERENCES

Worksheet	Questions
Worksheet 1	6, 7
Worksheet 2	3
Worksheet 3	7
Worksheet 4	3, 4, 5, 7

CHAPTER

8

Serious Issues

ome parents have serious issues, like domestic violence or substance abuse, that they must address in their parenting agreement. In some cases, these issues need to be addressed immediately, in the first parenting agreement. For others, these issues may never be relevant, or they may become relevant over time. Before you work on your parenting agreement, read through this chapter and include in your agreement anything that reflects your current needs or situation.

A. Issue 28: Domestic Violence, Child Abuse, and Child Neglect

#_____   **Domestic Violence, Child Abuse, and Child Neglect**

_____ If events such as _____ [specify] occur, _____ [parent] may seek a restraining order from the court that will [specify]:

_____
_____
_____

_____ Anyone providing care for our children other than a parent will be told about any existing restraining orders.

_____ _____ [parent] will seek counseling from _____ _____ [provider] regarding _____ _____ [specify]; also [choose all that apply]:

_____ Parent and provider will be permitted to determine when the need for counseling has concluded.

_____ At the conclusion of parent's counseling, provider will send a letter to _____ [other parent] indicating that counseling has concluded to the parent and provider's satisfaction.

_____ We will offer counseling and emotional support to our children as indicated in Issue # _____ [Psychiatric and Other Mental Health Care].

_____ If our children are exposed to a violent or otherwise dangerous situation, the parent in whose care they are will remove them from the situation and, if necessary, find another adult to provide care for them.

_____ Our children may call _____ [adult's name] if they fear for their safety while in _____ 's [parent] care. This adult will care for the children until he/she receives different instructions from the other parent.

_____ We will seek an independent evaluation regarding _____ _____ [specify] for help in how we might best address this situation.

_____ The time the children are with _____ [parent] will be supervised by _____ [other adult] to ensure the children's safety and well-being. The supervised visits will continue until [choose all that apply]:

_____ Our children feel ready to spend time alone with _____ .

_____ A counselor indicates that the supervision is unnecessary.

_____ Other: _____ [specify]

_____ From _____ until _____ , _____ [parent] will not spend time with our children.

_____ During that time, _____ [parent] will maintain contact with our children via [choose all that apply]:

_____ phone

_____ letter

_____ email

_____ other: _____ [specify]

_____ We further agree that [specify]:

_____

Domestic violence, child abuse, and child neglect are serious issues that affect all members of a family. Reports of violence, abuse, and neglect are on the rise nationwide. Domestic violence, child abuse, and child neglect happen in all kinds of families, in all parts of the country, and at all income levels. Domestic violence can be directed at women, men, and children. It may or may not be associated with drug or alcohol abuse. Some estimates show that approximately one in five marriages will experience at least five violent episodes each year. Other statistics estimate that in approximately 50% of the families where a mate is abused, the children are abused as well.

Get professional help if there is abuse in your home. Do not assume that violence directed at an adult does not affect the children. Children are very aware of their surroundings. Furthermore, violence, abuse, and neglect come in many forms. Hitting, molestation, name-calling, intimidation, abandonment, kidnapping, and neglect of basic needs for food, shelter, care, and protection all harm children—whether or not they are the intended targets.

Families with a history of violence, abuse, or neglect often use mediation, counseling, or attorneys to make their parenting decisions. Mediation can be a problem, however. A victim may be intimidated when making decisions with the batterer in the room. If your state requires mediation in custody and visitation disputes (see Chapter 16), ask for separate meetings with the mediator so that you can speak without fear or feeling intimidated.

In some states, judges appoint a social worker to evaluate both parents' homes and make a custody or visitation recommendation to the judge. In that situation, be honest about what has gone on and your concerns for the future. If you would feel more comfortable having a support person with you during an evaluation, ask the judge or social worker if it's possible. It's unlikely you'll be told no.

If your children are a target for a parent's uncontrolled anger, sexual advances, or violence, consider bringing in someone trained in assessing domestic abuse to help you decide whether your children will be safe in that parent's care. (We explain how to find domestic abuse experts in Chapter 17.) If violence or abuse against any family member was or is a fairly common event, the expert can recommend a treatment plan so the children are not placed in the same situations in that parent's new home or family setting.

KIDNAPPING IS A FORM OF CHILD ABUSE

Some 360,000 children are abducted each year in the United States. Only one in 750 of these is a stranger abduction. In cases involving a child abducted by a parent, the children are often under the age of six (implying that preschool children are easier to hide). For parents negotiating a parenting agreement, it is important to understand some of the most common reasons why parents abduct their children. These include:

- to exert control, power, or revenge in the parenting relationship
- to protect a child from physical abuse or sexual assault
- the abducting parent suffers from narcissistic personality disorder, or
- the abducting parent cannot accept responsibility for his or her own contributions to the marriage and divorce troubles.

Kidnapping, or child abduction, is a form of child abuse. Although it may happen in response to physical abuse or as a result of mental health problems, it is just as likely to happen when one parent feels powerless to influence his or her children's upbringing in the separate parenting arrangement. Quite simply, this means that parents who feel that they have nothing to gain by accepting little or no contact with their children are more likely to abduct those children.

If you were the target of violence or abuse in your family relationship, get help from a counselor or therapist to make sure the decisions you make for your children are not based on fear or intimidation. You should also find out what protective court orders might help you during the time when these decisions are being made and afterwards.

ISSUE 28 CROSS-REFERENCES

Worksheet	Questions
Worksheet 1	4, 8
Worksheet 2	3, 5, 6, 7, 8
Worksheet 3	1, 3, 4, 5, 6, 7, 9, 10, 11
Worksheet 4	1, 2, 3, 5, 6, 7, 12, 13, 14, 15

1. Make Protective Orders Work

If you are concerned about violence or abuse, you can get a protective order from a court that tells an abuser to stay away. Though a piece of paper is not a guarantee that the abuse will stop, most abusers adhere to the terms of an order.

Whether you are trying to negotiate or implement decisions regarding your children, protective orders can help:

- provide time and space to let a situation cool down
- keep specific people away from each other
- require supervised visits with the abuser, and
- limit telephone calls between the abuser and victims.

Be aware, however, that the time you decide to get a restraining order can be the most dangerous time of all. This is often because the other parent may want to scare you or hurt you to prevent you from getting help. It is important to talk with a professional to evaluate how dangerous your situation is and to plan for your family's safety.

A court may issue a temporary protective order that can be modified, extended, or made permanent, as needed. Some people change, or even drop, their protective orders if the restrictions later seem unnecessary. This might be the case, for example, if the violence happened only once at the time of separation and was not severe.

If you are considering dropping a protective order, consult with an attorney, counselor, or other domestic violence expert first. They may advise you to modify the order, rather than drop it altogether. This would keep the power of the court behind you but make it a little easier to handle visits or information exchanges about the children. Remember that your court order stands until it is formally changed by a judge's decision. That means that the restrained parent can be arrested or found in contempt of court if he or she does anything that is not allowed by the court order.

2. Require Counseling or Emotional Support

One way to stop violence, abuse, or neglect is to deal with the issue openly and honestly. Many parents agree to undergo counseling to learn how to change their behavior. (See Chapter 17 for more information.) A parent who doesn't volunteer may be ordered to counseling by a court.

The abusive or neglectful parent may not be the only one who needs counseling. Often victims need counseling as well. If the abuse or neglect has ended, the parents may need joint counseling to learn how to work together.

3. Looking for and Responding to Signs of Child Abuse

Many parents wonder what signs to look for in a child who has been a victim of abuse. This question is a difficult one, and not just because abuse is such an emotionally charged issue. One of the most difficult aspects of assessing whether abuse has occurred (unless, of course, you witness that abuse) is that the signs or cues you must look for can also indicate other problems—some psychiatric and others developmental.

Professionals in the American Association of Child and Adolescent Psychiatry (AACAP) caution that even severe abuse may not surface in the child's awareness until adolescence, or even later. There are, however, some common behaviors children often exhibit if they have been victims of abuse. Be careful not to jump to conclusions. These types of behaviors should alert you to the fact that the child may be experiencing some kind of problem, and that abuse could be one of the causes. The AACAP notes that regardless of whether the child reports abuse, he or she may exhibit one or more of the following behaviors:

- a poor self-image
- an inability to depend on, trust, or love others
- aggressive, disruptive, and sometimes illegal behavior
- passive or withdrawn behavior
- fear of entering into new activities or relationships
- school failure, or
- serious drug or alcohol abuse.

Most parents, or other adults, don't know what to do when they suspect that a child has been abused, or if a child tells them they have been physically or sexually abused. Commonly, the adult who encounters this kind of information feels shocked, angry, confused, skeptical, or even afraid. How you handle this situation, however, is critically important. Regardless of whether you believe that either the suspected or reported abuse has occurred, professionals recommend you communicate your support for the child first, and then try to understand the reality of the situation.

The first step in supporting the child who reports abuse is to allow him or her to convey as much information to you as they are able, with as little pressure from you as possible. Next, you must enlist the help of one or more trained professionals, such as a doctor, nurse, or other medical professional, police officer, domestic violence counselor, mental health professional, or other trusted advisor to help unravel the child's experiences and feelings and understand what further responses are appropriate to the situation. Specifically, the AACAP recommends adults respond to the child who reports abuse as follows:

- encourage the child to talk freely
- don't make comments that appear to judge the child or the situation
- show that you understand and take the child's comments seriously
- assure the child that they did the right thing by telling you about the situation
- tell the child that they are not to blame for the abuse
- offer the child protection, and
- promise to take prompt steps to end the abuse—and then do just that.

How can you know whether claims of child sexual abuse are true? Much has been made recently of false claims of child sexual abuse. As a result, many question whether children, or adults, can be trusted when they report child abuse—especially if these reports surface for the first time as part of divorce proceedings or modifications of existing custody and visitation orders. While some assert that claims made during divorce or custody battles are manufactured to ensure a "win," others worry that legitimate claims are dismissed because they cannot be proved not to have been manufactured. Unfortunately, there will probably never be any clear-cut formula for guaranteeing the legitimacy of each and every claim.

Most professionals underscore the fact that any allegations of child sexual abuse are serious and should be treated as such. Regardless of the validity of the particular claims, however, the child who is at the center of this whirlwind will be affected and will need help to deal both with his or her own feelings and with the investigations and battles that are sure to follow.

4. Get an Independent Evaluation

A trained professional can provide parents with an objective opinion about how to deal with violence, abuse, or neglect. Depending on the issues involved, parents can learn new strategies for dealing with stress, disciplining their children, and understanding their children's behavior. Unless you are low-income and qualify for financial help, you will probably have to pay for this kind of evaluation.

5. Require Supervised Visitation

Supervised visitation means that another adult is present when your children spend time with an abusive parent or a parent who presents a serious threat of kidnapping. The court may recommend a specific person who has been trained to perform this function. If not, you and the other parent must find your own supervisor. This can be a relative or friend, or a social worker or battered women's shelter employee whom you may need to pay. Some courts require the supervisor to file a report with the court, describing the visit and the children's reactions to the parent.

If you decide to have your children's visits with one parent supervised, be sure that you specify what "supervised" means. Any court order you get should include:

- who will supervise the visits and what kind of training this person will need (some states and courts insist on the use of trained volunteers or professional visitation supervisors)
- how long the visits will last
- whether the visits can take place at the parent's home or at another location, like a playground or visitation center
- whether there will be limits on the types of activities the children can do with this parent
- how you will know whether the supervised visits are succeeding—for example, are the children becoming more comfortable around a previously absent parent, or is an angry parent demonstrating more self-control?
- how often the need for supervised visits will be reviewed, and
- when the supervised visits can end.

You should also identify an adult whom your children can call if they ever fear for their safety while in a parent's care. Be sure your children know that they will never be punished for calling this adult, even if their fears were unfounded.

6. Take a Break

If the violence you're experiencing is the result of the stress of separation or divorce, take a break. After the parents have established new homes and you get some counseling, then slowly resume visits between the children and the abusive parent.

B. Issue 29: Alcohol or Drug Abuse

#_____ **Alcohol or Drug Abuse**

_____ _____ [parent] will attend a 12-step or similar program.

_____ _____ [parent] will seek counseling from _____

_____ [provider] to deal with the substance abuse; also [choose all that apply]:

_____ Parent and provider will be permitted to determine when the need for counseling has concluded.

_____ At the conclusion of parent's counseling, provider will send a letter to _____
[other parent] indicating that counseling has concluded to the parent and provider's satisfaction.

_____ _____ [parent] will modify his/her behavior around
our children so that he/she is "sober" as follows [choose all that apply]:

_____ Will not operate a motor vehicle within _____ hours of consuming drugs or alcohol.

_____ Will not consume drugs or alcohol for at least _____ hours before visits with the children.

_____ Will submit to a drug and alcohol screening test performed by _____
_____ [name of organization].

_____ The time the children are with _____ [parent] will be supervised
by _____ [other adult] to ensure
the children's safety and well-being. The supervised visits will continue until [choose all that apply]:

_____ Our children feel ready to spend time alone with _____ .

_____ A counselor indicates that the supervision is unnecessary.

_____ Other: _____ [specify]

_____ _____ [parent] will prevent others
from consuming drugs or alcohol while our children are in [his/her] care.

_____ During that time, _____ [parent]
will maintain contact with our children via [choose all that apply]:

_____ phone

_____ letter

_____ email

_____ other: _____ [specify]

_____ We further agree that [specify]:

_____

_____

_____

Many parents have alcohol or drug problems. For some, it is an ongoing problem. Others use alcohol or drugs to escape the pain of the separation or divorce. You and the other parent will be more successful in dealing with these issues if you allow the addicted parent to help define and control his or her own recovery.

ISSUE 29 CROSS-REFERENCES

Worksheet	Questions
Worksheet 1	3, 4, 7, 8
Worksheet 2	8
Worksheet 3	1, 6, 7, 10
Worksheet 4	1, 2, 3, 5, 7, 12, 14, 15

1.   Attend a 12-Step or Similar Recovery Program

There are many 12-step recovery programs, such as Alcoholics Anonymous, that meet daily throughout the country. (Chapter 17 provides information on how to locate these types of programs.) Some programs will provide a written record of a person's attendance to whoever needs to verify it. In some instances this will be the court, while in others it might be the other parent.

2.   Require Counseling or Emotional Support

Consider requiring a parent to get counseling. Some courts require the completion of a particular course of counseling or group therapy. If you agree to counseling without court intervention, check with a mental health agency, doctor, hospital, police department, community organization, or church to find a qualified counselor.

Your agreement will be more likely to succeed if it:
- describes what specific behavior must stop
- describes what issues must be covered (such as ending the substance abuse and dealing with feelings of anger, jealousy, and abandonment), and
- gives the addicted parent and the counselor a method of defining when the problem is under control.

3.   Structure or Limit Access to the Children

Getting a handle on a substance-abuse problem can take a long time. You may want to establish certain conditions before allowing the parent with the problem to care for the children, such as:

- The parent with the alcohol or drug problem will not operate a vehicle with the children in it within 12 hours of consuming any alcohol or nonprescription drugs.
- The parent with the alcohol or drug problem will not consume alcohol or nonprescription drugs within 12 hours prior to, or during, any visit with the children.
- The parent with the alcohol or drug problem will not allow any person to consume alcohol to excess or nonprescription drugs in the children's presence.
- The parent with the alcohol or drug problem will submit to alcohol or drug testing if the other parent requests it. If that parent passes the test, the other parent pays for the test. If the parent fails the test, he or she must pay for it and forfeits scheduled visits until he or she can pass a test. (Alcohol or drug testing might be available through your police department, hospital, or public health facility. You will have to investigate what services are available in your area. There is no universal way these services are made available to the public.)
- You can limit visits, or require them to be supervised (see Issue 28, earlier in this chapter), until the parent with the alcohol or drug problem successfully completes a rehabilitation program.
- Identify an adult whom your children can call if they ever fear for their safety while in a parent's care. Be sure to let your children know that they will never be punished for calling this adult, even if their fears were unfounded.

C. Issue 30: Undermining the Parent-Child Relationship

#_____   **Undermining the Parent-Child Relationship**

_____   We will encourage and support our children in maintaining a good relationship with the other parent. If either of us feels that the other is undermining our relationship with our children, we will proceed as follows [choose all that apply]:

_____   We will discuss the matter and try to reach an agreement.

_____   We will resolve the dispute through:

_____   counseling

_____   mediation

_____   arbitration

_____   other: _____ [specify]

_____   We further agree that [specify]:

_____

_____

_____

Many parents are uncomfortable with their children's relationship with the other parent. Children pick up on this quickly. When parents cry out in frustration, "You are just like your (mother/father) when you do that," children hear this as a warning that they possess a bad character trait or personality flaw.

Some parents try to undermine their children's relationship with the other parent in a more direct manner. For example, one parent might force the children to sit and listen to lectures about the other parent's faults. Sometimes (less commonly), a parent will punish the children for talking about the other parent or asking to see the other parent. Or a parent might try to prevent the children from talking to, spending time with, or accepting gifts from the other parent.

In some instances, a parent might physically inspect the children upon each return, looking for evidence of mistreatment. Unless you have real reasons for suspecting child abuse, do not examine your children in this way. You are likely to instill real, yet unwarranted, fear in your children that they must worry about their safety when they are with the other parent.

Whether your undermining efforts are indirect or direct, the effect on your children is the same. They will be torn between a desire to love both parents and the need to earn approval by saying they love one parent and hate the other.

ISSUE 30 CROSS-REFERENCES

Worksheet	Questions
Worksheet 1	4, 5, 7, 8
Worksheet 2	3, 4, 5, 6, 7
Worksheet 3	4, 5, 6, 7, 11
Worksheet 4	3, 4, 5, 7, 11, 12

D. Issue 31: Denying Access to the Children

#_____   **Denying Access to the Children**

_____ If either of us is denied physical access to our children, contact with them, or information about them, we will proceed as follows [choose all that apply]:

_____ We will discuss the matter and try to reach an agreement that will involve reinstating a visitation schedule.

_____ We will resolve the dispute through:

_____ counseling

_____ mediation

_____ arbitration

_____ other: _____ [specify]

_____ We further agree that [specify]:

_____

_____

_____

Some parents try to limit the relationship that their children have, or might have, with the other parent. It may be because of lingering anger or pain from the separation or divorce. Or, when communication breaks down and conflict heats up, one parent might stop adhering to the children's visitation schedule and not allow the children to have time with the other parent.

If you feel that your only recourse in a particularly troubling situation is to deny the other parent access to the children, you must obtain outside help. If you've already decided Issue 9—Resolving Disputes (discussed in Chapter 6)—follow your agreement. If you haven't, consult Chapter 4 for information on negotiating, Chapter 11 for information on mediation and arbitration, and Chapter 17 for ideas on finding appropriate resources.

ISSUE 31 CROSS-REFERENCES

Worksheet	Questions
Worksheet 1	3, 4
Worksheet 2	6, 7
Worksheet 3	1, 4, 5, 7, 11
Worksheet 4	1, 2, 3, 4, 7, 15

E. Issue 32: If Extended Family Members or Close Friends Are Fueling the Dispute

#_____   **If Extended Family Members or Close Friends Are Fueling the Dispute**

_____   We will encourage our children to have ongoing relationships with members of our extended family and with our close friends as long as those relationships are healthy and do not make disputes we have over parenting or adult relationship issues worse.

_____   If a family member or close friend is fueling our disputes over parenting or adult relationship issues, we agree that, as appropriate, either the parent who has the most frequent contact with this person, or both parents will:

_____   limit the information shared with this person

_____   schedule a "family meeting" to discuss the matter, and identify ways it can be addressed and resolved

_____   ask an attorney to explain the matter to the family member or friend, and to ask him or her to stop whatever behaviors are fueling the dispute

_____   schedule a mediation session with the family member or friend to discuss the matter and find ways it can be addressed and resolved

_____   create a talking circle among the extended family or among close friends to discuss the matter and find ways it can be addressed and resolved

_____   get a court order to have the family member or friend stop the behavior that is fueling the dispute

_____   We further agree that [specify]:

_____

_____

_____

Sometimes, dealing with "over-involved" grandparents, other family members, or close friends can be the greatest stumbling block parents face as they separate or divorce. Though you will want to encourage your children to maintain their relationships with other significant adults (see Issue 19: Grandparents, Relatives, and Important Friends), you do not want to allow these relationships to undermine your ability to make decisions and maintain control over the situation.

When parents ask for help in coping with a troubled marriage, separation, or divorce, that "help" can sometimes become a hindrance. Occasionally, grandparents, other relatives, or close friends decide that they have a stake in the decisions that you and the other parent make as part of your separation or divorce (or even that they would be the better custodian for your children). When this happens, their influence on your negotiations can be overwhelming—and it can make an already difficult situation even worse.

Grandparents or others may become overly involved—first with trying to save the marriage, and then in blaming one or the other parent when the marriage fails. Alterna-tively, the grandparent, other relative, or close friend may feel that the marriage or relationship is destructive, and that one partner is incapable of ending it on their own. This is often the case when domestic violence, child abuse, or child neglect has been involved.

In extreme cases, grandparents or other close relatives fear that the natural or adoptive parents are incapable of providing the care children need. The result can be a custody battle in which parents, grandparents, or others try to prove their fitness, the unfitness of the others, or that they have a significant relationship with the children. In the event someone other than the parents is trying to gain custody of the children, it often helps to get an opinion on the matter from a trained mental health professional.

Outside intervention, even if well-intentioned, can take on a life of its own. This can interfere with the parents' efforts to reduce conflict and negotiate child-focused agreements. While it can be difficult to ask an over-involved grandparent or other relative or close friend to stay out of the middle of the conflict, it may be the best way for parents to figure out their own priorities and negotiate their agreements.

Some of the ways that you can tell whether grandparents, other relatives, or friends are becoming over-involved include:

- receiving regular calls from the same person who is "just asking how everything is going" (translate—wants an update about the latest "horror story")
- receiving regular calls to report about the other parent's activities (especially activities that don't have much to do with parenting, like who the other parent went out with on Saturday night)
- hearing how many people are lining up "for" or "against" one or the other parent
- being told that others are willing to back you "if you want to get serious about it and sue," or
- being told that an outside party might sue for temporary custody if both parents can't make progress in their custody battle soon.

When trying to sort out the positive contributions by grandparents, other relatives, or close friends from the negative, consider who is:

- raising the key issues in dispute
- fueling the conflict surrounding those issues, or
- recommending against agreements that you and the other parent have been ready to reach on your own.

ISSUE 32 CROSS-REFERENCES

Worksheet	Questions
Worksheet 1	4, 7, 8
Worksheet 2	4, 5, 8
Worksheet 3	1, 4, 5, 6, 7, 11
Worksheet 4	1, 2, 3, 5, 7, 12, 15

1. Limit the Information You Share

One of the easiest ways to prevent others from fueling your conflict is to limit the amount of information you share. This may be difficult if these same folks are your primary source of emotional support, but it is often necessary. Consider holding back details of your parenting agreement negotiations. Think about what you would tell a casual acquaintance in the grocery store, and limit your comments to that. Detailed descriptions of difficult negotiations may lead those who care about you to want to intervene, rescue your children, or even try to solve the problem themselves. If, for example, you are used to turning to your mother for a sympathetic ear, this may be a good time to find a friend or counselor who can listen compassionately without offering lots of advice or choosing to get involved on your behalf.

2. Schedule a "Family" Meeting

Often, the simplest way to diffuse a difficult situation is to tackle it head-on. If you and the other parent believe that a significant source of your troubles is with over-involved grandparents, other relatives, or close friends, consider convening a meeting among the three or four (or more) of you during which you say politely, but firmly, "Thanks, but no thanks."

At the meeting, you should describe the problem and the impact it has on your and your children's lives. Depending on the details of your situation, this may have to be stated more or less bluntly—but under any circumstance, you need to be understood. For that to happen, you and the other parent need to agree to a number of things, including:

- how much outside input you are willing to accept as you negotiate your agreement
- whether you are willing to share information about your agreement with this grandparent, other relative, or close friend once it has been completed, and
- how unwanted intervention will be handled.

Introducing this subject at a "family" meeting feels scary, but it needn't be harsh. For example, you might say something like, "Over the past year each of us has turned to you for help while we tried to save our marriage. We both appreciate the fair hearing, moral support, and great ideas you offered. Though we know that the road ahead is going to be difficult, we also know that it will be harder if we have to find an agreement that satisfies everyone in the family. Recently, it has become almost impossible to resolve our conflict now that others in the family are so heavily involved. Our priorities are on figuring out what we need to do to meet the children's needs, while satisfying our own. We know that more than almost anything else, our children need to know that they can rely on their parents to make necessary decisions on their behalf—whether or not we are together as a couple. While we are not experts at this, we are both sure about what we are doing and why. We feel it is our responsibility to make the decisions that will make this divorce final. We will probably make some mistakes along the way, but we feel confident that we each have the children's best interests at heart, that we are willing to get help from experts as needed, and that we will be able to make whatever changes may be necessary as time goes on."

3. Use Mediation or Counseling

Sometimes it is difficult for an over-involved grandparent, other relative, or close friend to understand where their natural concerns for you, the other parent, or the children have become intrusive. It might help to discuss the problem, its impact, and possible resolution with the assistance of a mediator, counselor, or other trusted third party.

For some, confronting others directly is either too difficult or has already proven unsuccessful. For others, direct confrontation is pointless because they know they will not be taken seriously. If either of these describes your situation, you might consider bringing in another person who will be viewed as an "authority" because of their standing as a professional or expert. If this is an option you are considering together, talk it over first to determine:

- whose opinions or expertise would be best
- what the grandparents', other relative's, or close friend's reaction to this kind of contact is likely to be
- how the information should be delivered (that is, in person, in writing, or by telephone), and
- when the contact should be made in order to have the desired effect (that is, immediately or after the parents have made an effort to resolve the problem).

4. Get Protective Orders

In rare instances, over-involvement on the part of a grandparent, other relative, or close friend becomes so severe that it is significantly destructive. This may be especially true if this individual is trying to fight for custody of the children. Some extended family members may even threaten to kidnap the children "for their own good." Any of these scenarios can have a potentially damaging effect on the children, and may require court orders to protect the children, you, or the other parent until the matter can be sorted out and resolved. To get more information about these orders, contact an attorney or your local district attorney's office, battered women's shelter, police department, or children's protective services department. ■

CHAPTER
9

Special Circumstances

n this chapter, we cover special circumstances, like moving and military service, that some parents may want to include in their parenting agreement. As with the serious issues discussed in Chapter 8, these are matters that some people may need to address in their first agreement, while others can wait. Read through the topics in this chapter and think about whether you want to include any of them in your agreement. There may be issues that aren't relevant now but are likely to become relevant over time. If that's the case, decide whether you want to address the issue now while you are working through your agreement. Or, you may decide it's easier to wait and come back to these issues when you have had more experience negotiating and reaching agreement, or when your kids are older.

A. Issue 33: Moving

#_____ **Moving**

_____ We agree that in the event either parent plans to relocate from _____

_____ [describe community, county, state], that parent will provide

the other parent with at least _____ days' notice in order to allow us to assess the impact that this

move will have on our current parenting arrangements, and to renegotiate or modify the agreement accordingly.

_____ We agree that neither parent plans to relocate now, but in the event either parent wishes to relocate in the future,

we will consider the following [choose all that apply]:

_____ having both parents relocate

_____ changing physical custody of the children to the remaining parent

_____ allowing a move as long as our children are under age _____ / over age _____

_____ time a move with a change in schools

_____ allowing our children to chose whether they will move after age _____

_____ allowing the parent to relocate as planned

_____ finding new ways to meet both parents' needs and goals so that both parents can remain in the area

_____ We agree that _____ [parent] will move to

_____ [specify] on or after _____ [date],

and after that time, our parenting agreement will be as follows:

_____ It will remain as currently drafted.

_____ It will change as follows [specify]:

_____

_____

_____

_____ We further agree that [specify]:

_____

_____

_____

Some parents want to move away after a separation or divorce. A career change, job change, enrollment in school, new partner's job change, desire to be near a parent who can provide childcare, inability to afford to live in the community, or desire to just start over are common reasons for wanting to move.

1. Moving Is Stressful for Everyone

Although there may be many more good reasons for moving than for staying, moving almost always becomes an emotionally charged issue for parents, children, and the extended family. When children move, they may experience any number of stress-producing events, including:

- interrupting existing friendships
- forming new friendships, often after other age-mates have established social circles
- adjusting to different school curricula and teacher styles
- coping with either or both parents' stress or arguments over the move, and
- having considerably less contact with one parent.

Children who are allowed to remain in their neighborhoods because of a custody modification may be spared a change of schools, friends, and contact with extended family members, but they will certainly miss the level of contact they had with their previous custodial parent if that parent moves away.

Regardless of what happens with legal custody (decision making on behalf of your children), the further apart parents live, the more difficult it is for the children to spend significant amounts of time with both parents. Any parent who wants to move should, therefore, examine his or her motives and options carefully.

2. Moves Generate Conflict

In general, any proposal by a primary custodial parent to move away will trigger a dispute with the other parent if the move will either reduce the amount of time the other parent spends with the children, or increase the difficulty, time, or expense of maintaining the current level of visitation.

If you are thinking about moving, you should be aware that child support might change significantly if the move will change the amount of time your children will spend with each parent. Many child support formulas are based not only on what each parent earns but also the percentage of time the children spend with each parent. More often than not, this means that the parent who earns more income or spends less time with the children will end up paying a higher amount of child support.

In the typical dispute, custodial parents want to know whether they can move under the terms of their existing court order and the laws of their state, and noncustodial parents want to know whether they can prevent the move or have primary custody of the children change hands. Unfortunately, a definitive answer to these questions is hard to come by. Legislatures and courts around the country have wrestled with these questions—as have the parents whose struggles bring the issue to center stage.

Each state has its own criteria for determining whether one parent should be allowed to move with the children. In some states, the considerations are no more specific than deciding what is in the child's best interests. Other states offer more extensive guidelines. As a bell-weather state on this issue, California's Supreme Court has issued two landmark move-away decisions in the past eight years—each of which reached a different conclusion. Using similar lines of reasoning in each case, the court allowed the mother to make the move in the first case (*Marriage of Burgess,* 1996), but in the second case ordered primary custody to switch to the father if the mother decided to move (*Marriage of LaMusga,* 2004). Among the factors that California's courts have considered are:

- whether the move will be in the best interests of the child
- the child's attachment to each parent
- the degree to which each parent is involved in their child's daily life
- the distance of the move
- the reason for the move
- the child's wishes (often children 12 and older can at least express their opinion or preferences), and
- the degree to which the child will be able to sustain an ongoing relationship with the parent who remains.

Because mothers are often the primary caretakers, mother's and father's rights groups each have their own positions on and interpretation of these questions. The Internet is full of articles, blogs, discussion groups, and websites that offer platforms for the debate. Bookstores and libraries have any number of publications that lean one way or the other. Researchers are also divided on whether children whose parents move become more vulnerable to mental health or behavioral disturbances—or whether the conflict between the parents is just as (if not more) influential in the problems that some children experience after a move.

One fact that remains crystal clear is that this is an issue that will not be going away anytime soon. While the path ahead is still being blazed, there are some factors that seem to make it easier for courts to make a decision about whether to approve or prevent a parent's ability to move the children. When courts approve a move, it is often because the moving parent:

- has been the primary caretaker
- previously discussed his or her intent to move with the other parent
- has never hidden the child or prevented or frustrated the child's visitation schedule with the other parent (except for instances of child abuse or other violence)
- is willing to share in transportation costs so that the child can spend as much time as possible with the other parent
- is willing to allow visitation with the other parent at every reasonable opportunity
- supports the child in maintaining an ongoing relationship with grandparents, other relatives, and close friends, and
- has not tried to coach the child to convince the judge, mediator, custody evaluator, or other professional to approve the move.

When courts either prevent a proposed move or switch custody to the parent who will remain, it is often because the moving parent has engaged in one or more of the following behaviors:

- has already tried to restrict or eliminate visits with the other parent by hiding the children or fabricating excuses about why visits cannot take place
- has tried to coach the children into convincing the judge, mediator, custody evaluator, or other professional that they do not want to remain behind
- is unwilling to find ways to accommodate the other parent's visits with the children in view of the increased distance between the parents' homes
- ignores the wishes of teens who wish to switch custody arrangements in order to remain in familiar surroundings, or

- wants to move solely for the purpose of getting a fresh start.

3. "An Ounce of Prevention …"

Clearly, a move can be one of the most volatile issues parents face as they live with the demands of parenting after a separation or divorce. Dealing with these issues after a move has been planned, however, makes it even harder.

By taking the time to plan for how you will resolve these kinds of issues in the future, including how much notice the moving parent must give if he or she is planning a move, you and the other parent can avoid many of the traps that other parents encounter when they try to tackle these issues after things have been set in motion. Other ways parents can plan ahead to minimize the difficulty in handling a potential move include:

- making decisions about how far away a parent can move (measured in miles, travel time, etc.) without triggering the need to review the parenting agreement
- postponing possible moves until the children have reached pre-agreed ages
- identifying situations under which custody of the children might fall to the parent who remains, and
- identifying the strategies you will use to address these issues (such as mediation) if your own negotiations fail to produce an agreement.

In thinking about the reasons a parent might be able to move away with the children, or reasons why custody might be switched to the parent who remains, you might consider several factors, including:

- your children's ages and grade level in school
- your children's involvement with extended family members, the community, and friends
- the amount of time the children are spending with each parent and the depth of these relationships, and
- the reasons one parent wishes to leave, or the reasons the parent who remains might wish to block the move.

If one parent does move—with or without the children—both parents will need to consider how current court orders will have to be changed. For example, in addition to needing to modify the visitation schedule, you will probably need to refigure child support, as this amount is often tied to the time your children spend with each parent. To help your children maintain contact with the distant parent, you may want to refer to Issue 37 later in this chapter.

⚠ This information is intended to help you and the other parent understand and anticipate some of the issues that are often associated with a move. The laws in each state vary regarding how move-away issues will be decided. To get more information about these issues in your state, refer to Chapter 16, Section A.

ISSUE 33 CROSS-REFERENCES

Worksheet	Questions
Worksheet 1	3, 4, 5, 6, 7, 8
Worksheet 2	1, 4, 5, 6, 7
Worksheet 3	3, 4, 5, 6, 7, 8, 11
Worksheet 4	1, 2, 3, 4, 5, 6, 7, 12, 15

4. Both Parents Relocate

In some parts of the country, the economy is so depressed that both parents may have to leave following a separation or divorce. Or, if both parents are originally from the same area, both may want to move back to that area after the divorce or separation to take advantage of the support that may be forthcoming from family members or old friends who have remained there.

You and the other parent can consider several options, including relocating together to a city or other area large enough to support you both and let you pursue your own lives. Many parents consider this alternative when they agree that their children need to have frequent contact with both parents, and feel that they might each benefit by making a move.

5. One Parent Relocates, Physical Custody Changes to Remaining Parent

For some parents, relocation is a necessity if they are to earn a living, gain an education, or meet other pressing needs. Children don't always make the move with their parents, however, even when it is the primary custodial parent who needs to relocate. Some families prefer to raise their children in a particular community and will alter the physical custody arrangements to ensure that the children can stay in that community as long as one of the parents is able to remain.

6. Allow a Move If Children Are of a Certain Age

Mental health professionals note that both kindergartners or first graders and teens are particularly vulnerable during a move. This is because the five- to seven-year-old is learning to separate from their parents' authority and to accept direction from other adults, and teens are increasingly dependent on their peer groups and may resent losing this support and social resource. Accordingly, some parents choose to either delay or time a move so that they can avoid moving their children during these critical age ranges.

7. Time a Move With a Change in Schools

Some parents choose to delay a move until children are either ready to start school, or will otherwise be changing schools (for example, moving between elementary and middle school, or between middle school and high school).

8. Allow Children to Choose Whether They Will Move

Some parents agree that they will allow their children to decide whether they will move with a parent after they have reached a certain age. Many parents decide to allow their children to choose whether they will move with a parent when the child is between the ages of 12 and 15, because that is when their children are either approaching high school or entering their sophomore year (the one that really starts to count for college applications).

9. One Parent Relocates

With this option, the parents agree that there is no compelling reason for both parents to either remain in the same area or move to the same new area. You must choose a living arrangement that accommodates the distance

between your homes. Issues 1 and 18 (discussed in Chapter 6 and 7, respectively) suggest options.

10. Parents Remain and Find New Ways to Meet Their Goals

You may decide that, although you or the other parent might prefer to relocate, the children's interests would be better served if both parents remain in the area. You'll need to adopt some creative solutions to address the concerns of the parent who considered moving. Here are a few suggestions:

- The parent who wanted to move could return to school to gain new job skills to find employment in the area.
- The parents could alter the living arrangements to allow the parent who wanted to move to "commute" between two cities to work.
- The parents could alter the living arrangements (and child support payments) so that the parent who wanted to move becomes the primary caretaker for the children.

B. Issue 34: When Parenting Styles and Values Differ

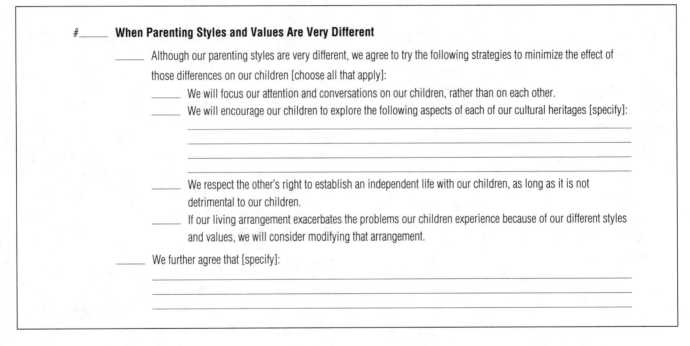

Parents frequently differ in beliefs, values, and expectations for themselves and their children. Children whose parents have substantially conflicting child-rearing rules and disciplinary styles sometimes feel as though they are two different people—one to please each parent. You can guard against this by not criticizing the other parent's style and, if possible, finding some common ground.

Differences are not necessarily bad—in fact, they are what make the world go 'round. While some children tolerate the variety, others find it overwhelming. You need to tailor your agreement on this issue to fit what best suits your children.

If the differences between you and the other parent come from differences in cultural backgrounds or religious beliefs, see Chapter 14 for more information. If your differences are because one of you recently came out as a lesbian or gay man, or have chosen a non-mainstream way of living, read Chapter 15.

ISSUE 34 CROSS-REFERENCES

Worksheet	Questions
Worksheet 1	3, 4, 6, 7, 8
Worksheet 2	2, 3, 4, 5, 6, 7
Worksheet 3	4, 5, 6, 7, 8, 9, 10, 11
Worksheet 4	1, 2, 3, 4, 5, 6, 7, 12, 13, 14, 15

1. Focus on Your Child

Some parents can only agree that they both love their children. If this is true for you, use it as a starting point for a new partnership with the other parent. The key to making this option work is to recognize your children's skills, interests, and personalities and find ways to complement them.

Children's needs and interests depend a lot on their ages. Young children often find security in being with or near a close extended family. By contrast, teens often like to "hang" with their friends and need a parent who can supervise from a distance. (For more information on how differences in parenting styles affect children of various ages, see Chapter 13.)

Sometimes, parents are able to resolve these issues on their own. But often they need help refocusing their energy from trying to change everything about their former partner to finding ways to work together. First, each parent must decide and then articulate what they think isn't working well. Then each parent must find a way to make the situation better, or at least less bad. For a step-by-step approach, parents with different parenting styles or values should try to:

- define the problem
- propose solutions
- identify areas of agreement
- evaluate any disagreements
- decide whether more help (or help from a different professional) is needed
- decide how they will know whether the situation has improved
- make the agreed-upon changes
- measure their progress in accomplishing their goals, and decide whether any further changes are needed.

If you and the other parent come from different cultural or religious backgrounds, teaching your children about who they are can give parents a way to focus on their children. In particular, consider having your children:

- hear stories from grandparents or other elders
- attend special religious or cultural functions
- learn skills unique to a particular culture, or
- attend special camps.

2. Structure the Living Arrangements or Transition Times to Reduce Conflict

If the lives your children lead are radically different in each parent's home, then you may find transition periods are particularly difficult for your children.

Several researchers have found that children adjust better to two homes with very different rules and standards than to open conflict between the parents. Nevertheless, it may be very difficult for your children. To ease the contradictions, you have two options. One is to modify the living arrangements (Issue 1) so that your children go back and forth infrequently. For example, one parent can have the children during the school year and the other in the summer, with frequent communication but no physical exchanges.

Your other option is to improve transition times. (For suggestions, see Issue 17, discussed in Chapter 17.)

3. Agree to Disagree

For some parents, the differences are so great that they do not try to bridge the gap. If you are in this situation, do your best to have some consistent standards for your children's conduct and to respect your children's right and desire to know, understand, and love the other parent. Beyond that, each parent must be willing to let the other parent enforce his or her rules in his or her own home.

4. Take These Issues to Counseling

Communication is often the first casualty in a failing relationship. But it is communication that will save the children (and both of you) from emotional pain and suffering. If each parent can spend a little time trying to see the world through their former partner's eyes, they may gain insight into why they do the things that they do. Each parent may also be more able to modify his or her behavior to suit the other parent's needs if they understand why the other parent desires the change. But this type of role-playing can be difficult alone. For all these reasons, counseling can sometimes take the edge off a certain set of conflicts—or even help parents find new strategies that help the sources of conflict go away. For example, parents might agree to disagree on bedtimes and eating times, as long as each is satisfied that the children won't go hungry, will eat nutritious foods, and will still be in bed at a reasonable time.

C. Issue 35: When a Parent Needs to Develop Parenting Skills

#_____   **When a Parent Needs to Develop Parenting Skills**

_____ _____ [parent] will work on improving

his/her parenting skills as follows [choose all that apply]:

_____ will attend parenting classes through _____

_____ will review written materials on parenting

_____ will attend counseling with _____

to deal with and resolve these issues

_____ We further agree that [specify]:

_____

_____

_____

Many parents need help with their role as a parent. For parents who were previously uninvolved in the day-to-day care and discipline of the children, having full responsibility for their children, even for relatively short periods of time, can be overwhelming. A parent who has abused or neglected his or her children in the past needs special help so that discipline and other child-rearing situations do not further harm the children. Fortunately, many agencies and other resources offer help in honing or developing parenting skills. (See Chapter 17.)

ISSUE 35 CROSS-REFERENCES

Worksheet	Questions
Worksheet 1	1, 2, 4, 7
Worksheet 2	1, 2, 3, 4, 5, 8
Worksheet 3	7, 9, 10, 11
Worksheet 4	3, 4, 5, 7, 13, 14, 15

D. Issue 36: When Parents Have New Partners

#_____   **When Parents Have New Partners**

_____ We will resolve issues surrounding a parent's new partner as follows [choose all that apply]:

_____ Our children will always know that we are their parents, regardless of their attachment to a parent's new partner.

_____ Our children will refer to new partners as _____.

_____ The adults and the children will have separate sleeping quarters.

_____ Any new partner will participate in decisions regarding the children as follows [specify]:

_____

_____

_____ We further agree that [specify]:

_____

_____

_____

When a separated or divorced parent develops a new intimate relationship, both parents and the children are likely to have fairly intense feelings about the situation. The other parent may be jealous, even if he or she has no desire to get back together. That parent may also be afraid that the children will get attached to the new partner and lose their bond with their parent.

These feelings can be very powerful and can seriously disrupt your parenting relationship. Although you both know that you cannot tell the other parent whom to choose as a partner, you still must address certain issues, such as:

- how the children will relate to the new partner—in particular, whether that person will supersede the children's relationship with the other parent
- what the children will call the new partner
- ensuring that the children have their own sleeping quarters, and
- whether the new partner will make parenting decisions.

One of the most challenging problems is to figure out the new partner's role in discipline. Many parents want new partners to have nothing to do with discipline at all. But children can become confused and difficult to handle if there is an adult in their lives who does not set any limits or who fails to support the rules or disciplinary practices of the household. For these reasons, it makes sense to carefully discuss what issues the new partner should deal with and what should be left to the parents alone. Depending on the situation, this conversation can be handled best if all of the adults can talk these issues out together. Often this kind of conversation is most successful if you involve a mediator or counselor.

If the new partner has children, the situation is even more complicated. Blended families are common, and children whose parents have parted ways are likely to live in one at some point in their lives.

For children, this can be an especially complex situation. Not only did they not choose their parent's new partner, they often do not want another parenting relationship in their lives. The older the children are when their parent's new partner enters the picture, the harder it is to establish a positive relationship. When there are stepsiblings in the mix, it is harder still.

Planning for how to address your children's needs following divorce is difficult. But just as it is critical to help them deal with the divorce, it is equally important to help them navigate the unfamiliar waters of building a new family with people that they may or may not know all that well. No small task indeed!

Viewed through your children's eyes, there are probably four key areas to address where stepfamilies or blended families are concerned. These include:

- dealing with the loss of their first family
- dealing with the conflicting emotions that emerge from forming a new family (especially if there will be stepsiblings)
- developing the ability to build strong relationships and resolve conflict in their new family, and
- maintaining ties with their other parent (and potentially that parent's new partner and children).

To help your children bridge the divide between their newly forming families, you will need to work diligently with the other parent and the new partner(s) to:

- arrange time when your child can be with both of his or her new families
- resolve conflicts that are likely to emerge between the three or four adults regarding disciplinary, emotional, or financial issues
- nurture the growth of new stepparent and sibling relationships, while preserving each child's tie to their natural parent, and
- deciding whether and when stepparents will help with exchanges.

Following are strategies you can consider when dealing with the realities of stepfamilies and blended families.

1.   Describing the New Partner's Role

This issue can lead to some pretty heated arguments. But it is often easier to tackle them directly than to let negative feelings about a new partner infect all aspects of a parenting plan. Issues should include what the children will call the new partner and how the new partner will be involved in daily decision making and discipline, as well as in the larger decisions such as where the children will live or where they will go to school.

2.   New Partners, Decision Making, and Conflicts

Parents must consider how the new partner will (or will not) be involved in altering or updating the parenting agreement and what types of issues the other parent can legitimately raise about the new relationship.

3. Talk Before Problems Come Up

If it looks like a new partner will be around for a while—either through marriage or just a committed relationship—it helps if there is good communication with the other parent. Because the new partner and the other parent will likely be working together, it helps if they get to know each other before any problems crop up. Then, when conflicts do come up, there is some framework for working together to find a solution.

Even if neither of you has a new partner, you can include this provision in your parenting agreement in anticipation of that time. Or, you can skip this issue now and modify your agreement when necessary.

(Additional information on new partners is in Chapter 13, Section A4, and Chapter 15.)

ISSUE 36 CROSS-REFERENCES

Worksheet	Questions
Worksheet 1	3, 4, 5, 6, 7, 8
Worksheet 2	1, 3, 5, 6, 7
Worksheet 3	2, 3, 4, 5, 6, 7, 11
Worksheet 4	3, 4, 5, 7, 11, 15

E. Issue 37: If Our Homes Are Far Apart

#_____   **If Our Homes Are Far Apart**

_____ If there is a considerable distance between our homes, we agree as follows [choose all that apply]:

_____ The children will spend the school year with _____ [parent] and the summers with _____ [other parent].

_____ The children will live with _____ [parent] for _____ [specify grade or school level] and with _____ [other parent] for _____ [specify grade or school level].

_____ The children will reside at _____ [name of school] and will visit with each parent as follows [specify; be consistent with the options you choose under holidays and vacations]:

_____

_____

_____

_____ We further agree that [specify]:

_____

_____

If one parent moves a significant distance away, the parents face the challenge of helping the children maintain a close relationship with both parents. Transporting the children is covered in Issue 16, discussed in Chapter 7.

ISSUE 37 CROSS-REFERENCES

Worksheet	Questions
Worksheet 1	3, 4, 5, 6, 7, 8
Worksheet 2	1, 3, 4, 5, 8
Worksheet 3	3, 5, 7
Worksheet 4	3, 4, 5, 7

1. School Year With One Parent, Summer With the Other

The most common solution parents choose when they live far apart is for the children to spend the school year with one parent and the summer with the other. If your children's school district is on a year-round calendar, however, this option isn't feasible.

2. Change Primary Residence With Change in Schools

Some parents consider alternating each school term—for example, third grade with one parent and fourth grade with the other. Few professionals would recommend this, however, because it provides little continuity in the children's education and social life. Instead, the children could live with one parent during elementary school, the other parent during middle (or junior high) school, and then choose where they live during high school. These transitions often involve minimal disruption because so many children change school districts at these times.

3. Children Attend Private Residential School

A few families send their children to a private residential school. The children alternate vacations with their parents according to a predetermined schedule. See Issue 5, Holidays, discussed in Chapter 6, for suggestions on alternating times with parents.

F. Issue 38: When Nonrelatives Live in the Home

#_____   **When Nonrelatives Live in the Home**

_____ If either of us lives with nonrelatives, our children will have separate sleeping quarters from the adults.

_____ _____ [parent] will be responsible to make sure that no one in the house consumes nonprescription drugs or becomes a danger to our children because of intoxication.

_____ _____ [parent] will be responsible to make sure the number of other visitors is kept reasonable.

_____ A nonrelative may not care for our children in the parent's absence.

_____ A nonrelative may not discipline our children in the parent's absence.

_____ We further agree that [specify]:

_____

_____

_____

Housing is expensive, especially on one income. After a divorce or separation, you (or your ex) may need to share your home, especially if it means you can afford to live somewhere large enough to accommodate your children overnight.

You or the other parent may imagine the worst when you hear that one of you has roommates. Any concerns about roommates should be included in your parenting agreement. For example, you can:

- require the children to have separate sleeping quarters
- bar the roommates from having or using drugs in the home
- prohibit the roommates from disciplining the children, or
- restrict the number of outside visitors.

ISSUE 38 CROSS-REFERENCES

Worksheet	Questions
Worksheet 1	4, 7
Worksheet 2	3, 6, 7, 8
Worksheet 3	4, 5, 6, 7, 9, 10, 11
Worksheet 4	3, 5, 12, 13, 14, 15

G. Issue 39: Reinvolving a Previously Absent Parent

#_____ **Reinvolving a Previously Absent Parent**

_____ _____ [parent] has been absent
from our children's life for _____ [period of time], and now wishes to become
reinvolved. To make this transition easier for all of us, we agree as follows [choose all that apply]:

_____ We will both seek counseling.

_____ Our children will receive counseling.

_____ We will focus our attention and conversations on our children.

_____ We will build up the amount of time _____ [parent]
spends with our children as follows:

_____

_____

_____ _____ [parent] will retain the support systems and schedules
he/she established while _____ [parent] was absent, as follows:

_____

_____

_____ To make sure that _____'s [parent] reentry into
our children's lives is for the long term, we will make necessary modifications to this agreement on or
before _____ [specify date].

_____ We further agree that [specify]:

_____

_____

Parents drop out of their children's lives for a variety of reasons. Some parents are better able to cope with the separation or divorce if they have little or no contact with their family. Others leave or are kept away because of substance abuse, violence, child abuse, or incarceration. Regardless of the reason, reinvolving a parent is often a difficult task.

Although children are remarkably adaptable, flexible, and loving, they typically experience a mixture of hurt, anger, happiness, confusion, hope, jealousy, anxiety, and anticipation as a result of a parent's absence and return. So does the parent who remained. In short, the whole family will need a lot of time to get used to the absent parent's return. Consider incorporating many of the options below into your parenting agreement.

1. Deal With Your Feelings

Everyone—the children, the parent who remained, and the returning parent—can benefit from counseling. The children and the parent who remained may need to talk about their fears and hopes. The returning parent may need help in understanding both his or her own feelings, and the feelings of the children and the other parent.

2. Develop a Businesslike Relationship With the Other Parent

When a parent returns, tension with the other parent is both natural and common. Parents need time to develop trust, resolve the issues that existed before the parent left, and come to terms with the changes that are inevitable.

Often, returning parents want to pick up where they left off. A parent who remained often resents the underlying assumption that the returning parent can just "waltz back in, become an instant parent, and be a hero!"

To help ease this transition, you and the other parent can behave like business partners. Maintain your separate adult lives, but work together to raise your children. As with all good business relationships, the partnership works best when the parents can exchange information, respect each other's privacy and relationship with the children, and keep a cool head when conflicts arise.

3. Go Slowly and Respect the Children's Feelings

Children often act out to avoid being hurt again. Young children may feel that they can't get enough of the returning parent, and not let that parent out of their sight. Older children, on the other hand, may test the parent's commitment through weeks, or even months, of short, tense visits before resuming a normal relationship. The returning parent may develop a deep and satisfying new relationship with the children if he or she respects the children's feelings. You might ask your children how much contact they can handle.

If you are the parent who has been absent, be prepared to talk honestly about what happened and to answer your children's questions—even if it takes a while for the questions to surface.

4. Keep an Open Mind

If you are the parent who remained, you probably have mixed feelings about the other parent's return. Depending on the length of the absence, your life and your children's lives may have changed considerably.

You need to maintain an open mind about the possible ways in which the other parent might reenter the children's lives. At the same time, be realistic and keep your support systems in place. The other parent may find the transition back too hard and may leave again or assume a very limited parenting role. If, however, the other parent wants to take an active role in your children's lives, consider ways to accommodate this request, as long as it is not harmful to the children.

5. Negotiate Short-Term Agreements

When a parent reenters his or her children's lives, it is a good idea to negotiate simple, short-term agreements. These agreements allow both parents and children to test the waters and learn what works best.

Trust, a critical element of any parenting relationship, is built over time. By adhering to these short-term agreements, returning parents demonstrate trustworthiness—and make more reliable negotiators for long-term agreements.

6. Consider Reevaluating Your Sole Custody Arrangement

Parents who remain behind have de facto sole custody of their children, whether or not a court makes such an order. If the returning parent appears to be reestablishing a long-term parenting role, you might consider modifying the custody arrangement.

Knowing whether a parent is back for good can be difficult. One way to test this is to negotiate and adhere to several temporary agreements, as described above. After everyone is satisfied that the returning parent is reliable, it may make sense to give that parent a larger parenting role.

The parent who remained behind may balk. But researchers repeatedly find that parents who are actively involved in their children's lives maintain regular visitation schedules, pay a higher percentage of court-ordered support, and have more satisfactory relationships with their children than do parents who are less involved in their children's lives.

H. Issue 40: Driving and Owning a Car, Motorcycle, or Off-Road Vehicle

#_____   **Driving and Owning a Car, Motorcycle, or Off-Road Vehicle**

_____ We will permit our children to own a car.

_____ We will not permit our children to own a car.

_____ We will permit our children to drive a car under the following conditions [choose all that apply]:

    _____ After completing a certified training course.

    _____ With the consent of _____ [one or both parents].

    _____ With adult supervision.

    _____ Driving only on unpaved roads.

    _____ Using a family car.

    _____ After buying a car.

    _____ After being given a car.

    _____ After paying their own car insurance.

    _____ They must pay for any tickets received while operating the car.

_____ We will permit our children to own a motorcycle.

_____ We will not permit our children to own a motorcycle under any circumstances.

_____ We will permit our children to drive a motorcycle under the following conditions [choose all that apply]:

    _____ After completing a certified training course.

    _____ With the consent of _____ [one or both parents].

    _____ With adult supervision.

    _____ Driving only on unpaved roads.

    _____ Using a family motorcycle.

    _____ After buying a motorcycle.

    _____ After being given a motorcycle.

    _____ After paying their own motorcycle insurance.

    _____ They must pay for any tickets received while operating the motorcycle.

_____ We will permit our children to own an off-road vehicle.

_____ We will not permit our children to own an off-road vehicle under any circumstances.

_____ We will permit our children to drive an off-road vehicle under the following conditions [choose all that apply]:

    _____ After completing a certified training course.

    _____ With the consent of _____ [one or both parents].

    _____ With adult supervision.

    _____ Driving only on unpaved roads.

    _____ Using a family off-road vehicle.

    _____ After buying an off-road vehicle.

    _____ After being given an off-road vehicle.

    _____ After paying their own off-road vehicle insurance.

    _____ They must pay for any tickets received while operating the off-road vehicle.

_____ We further agree that [specify]:

_____

_____

_____

Parents often disagree about when their children will be allowed to drive or own a car, motorcycle, or off-road vehicle. Though most parents let their teens take driver's education with their peers, the rules regarding when, how far, and under what circumstances they may drive without an adult vary. Parents often disagree on the following issues:

- whether or not their teens may own a car, motorcycle, or off-road vehicle
- under what circumstances the teens may own a vehicle (for example, only if it is brand new, if it is formerly the "family car," or if a teen pays for it), or

- who will pay the insurance, tickets, repairs, and other costs—the parents or the teens.

Because driving and owning a vehicle can be very important for your children in their teen years, this decision is especially worth thinking through in advance.

ISSUE 40 CROSS-REFERENCES

Worksheet	Questions
Worksheet 1	3, 4, 5
Worksheet 2	6, 8
Worksheet 4	6, 7, 12

I. Issue 41: International Travel and Passports

#_____   **International Travel and Passports**

_____ Our children may obtain a passport under the following conditions [choose one]:

_____ Either parent may obtain a passport if it is necessary for travel.

_____ Either parent may obtain a passport, but our children may travel out of the country only if the other parent approves of the itinerary and the dates of the trip.

_____ Either parent may obtain a passport, but our children may not travel out of the country unless _____ _____ [adult's name] travels with them.

_____ A passport may not be issued to our children under any circumstances.

_____ Only _____ may obtain a passport for the children.

_____ We further agree that [specify]:

_____

_____

_____

Some families want or need to travel out of the United States with their children. Almost all foreign travel requires a passport—even for children. This issue may concern you if you fear that a trip abroad will turn into an attempt to change custody or take the children away from you. If your children have dual citizenship, it may be difficult for you to enforce your U.S. court order in another country, because there might be a question about which country has legal authority to make decisions.

Some U.S. courts are beginning to order economic sanctions against a parent who tries to change a custody agreement while outside the United States. Some courts have cut off child support if a parent has tried to live permanently, and have jurisdiction transferred to, a foreign

country. Judges have also required a parent to post a bond before taking a child out of the country.

ISSUE 41 CROSS-REFERENCES

Worksheet	Questions
Worksheet 2	3, 4, 5
Worksheet 3	6, 8
Worksheet 4	1, 2, 6, 7, 12

⚠ This book assumes that neither parent intends to take the children out of the country to steal them from the other parent. If this is a concern, see a lawyer for help in securing a court order that will minimize this possibility.

1. Issue Passport but Set Limited Travel Time or Destination

With this option, parents might permit travel out of the United States but incorporate restrictions specifying permitted countries or the amount of time their children can be abroad, or both. As a practical matter, most international travel with children now requires that the adult traveling with the minor show proof that both of the children's legal parents approve of the travel plans.

2. Issue Passport but Require Supervised Travel

Your parenting agreement might require that an adult nonparent accompany your children and the other parent for international travel. If this is your inclination, you might seriously rethink whether issuing a passport is advisable at all, given that it might not be possible for a travel "supervisor" to prevent child snatching under all circumstances.

3. Require Both Parents' Permission to Obtain a Passport

If one parent fears flight or abduction of a child, then that parent should probably require that both parents give permission for a passport to be issued for their children. Withholding the passport in the first place is the most effective way to deal with the problem of flight.

4. Instruct the State Department to Withhold a Child's Passport Unless Requested by the Custodial Parent

If one parent has sole custody, he or she can inform the State Department not to issue a passport for the children unless it is the custodial parent who applies for it.

J. Issue 42: Military Service

#_____   **Military Service**

_____ Our children may enter military service if they are under the legal age as follows [choose all that apply]:
 _____ if they so choose
 _____ in the event of a war
 _____ if they are at least age _____
 _____ if we both agree
 _____ if _____ [parent] consents
 _____ never
_____ We further agree that [specify]:
_____
_____
_____

Minor children need a parent's permission to enter the military. Some options you can consider would allow your minor children to enlist as follows:

- without restriction
- in the event of war
- after a certain age
- with the approval of one or both parents, or
- never.

K. Issue 43: Allowing Underage Marriage

#_____ **Allowing Underage Marriage**

_____ Our children may marry if they are under the legal age as follows [choose all that apply]:

_____ if they so choose

_____ in the event of a pregnancy

_____ if they are at least age _____

_____ if we both agree

_____ if _____ [parent] consents

_____ never

_____ We further agree that [specify]:

_____

_____

You may wonder why underage marriage has been included as an issue you should consider when negotiating your parenting agreement. The reason is simple: Underage marriages are increasing, and you are now more likely than ever to have a child who considers this option. The divorce rate for these underage marriages is also staggering. Although underage marriages tend to last for an average of 7.1 years (slightly longer than the 6.8-year average for adult marriages), these marriages are just as likely to include children, and generally include more than one child.

You have at least five options when considering whether you will let your minor children get married, including:

- allow it at the child's discretion
- allow it in the event of a pregnancy
- allow it after a certain age
- allow it with consent of one or both parents, or
- not allow an underage marriage.

Because teenage pregnancy and underage marriage are such emotionally charged issues, you might make a tentative decision now and reevaluate that decision if the issue actually arises.

ISSUE 42 CROSS-REFERENCES

Worksheet	Questions
Worksheet 2	3
Worksheet 3	1, 6, 7, 11
Worksheet 4	1, 2, 3, 6, 7, 15

■

Part III

Beyond Your Parenting Agreement

Child Support, Alimony, and Jointly Held Property

This book is primarily about how to create an effective parenting agreement. However, if you are separating or getting a divorce, child custody is but one of the issues that you may be facing. Other issues typically include child support, alimony (also commonly called "spousal support"), and the division of jointly owned property. Though it is certainly possible to keep these issues separate, many parents find these issues overlap. For instance, deciding who gets the family home may depend on which parent can best afford its upkeep and mortgage. Alternatively, if your goal is for the children to continue living in the family home, then the parent who becomes the children's primary caretaker will probably be the parent who remains in the family home even if they're not the higher earner.

Child support and alimony can also affect custody arrangements. A parent who receives substantial child support and alimony may have an easier time caring for young children than a parent who has to earn the entire family's income. How property (other than the house) is divided may affect a parent's ability to raise the necessary money to purchase a home or move to a neighborhood that is more attractive, offers a better public school system, offers more social and cultural amenities, or allows that parent to be closer to extended family members or pursue education or employment opportunities.

Fortunately, if you truly focus on the best interests of your children—issue by issue and option by option—you will find that most decisions about how the children are to be raised can be made prior to, and independently of, the money issues. By basing your custody decisions squarely upon what is best for the children, you may even find that you will also be able to resolve such fundamental and potentially divisive issues as who keeps the house and how much alimony or child support, if any, should be paid. For example, some parents are tempted to argue for custody in order to receive or avoid paying child support. For most parents, however, this is faulty reasoning, because the actual costs associated with being a custodial parent are almost always higher than any child support payment a court is likely to order.

The balance of this chapter will provide you with some basic information about divorce-related money issues that may help you negotiate a mutually acceptable parenting agreement. As you review this information, you should understand that each of these matters is likely to involve legal or other issues, including some with tax consequences. For this reason, you should consider consulting an attorney, accountant, or other advisor before finalizing any agreement.

A. Understanding Child Support

What follows is a brief introduction to the subject of child support. If you want more detailed information, refer to Chapter 17, Help Beyond the Book, for a bibliography of more detailed information and resources.

Every parent is legally responsible for supporting his or her children until:

- the children reach the age of majority (and sometimes longer, particularly if a child is disabled or still in school)
- the children go on active military duty
- the children are declared emancipated by a court, or
- the parents' rights and responsibilities are terminated (such as when a child is adopted).

Separated or divorced parents must satisfy this legal obligation in one of two ways. Either:

- the parent who has the children most of the time satisfies his or her obligation by becoming the primary caretaker, or
- the parent who has the children the least amount of time satisfies his or her obligation through monthly child support payments.

When the time that the children spend with each parent is more or less equal, the parent with the larger income will be expected to pay at least some support to the parent with the smaller income.

1. How Child Support Payments Are Calculated

Each state has its own method for calculating the amount of child support that one parent will pay to the other after separation or divorce. States generally consider the following factors in determining child support formulas:

- how much time each parent spends caring for the children
- each parent's income and necessary expenses
- each parent's earning potential
- each parent's eligibility for public benefits, and
- the number and ages of the children.

Most states allow the parents to negotiate a support payment that is higher or lower than the statutory amount but also allow the family court judge to reject the parents' agreement if it does not provide adquate support for the children. (A few states require the parent paying the child support to pay at least a minimum amount.)

In addition to the guidelines imposed on them by state law, judges are supposed to strive for fairness in establishing child support obligations. They are thus given at least some discretion to apportion child support responsibility between parents according to their relative financial circumstances. Some states' laws specify additional factors that must be considered in determining how much child support parents will pay. These factors include the needs of the child—including health insurance, educational needs, day care, and special needs—the needs of the custodial parent, the payer's ability to pay, and the children's standard of living before the divorce.

a. Relative Financial Circumstances

When determining child support orders, a court usually considers the relative income and assets of both spouses. If the custodial parent earns more than the noncustodial parent, child support may be very low. Accordingly, when courts consider the relative assets and income of the parties, they usually end up awarding at least some child support to the custodial parent. In general, the statistics show that mothers are most often the custodial parent and fathers generally pay child support. In general, custodial mothers have considerably less household income than noncustodial fathers.

b. Ability to Pay

Courts always consider a person's ability to pay when establishing child support obligations. To do this, a court totals the payer's income from all sources (such as wages, public benefits, interest and dividends on investments, rents from real property, and profits from patents or other intellectual property), then reduces that total by the amount of any mandatory deductions (such as income taxes, Social Security, health care, and mandatory union dues) to calculate the payer's net income.

In most states, deductions for credit union payments, wage attachments, and the like are not subtracted when calculating net income. For example, John makes $3,000 per month, and his income tax, Social Security, unemployment insurance benefits, and other government deductions reduce his income by $500 per month. John's net income for purposes of calculating child support is now $2,500 per month. The court will not further reduce John's net income to acknowledge the $300 per month automatic

deduction that John takes to repay his credit union loan. The law accords support payments a higher priority than other types of debts and would rather see other debts not paid than deprive a spouse or child of adequate support.

When calculating a child support payer's living expenses, some states permit the court to consider the basic necessities of life (such as rent or mortgage, food, clothing, and health care) but not extraneous expenses such as school tuition, dining outside the home, and entertainment. Again, courts consider family support obligations to be more important than many personal expenses.

c. Ability to Earn

When a court computes the amount of child support to be paid by a parent, the judge usually factors in both parties' ability to earn. Although actual earnings are an important factor in determining a person's ability to earn, they are not conclusive when there is evidence that a person could earn more if he or she chose to do so. For example, assume a parent with an obligation to pay child support leaves his current job and enrolls in medical school or law school, takes a job with lower pay but good potential for higher pay in the future, or takes a lower-paying job that provides better job satisfaction. In each of these situations, a court may base the child support award on the income from the original job (ability to earn) rather than on the new income level (ability to pay). In this situation, courts often reason that the children's current needs should take priority over the parent's career plans and desires.

d. Standard of Living

When a court sets child support, it often considers the family's predivorce standard of living and attempts to continue this standard for the children. Courts, however, are aware of the difficulty of maintaining two households on the income that formerly supported one home. Therefore, maintaining the predivorce standard of living is often more of a goal than a guarantee.

2. Tax Consequences of Child Support

Child support is tax-free to the recipient but cannot be deducted by the payer. When ex-spouses had more flexibility in negotiating the amount of child support and alimony, many chose to pay more alimony (which can be deducted by the payer and must be reported as income by the payee) and less child support because of the tax advantage to the payer. Because states now use a formula to determine the basic child support obligation, shifting the amounts of child support and alimony to take advantage of tax deductions is increasingly difficult.

3. Children May Not Be Traded or Withheld for Child Support

Some noncustodial parents equate their obligation to pay child support with the "right" to visit the child, while some custodial parents conclude that the payer loses the "right" to visit the child if he or she falls behind on support. In fact, neither position is accurate, and neither position reflects the children's best interests.

Although some parents negotiate privately to trade child support for visitation with the children, no state condones this practice, and all states specifically prohibit parents from withholding visitation because the other parent owes support, or from withholding support because of disputes over custody or visitation. Quite simply, children need financial, physical, and emotional support, but children are not to be traded or withheld for money.

4. Modifying Child Support Orders

A child support obligation under a court order may be modified if financial circumstances change. However, child support obligations must be paid, no matter what the payer's circumstances, until the court makes a new support order. For example, Noah is required to pay $300 a month child support. If Noah loses his job, he must still pay $300 a month until the court order is modified. If Noah goes to court to get the order modified because of his decreased income, Noah will be liable for all payments owed prior to the modification date, because the courts will not reduce a support order retroactively. Even if Noah's ex informally agrees to let Noah pay less, Noah still technically owes the support because the underlying court order wasn't modified.

Most child support orders can be modified upon a showing that circumstances have changed. Some examples of these changes include:

- the existence of an additional financial burden (such as a medical emergency)
- additional income that becomes available because of remarriage
- a change in the law

- change in employment
- an increase in the cost of living
- an increase or decrease in income
- disability
- medical or financial emergency
- hardship, and
- an increase or decrease in the children's needs.

B. Understanding Alimony or Spousal Support

The following is a brief introduction to the subject of alimony (also called spousal support). If you want more detailed information, you can refer to Chapter 17, Help Beyond the Book, for a bibliography of resources.

Alimony is money one spouse pays to the other spouse for support as part of a court order or marital settlement agreement after a divorce. Until the 1970s, alimony was the natural extension of a wife's financial dependence on her husband in "traditional" marriages. These traditional marriages presumed that the husband was the breadwinner and the wife stayed home, caring for the house and children but not earning any income. Alimony was paid only by the husband to the wife. The amount of alimony was determined by a number of factors, including the needs of the parties, their status in life, their wealth, and their relative fault in causing the divorce. If a husband committed adultery or treated his wife cruelly, he would generally pay more alimony than if the wife was having an affair or treating her husband cruelly. Today, except in marriages of long duration (roughly ten or more years), or in the case of an ill or ailing spouse, alimony usually lasts for a set period of time, with the expectation that the recipient spouse will become self-supporting.

Alimony payments can be modified if the spouses agree, or if the spouse who wants the modification petitions the court. The court can change the amount to be paid or the duration of the payments. The only time alimony cannot be modified is when the spouses specifically agree that the alimony is nonmodifiable, or when alimony payments are part of an integrated property settlement agreement (that is, where alimony is paid as part of the property division. See "Integrated Property Settlement Agreement," below.)

When alimony and child support are combined into one payment without specifying what portion is alimony and what is child support, this total payment is sometimes called "family support." Because of tax issues and increased concern over enforcement of child support orders, however, most courts require that child support and alimony be identified separately.

INTEGRATED PROPERTY SETTLEMENT AGREEMENT

Upon divorce, couples commonly enter into a divorce agreement that divides marital property and sets alimony, if applicable. This agreement is "integrated" if the property settlement and alimony payments are combined into either one lump-sum payment or periodic payments. Integrated agreements are often used when the marital property consists of substantial intangible assets (for example, future royalties, stock options, or pension plans that will vest in the future) or when one party is buying the other's interest in a valuable tangible asset (for example, a home or business). If a spouse is entitled to little or no alimony but is not financially independent, periodic payments may help that spouse gain financial independence.

Courts typically use several basic criteria when setting alimony amounts:

- **Ability to pay.** Courts measure ability to pay based upon net income. Net income is calculated by totaling the payer's gross income from all sources (such as wages, public benefits, interest and dividends on investments, rents from real property, and profits from patents), and then subtracting any mandatory deductions (such as income taxes, Social Security, health care, and mandatory union dues).
- **Ability to earn.** Some states calculate the spouse's ability to earn by comparing actual earnings and estimated earnings if there is evidence that a person could earn more if he or she chose to do so. Others, however, set alimony payments based only on actual earnings. For example, Jane Doctor earned $150,000 a year from medicine for the past three years while married, then quit her job when she and her husband separated and became a TV repairperson with an annual income of $40,000. During the divorce trial, Jane's husband, Lionel, requested alimony from Jane. Because Jane abruptly changed her income, the court

imposed a larger alimony obligation on her than she would normally have to pay with a salary of $40,000 a year. The court reasoned that Jane could return to the world of medicine if she needed to and that her ex-husband should not be penalized because of her employment decision. In some states, however, the court would reason that ability to earn is too speculative and would instead base alimony on Jane's $40,000 income.

- **Ability to be self-supporting.** Courts normally calculate an ex-spouse's ability to support himself or herself by considering whether the ex-spouse has marketable skills and whether he or she is able to work outside the home. (Having custody of preschool children and not having access to day care could make this impossible.) If a spouse has marketable skills and is able to work outside the home, but has chosen not to look for work, the court is very likely to limit the amount and length of alimony. In many states, courts do not award alimony if the marriage is of short duration or both spouses are able to support themselves. If, however, one spouse was dependent on the other for support during the marriage, the dependent spouse is often awarded alimony for a transition period or until he or she becomes self-supporting. If a spouse receiving alimony becomes self-supporting before the time set by the court for the alimony to end, the paying spouse can go to court and file a request for modification or termination of alimony based upon these changed circumstances. Although it is difficult to obtain, ex-spouses are sometimes awarded an extension of alimony if, at the end of the support period, they are still unable to support themselves.
- **Standard of living during the marriage.** When a court sets alimony, it often considers the family's pre-divorce standard of living and attempts to continue this standard for both spouses. But whether or not both spouses worked outside the home during the marriage, it is often impossible to continue the same standard of living for both people after the spouses have gone their separate ways. This means that courts try, but cannot guarantee, to continue the predivorce standard of living for each parent.
- **Length of the marriage.** When a marriage is relatively short (for example, five years or less) and no children were born or adopted during the marriage, courts

often refuse to award alimony. If there are children under school age, however, the court may award alimony to allow the primary custodial parent to provide full-time care for the children. For federal income tax purposes, alimony paid under a written agreement or court order can be deducted by the payer and is taxable to the recipient. Child support, on the other hand, is tax-free to the recipient but not deductible by the payer.

- **Marital debts.** Upon divorce, the court considers who can pay any debts that have accumulated, as well as who benefits most from the asset attached to the debt, and allocates those debts accordingly. If the court orders a spouse to pay a large portion of marital debts, it often reduces the amount of alimony that spouse is ordered to pay.

- **Acquisition of a professional degree or license during the marriage.** Some spouses support their mates financially as well as emotionally through professional, graduate, or trade school. Alimony is rarely awarded to the spouse who supported the couple, even though he or she often made sacrifices, such as delaying his or her own education, in order to support the other. Some states, however, try to compensate the spouse who put the other through school through the alimony award.

- **Existence of an agreement before marriage.** Some couples enter agreements before their marriage about whether alimony will be paid in the event of divorce. Whether they are called antenuptial, prenuptial, or premarital agreements, these agreements are usually upheld by the court unless one person can show that the agreement was likely to promote divorce (for example, by including a large alimony amount in the event of divorce), was written and signed with the intention of divorcing, or was inherently unfair because one spouse took advantage of the other.

C. Negotiating Child and Spousal Support

How should you approach your child or spousal negotiations? Quite simply, you should go back to the basics. This means understanding what makes issues difficult and finding ways to address each concern, one at a time, with the intent of finding child-focused solutions that both parents can accept.

Many parents resent paying child support. Often these resentments are based not on how much money the children need but on the fact that the parent who receives the money controls how it is spent. For example, the paying parent may feel:

- The money isn't being spent directly on the kids.
- The receiving parent gains an unfair benefit by being able to use child support monies to pay rent.
- The parent receiving child support doesn't have to account for how the money is spent.
- The child support allows the parent who receives it to be "lazy" about supporting him- or herself and working to provide a living for the children.

MOTHERS FARE WORSE AFTER DIVORCE THAN FATHERS

Much has been made of the changed circumstances, financially, when families separate or divorce. Initially, both parents experience substantially reduced economic resources. Over time, this may change significantly as a result of new jobs, better pay, remarriage, public assistance, the sale of property, or other factors. One disturbing fact, however, emerges consistently. Although the economic well-being of divorced mothers and their children increases over time, the income of mothers who do not remarry remains substantially below the father's income. By contrast, the economic well-being of divorced fathers (over time) remains substantially above preseparation levels. Despite this discrepancy, custodial mothers remain the primary support for their children in the years after divorce. Even if paid in full, child support and alimony represent only a fraction of the mother's postdivorce household income.

Although child support issues are critically important for everyone, they are adult issues not to be shared with children. Though it is often necessary for one parent to explain that they cannot provide the same things that the other parent can because of their finances, it is equally important that neither parent puts the children in the middle of financial issues.

Child support involves first getting the court order and then collecting the support. Although states offer child support recipients a number of techniques for collecting it, probably the most effective approach to enforcement is to prevent a problem from arising in the first place. Involving both parents at a significant level in their children's lives is one of the most effective ways to head off a dispute over child support or to repair a situation that has deteriorated. If you are already in a dispute over child support, there are a number of ways to approach the situation, including:

- talking to the other parent directly to find out why he or she isn't paying
- discussing how support payments are used, and the value of spending it in those ways

- asking whether the other parent wants a more substantial role in the children's lives
- assessing whether the paying parent's economic circumstances have changed, thereby warranting a change in the order for support
- taking the matter to mediation and, if necessary, reviewing the entire parenting agreement to see whether changes might make the parent feel better about paying
- investigating options for providing better support through medical, dental, and vision care insurance, or
- investigating options for both parents to move to another area where both might find work, or work that pays better.

Happily, one approach to child support negotiations tends to produce consistently superior results. This strategy is to make sure that both parents are actively involved with the children. There is a strong correlation between the amount of time a parent spends with his or her children and that parent's willingness to pay child support. Maccoby and Mnookin, in their book *Dividing the Child* (Harvard Press), reported that most families opt for custody with the mother while the father pays child support. On average, fathers paid between two-thirds and three-fourths of the awarded support, but their compliance with support orders fell off over time.

The researchers discovered that fathers tended to continue paying child support when they had regular and frequent visits, both daytime and overnight, with their children. The less involved with their children's lives they became, the less apt they were to keep paying support.

D. Dividing Jointly Owned Property

In all states, a divorce or separation requires the division of property that the spouses own jointly. In the community property states (California, Nevada, Arizona, New Mexico, Texas, Washington, Idaho, and Wisconsin) this usually consists of property that was acquired after the marriage but before the spouses separated. Common exceptions to this rule are gifts and inheritances received by one spouse and kept in a separate account, and income earned on a spouse's separate property. In all other states, jointly owned property is property acquired jointly by both spouses.

Different types of property can raise different issues when it comes to dividing it in a divorce or separation. This is especially true when the property is a mix of one spouse's separate property and community or marital property. For instance, a house purchased with one spouse's separate property (assets) is that spouse's separate property upon divorce. However, if jointly owned property was used to increase the value of the house, figuring out who owns what can be tricky, especially if the house's value has appreciated significantly. Similarly, if one spouse owns a business as his or her separate property but both spouses work in the business, it can be difficult to decide how the appreciated value of the business should be divided.

These and other property division issues are covered in detail in *Divorce & Money,* by Violet Woodhouse with Dale Fetherling (Nolo).

RELEVANT ISSUES

Issue	Number
Medical, Dental, and Vision Care	2
Surname	22
Making Decisions	8
Resolving Disputes	9
Exchanging Information	11
Reinvolving a Previously Absent Parent	39
Moving	33
If Our Homes Are Far Apart	37
Holidays	5
Vacations	14
Special Occasions and Family Events	13
Improving Transition Times	17
When Parenting Styles and Values Differ	34
Disparaging Remarks	3
Undermining the Parent-Child Relationship	30
Denying Access to the Children	31
When Nonrelatives Live in the Home	38
When Parents Have New Partners	36
Making Changes	25

ntil recently, when parents could not agree on custody and visitation during or after a divorce, they would bring the issues to court for a judge to decide. Now, many parents seek help from a neutral third party who is trained to work with people so they can come to an agreement on their own. This process is called mediation, and the third party is known as a mediator.

Mediation has become such a well-accepted method of resolving custody and visitation disputes that most states encourage judges to order it in appropriate circumstances. Indeed, a few states require it before a judge can get involved. Even if a judge doesn't order mediation, you can voluntarily choose it if you need help in reaching an agreement. Although voluntary mediation usually costs money, the price is trivial compared to what you would have to pay lawyers to fight out custody and visitation issues in court.

You can use mediation in several different ways. Some parents use it to start the settlement process, then stop mediation once they are able to negotiate on their own. Other parents use mediation now and then—an hour here, and an hour there—throughout the negotiation process to resolve particularly difficult issues. Still other parents mediate their entire parenting agreement. The point is this: Mediation is a flexible tool that you can use to meet your family's needs as you develop your agreement.

A. How Mediation Works

Mediators facilitate discussions so parents can voice their concerns, identify important issues, and focus their efforts on meeting their children's needs. Almost every mediation has the characteristics listed below:

- **The mediator is neutral.** The mediator has no personal or business ties with either parent, has no past knowledge of the family, is not aware (in advance) of the specific issues to be mediated, and has no preconceived ideas about what type of parenting plan would be best for that family.
- **The process is confidential.** The mediator will not disclose to a court or anyone else what either parent says during the mediation. Furthermore, no one will know about the mediation or its results unless the parents agree or submit their agreement to a court to be incorporated into a court order. In rare circumstances, a mediator may be subpoenaed by a court and compelled to testify about the mediation if the mediator made a recommendation to the court and that recommendation is contested by a parent.
- **Mediation is focused on the future.** Most mediators ask parents to focus on what they'd like to have happen in the future. This means that the mediator spends little time on who said or did what in the past, but significant time on what can be done to control or prevent these problems in the future. The mediator's goal is to help parents build agreements that are likely to succeed by avoiding past problems.
- **Agreements are voluntary.** An agreement is reached only when both parents say that the terms are acceptable.

B. Why Mediation Works

The reasons why mediation works and why parents prefer mediation over litigation are many, including:

- Mediation offers access to a trained neutral person who can help parents focus their attention on the issues to be resolved, instead of blaming each other for the problems they face.
- Mediation is confidential, which allows parents to discuss the issues freely and evaluate possible solutions without fear that the other parent might use the discussions or the mediator's statements to build a court case.

- Parents decide for themselves whether to accept or reject any particular agreement.
- Parents control the time, costs, and degree of acrimony associated with finding a resolution.
- Mediation helps parents improve their communication skills—an important part of successful separate parenting.

Mediators are especially skilled at generating ideas and helping parents overcome impasses. Mediators can also review a parenting agreement to point out potential problems such as:

- vague language—(reasonable visitation)
- vague action plans—for example, a plan that doesn't include specific pick-up and drop-off times for visits, vacations, or holidays, and
- arrangements that might leave one parent feeling excluded from the children's lives—such as a sole custody arrangement with unspecified visitation.

Although mediators don't provide legal advice, they often can give general information about your state's custody and visitation laws, and suggest resources for information on child development and parenting theories. If your mediator is also a family law attorney, you may be able to get the legal information you need to make sure your agreement includes everything a court will want to see.

Even if your mediation sessions do not result in a complete parenting agreement, you probably will still benefit from the process. Partial agreements can narrow the issues to be negotiated or litigated later, and mediation can help open and improve lines of communication.

C. Proposing Mediation

For some families, the hardest task in mediation is to get it started. Many parents are reluctant to suggest mediation to the other parent because they:

- are convinced the other parent will refuse, or
- fear they will appear weak to the other parent.

In fact, once you (or a mediator) explain mediation to the other parent, that parent is likely to see its advantages over litigation and go along with it. And once mediation is under way, any suspicions about the process or the motivation for suggesting it are usually rapidly dispelled.

Mediation can be suggested in several ways: by one parent, a counselor, a lawyer, or the mediator. Here are some sample conversations that illustrate how each person's proposal for mediation might sound:

ONE PARENT PROPOSES MEDIATION:

I have heard about a process called mediation that might help us get these things resolved. From what I understand, the mediator would help us talk about our parenting situation—without fighting—so that we could see whether we can make the decisions on our own. We wouldn't have to spend any more time than we need to cover the issues and reach agreements. We could choose whether or not to involve attorneys, we might be able to avoid a court hearing, and we wouldn't have to drag ourselves or the children through any more bitterness than is absolutely necessary. The mediator wouldn't tell us what to do, and each of us could decide for ourselves whether any particular agreement was fair before we agreed to, or signed, anything. If the mediation doesn't work, we can still try to negotiate things on our own, or we can go to court—but at least we will have tried one more way to make our own decisions about how our children will be raised.

A COUNSELOR OR ATTORNEY PROPOSES MEDIATION:

At this point, I'd like to suggest that you consider a process called mediation. Mediation can be very effective for starting the dialogue on some of these difficult issues, and may allow both of you to find things that you can agree on. The mediator cannot impose a settlement on you—you and the other parent will be the ones to make all of the decisions. What the mediator can do is help you discuss your children's needs and how you plan to meet those needs—without allowing the discussion to deteriorate into an argument. When it works—and it works in the majority of cases—parents are in a better position to communicate and work together in the future. If mediation doesn't produce a full agreement, then you can go forward with negotiations on your own or through me, or you can take the matter to court.

THE PROSPECTIVE MEDIATOR PROPOSES MEDIATION:

_____ (name of parent, counselor, or attorney) has asked me to contact you to discuss how mediation might help you and the other parent resolve custody and visitation decisions on behalf of your children. The focus of mediation is your children, and making decisions in their best interests. If possible, we will work toward creating a comprehensive plan that describes all of the key elements of your parenting relationship. As a mediator, I am a neutral third party, which means that I have no previous relationship with either of you, and that I have no preconceived ideas about what decisions you should make. Although I will be happy to offer general information about the legal process and child development, I will not be making any recommendations about which options you should choose, and I will not provide legal advice of any kind. I will help the discussion remain civil, even when one of you is describing difficult or angry feelings.

As you begin to develop your parenting plan, I will help you make sure that it is clear, detailed, and easy to understand and live with. Because mediation is confidential, you can be candid and don't need to worry that what you say will be repeated in court. Because an agreement results only when both parents say it is acceptable, mediated agreements generally last longer, and result in fewer arguments or court battles, than nonmediated agreements.

D. Understanding Basic Mediation Techniques

One of the best ways to understand why mediation works is to look at a sample mediation session.

FAMILY PROFILE
Matthew and Brenda are divorced parents who live in neighboring communities and want to renegotiate their parenting plan, which has been in place for three years. Their children, Jason and Amy, are ages nine and seven, respectively.

1. The Mediator's Introduction

In addition to introducing themselves, mediators help parents articulate their own needs, interests, and concerns and focus their attention on how to best meet their children's needs, interests, and concerns. This is also the time when the mediator sets the ground rules for discussion and answers any questions the parents might have.

MEDIATOR: *Now, I will ask each of you to describe your children, their needs, the current arrangements, any concerns that you have, and your proposal for how you will share and divide your parenting responsibilities. As each of you speaks, I will ask that there be no interruptions, and that neither parent make derogatory remarks about the*

other. *Once we have done that, we will take each issue in turn and discuss how it might be resolved so that you are meeting your children's needs. As you start discussing and evaluating your various options, I will be happy to offer information about some of the choices that other parents have considered, and will help you generate ideas about solving difficult problems whenever it seems necessary. If either of you, or I, feel that discussion might be more productive if we meet separately, then I might take time to meet with each of you in private. Should either of you feel that you need advice from your attorney, just let me know and we will take a break.*

2. Parents' Opening Statements

The parents' opening statements give each parent an opportunity to hear how the other sees the issues, and what each proposes as a solution to meet their children's needs. Mediators use this time to learn about a family and get an idea about what an agreement will have to do to be acceptable to both parents. By using techniques such as "reflective listening" (verifying that the listener has an accurate understanding of the speaker's meaning), mediators can be sure that they are developing a complete list of all the issues to be resolved.

BRENDA: *Right now, the children live with me during the week, and they see their father on alternating weekends. We split all of the big holidays, like Christmas and Easter breaks, and alternate who gets the shorter holidays such as Thanksgiving, President's Weekend, and Memorial Day. I think that everything is working just fine. So do the kids. Matthew is the one who wants to change this.*

MEDIATOR: *Can you tell me something about the children's activities, how they are doing in school, and the things that you do together?*

BRENDA: *Both children are doing fairly well in school, they are involved in after-school sports, they do homework most days, and they have soccer games on the weekends. I try to carpool with some of the other parents to get them to practices and games. I help them with their homework each evening.*

MEDIATOR: *Do both you and Matthew live in the same school district?*

BRENDA: *No—and I don't particularly like the schools in Matthew's district.*

MEDIATOR: *Thank you, Brenda. From what I understand, you and the children have developed some routines that accommodate their schoolwork and sporting activities, and you are basically happy with the overall arrangements. Additionally, you don't see any advantages in considering a change in schools. Is this correct?*

BRENDA: *Yes.*

MEDIATOR: *Do you have anything that you'd like to add at this point?*

BRENDA: *No.*

MEDIATOR: *Now, Matthew, can you give me the same kind of information from your point of view?*

MATTHEW: *I feel like I'm losing touch with the kids. I want more time with them, and Brenda refuses. I am a good parent, but I gave in last time and let the kids live with her. Now it's my turn. I want them to live with me, and they can see Brenda on alternating weekends. Jason says he wants to live with me, and Amy says that she doesn't care who she lives with, but I think that the kids should stay together.*

MEDIATOR: *Thank you, Matthew. As I see it, you feel that you would like to play a greater role in both children's lives, and that Jason, at least, has expressed a preference for living with you. You also feel that it would be best if the children stayed together—regardless of the actual living arrangements. What do you know about the children's activities and school performance?*

MATTHEW: *Not enough. I often don't hear about their soccer games if it's not my weekend, and I almost never hear about their school activities or performance—except for getting a copy of their report cards. I'd like to know more about both things. Although our school district may not offer all of the same programs as the one the children are in now, it is still a good school. Jason will be transferring into the middle school in two years, and the middle school in our area is just as good, if not better, than the one he would go to in his current district.*

MEDIATOR: *Clearly, you would like to spend more time with Jason and Amy. Have you discussed this with them?*

MATTHEW: *Yes I have. Jason, especially, would like me to come to his games and practices. Amy has said that she'd like the same thing. If I at least knew something about the practice and game schedule, I could play a much bigger role in their lives—at least as far as sports goes. On the week-ends, they never bring home any schoolwork, so I have very little information about how they're doing. I didn't want to sit in the same room as Brenda to have our parent/teacher conferences, so I missed out on that this year.*

MEDIATOR: *Have you asked the children whether they want to change schools?*

MATTHEW: *Yes, and they're not happy about it, but they would do it as long as it happened over the summer.*

MEDIATOR: *Okay. Are there any other issues that you'd like to bring up at this time?*

MATTHEW: *No.*

3. Negotiating the Agreement

Once a mediator has an idea of the issues each parent wants to address, he or she works with the parents to see whether it might be possible to find areas of agreement. From the conversation above, a list of issues might include:

- improving Matthew's access to information about school and sporting events
- increasing Matthew's time with the children
- evaluating how and when decisions should be made regarding which school the children will attend, and
- evaluating which should be the children's primary home during the week.

MEDIATOR: *Turning to one of the issues raised during your opening remarks, I am curious about what each of you thinks about finding ways that Matthew might increase the amount of time he spends with the children?*

BRENDA: *If Matthew wants to take over my turn in the carpool, he could get to know more of the children's friends and could attend some of the practices or games. In fact, I could give him a copy of the game schedule, and he could attend any of the games, whether I am there or not.*

MATTHEW: *I'd like to do that. What about school, though? I should get a copy of their school calendar, too, and maybe they should be bringing some of their work to me when they come to visit on the weekends.*

MEDIATOR: *Brenda, would you be willing to give this information to Matthew?*

BRENDA: *Sure.*

MEDIATOR: *Now, how about parent/teacher conferences? How do each of you suggest that these be handled?*

BRENDA: *I think that Matthew should take the time to set up his own conferences. I don't want to have them together. All he has to do is call the school and arrange to meet with each teacher.*

MEDIATOR: *Matthew, is this something that you'd be willing to do?*

MATTHEW: *Yes.*

4. Turning Negative Feelings Into Positive Actions

Mediators recognize that it is hard to express negative feelings positively, and so a big part of their job is looking for ways to take anger, fears, or problems and transform them into potential solutions. If mediators have a strong suit, it is turning "fighting words" into productive conversation.

> **EXAMPLE:** *A parent says something like: "He/she is such a flake that you can't expect him/her to follow through with any agreement." The mediator might help the parent to rephrase the objection as follows: "Do you mean that you don't trust him/her to follow through with agreements based on his/her past behavior? Can you describe the behavior that bothered you? What could he/she do to demonstrate trustworthiness in the future?"*

5. Joint Versus Separate Meetings

Usually, both of the parents and the mediator are in the same room. Most mediators favor this approach because it helps the parents communicate with each other about their children—a skill they will need to work together in the future. If, however, the mediator feels that separate sessions might work better, the mediator places the parents in separate rooms and shuttles back and forth.

Many mediations end up a blend of same-room and separate-room sessions, depending on how high the tension is and whether the mediator thinks a parent might be more forthcoming about an issue if the other parent isn't present. If there's a history of violence between the parents, the mediation may consist entirely of separate meetings between the mediator and each parent. This can help prevent one parent from intimidating the other.

6. Overcoming Impasses

Impasses, or seemingly unresolvable differences of opinion, need not bring mediation to a halt. Mediators have many "tricks of the trade" they can and do use to help parents over rough spots. Many of the strategies that were described in Chapter 4 have their parallel in mediation. Additional strategies are outlined below.

Some of the ways parents can help each other, and the mediator, to understand what it would take for them to trust the other parent include:

- listing the specific things the parent should do or not do, such as be on time or don't have the child deliver the child support check
- listing the specific things the parent should say or not say during conversations between the parents, around the children or to friends or family members, and
- explaining what "pushes their buttons" and how the other parent can avoid it.

a. Reframing Statements

When one parent makes a statement that seems likely to make the other parent respond aggressively, mediators can diffuse the tension by reframing the statement.

> **PARENT SAYS:** *If that is the way you are going to treat me, then you can just forget about seeing the kids for half of the summer—we can just stick to the alternating weekend schedule all year long!*

MEDIATOR RESPONDS: *It seems that _____ (parent's name) has a difficult time feeling cooperative about finding ways to expand the amount of time that you and the children spend together when you make statements such as _____. Do you think there are any other ways you could get that point across without it leading to conflict?*

b. Focusing the Discussion on the Children

When the level of tension rises, mediators can try to diffuse it by asking the parents to focus less on themselves and more on their children's best interests.

EXAMPLE: *Matthew and Brenda are arguing heatedly over which home the children will live in during the school year. The mediator asks each parent to describe the school-age child's interests, attachment to friends, activities, and special needs. The mediator then suggests that the parents analyze the relative advantages of each school and choose a residence that provides access to the school that best meets the children's needs.*

c. Insisting on Clarity

If a parent makes blanket statements about the other (such as, "He/she can't be trusted!"), the mediator can insist that this parent describe the events that led to a lack of trust, and ask what that parent could do to demonstrate trustworthiness in the future.

d. Balancing the Power

Sometimes an impasse is the result of a power imbalance between the parents. The power imbalance may be for any number of reasons, but it is often evident when one parent:

- is more articulate than the other
- has traditionally dominated the other in making decisions
- has more experience in caring for the children, or
- has been violent, or has threatened to do harm to the parent, the children, friends, other family members, or a family pet.

A mediator confronted with a power imbalance will try to "level the playing field" by:

- moderating one parent's dominating style and boosting the other parent's self-confidence
- allowing both parents equal time to speak, and
- insisting that parents take the time to be specific about their concerns and their proposals for the future.

Sometimes, the best way to balance power is to get outside help. A parent feeling at a disadvantage might turn to a counselor to improve self-esteem, consult a lawyer to understand his or her rights, speak with a child development specialist to understand the children's best interests, or consult someone trained in domestic violence or child abuse to understand the impact of these events on all parties.

7. Recording the Agreement

When the parents reach agreement on a particular issue, the mediator takes careful notes. Typically, at the end of the sessions, the mediator will provide the parents with a summary of their entire agreement. It is each parent's responsibility to review that draft (with or without the help of an attorney) to make sure that it is accurate and complete.

E. Why Mediation Works in Very Difficult Cases

You may still be convinced that your conflicts with the other parent are unresolvable and that mediation will never work because:

- the conflicts are too intense
- each of you is entrenched in your position, or
- the conflicts involve domestic violence, child abuse, or substance abuse.

First, understand that all family law mediators assume there is substantial conflict between you and the other parent, and are prepared to use their facilitation skills to diffuse the tension and to refocus you on your children's best interests. Be encouraged by the fact that disputing parents reach agreement in approximately 70% of all cases that go to mediation. To understand how serious conflict might be handled in mediation, consider a mediation between two divorcing parents, Joseph and Elizabeth.

FAMILY PROFILE
Joseph and Elizabeth are confronting the serious conflicts—domestic violence, child abuse, and substance abuse—that were part of their marriage and separation.

MEDIATOR: *Now that we have agreed that there will be no interruptions while one parent is speaking, and that each of you will focus on the issues rather than on making derogatory remarks about the other, I'd like each of you to help* *me understand the situation from your point of view. First, I will need you to describe your children, then I would like to hear how you propose to structure your parenting relationship to best meet your children's needs. Who would like to start?*

JOSEPH: *I'll start. Our kids have been through a lot. Joey and Mary are basically happy children, but this whole thing has been hard on them. Elizabeth's lifestyle has been so unstable. Her drinking problem ruined everything. First, she started hanging out at bars, and had a few boyfriends. Then, she was upset at every little thing, and a few times she really took it out on the kids. Once, the kids ran away to a neighbor's house because they were afraid that she was really going to hurt them. I think that the kids should live with me and see their mother one afternoon a week until she can prove that she can take care of them.*

ELIZABETH: *My drinking! Big Joe has been an alcoholic ever since I've known him! When I wanted to separate, he beat me in front of the kids. That's when I knew for sure that I couldn't live with him anymore. Now, I have my own life, and no one to beat me, and I want them to live with me. I may have had my problems in the past, but that's all over now. I'm going back to school to get myself to a point where I can earn a good living and support myself and my kids. Pretty soon, I'll be able to afford my own place. He can be the one to see the kids one afternoon a week. The kids have told me that they want to live with me, and I said they could.*

MEDIATOR: *Okay. It sounds as though both you and your children have been through some tough times and have been dealing with some difficult issues. What do each of you think would be important for your children as you make plans for the future?*

JOSEPH: *For the future? Well, I suppose that the most important thing is to make sure that the children aren't around Elizabeth or her friends when they are drinking and partying. They do miss her, I know that, but I just don't know how I can trust her to take care of them given the way she is behaving.*

ELIZABETH: *I agree that they shouldn't be around in the wrong situations, especially the violence. I'd like to find some way that we could be sure that they'd be safe and cared for in both homes.*

As this mediation progressed, the mediator helped the parents explore the issues they had raised, and began looking for available resolution options. After some discussion, Joseph and Elizabeth disclosed that they had never tried to get help with substance abuse, domestic violence, or parenting skills, but that each was willing to try if the other agreed to do the same.

Elizabeth conceded that while Joseph might benefit by learning new parenting techniques for disciplining the children, he had never beaten or abused them in any way. Both Joseph and Elizabeth agreed that her few episodes of "taking it out on the children" happened after Joseph had beaten her during the separation and were not part of her normal parenting style. Neither parent feared for the children's safety while they were in either parent's care, but Joseph felt strongly that Elizabeth's new friends and frequent partying created an unhealthy environment for the children.

Joseph and Elizabeth acknowledged that they did not want their children exposed to the violence, alcohol, partying, or anger that they had experienced in the past. Elizabeth acknowledged that although she had come a long way in establishing a new life for herself, she still had some work to do before she would feel confident about caring for the children for more than short periods of time. Joseph agreed that he needed to get help in learning how to control his anger, but both agreed that for the moment, at least, he was probably better able to care for the children for longer periods of time. Both parents planned to remain in the same community.

MEDIATOR: *To recap what you have decided so far, you would like to make a temporary agreement that will carry you through the balance of the school year. Each of you agrees to meet together again at the start of the summer vacation to review this agreement and to negotiate any necessary changes. Either of you may request mediation for your next meeting, but it is not required.*

Here is the agreement as I understand it: Elizabeth and Joseph each agree to seek independent counseling or other support to deal with alcohol abuse. Each of you will continue with this counseling or support until such time as both you and your counselors agree that you can handle these issues on your own. Joseph agrees to seek counseling and support for dealing with anger. He will continue with this counseling until he and the counselor agree that he no longer needs this assistance. When his counseling has concluded, his counselor will write a letter to Elizabeth explaining the general issues covered in the counseling and that those issues have been dealt with or resolved. The children will be offered a chance to talk to a counselor, and may choose to continue counseling if they so desire. Both parents agree to identify at least one adult that the children can contact if they ever fear for their safety, or are concerned that their parent is too inebriated to provide adequate care. Neither child will be punished for contacting this "safe" adult—even if they misjudge the situation.

The children will live with Joseph during the week, and with Elizabeth two weekends out of the month. Elizabeth will arrange to take the children after school at least one afternoon a week, and will return them to Joseph's home by 7:00 p.m. Joseph will call Elizabeth each Monday evening between 4 and 6 p.m. to arrange for her midweek time with the children and a weekend visit, if appropriate, and to discuss the children's activities so that she can decide whether she will attend or otherwise participate. Each parent will be responsible for handling day-to-day decisions for the children when they are the primary caretakers, and each agrees to consult the other if important decisions are needed, and there is some lead time before the decision must be made. In the event of an emergency, either parent may seek whatever emergency attention is required, and will inform the other parent of the steps taken at the earliest practical time thereafter.

F. What Mediators Don't Do

Although some courts require mediators to make recommendations about how a custody or visitation dispute ought to be resolved when the parents can't agree (in California, for example), most mediators expect that only the parents can decide what kind of parenting plan they will accept. A mediator's sole mission is to help you and the other parent build your own agreement about how you will meet your children's needs. Sometimes, you may want to give in and have someone else decide an issue for you. To get an outsider to make these decisions, however, you must choose a forum other than mediation. This usually means an expensive and divisive court hearing.

Mediators can offer general information, but they don't provide legal advice or counseling—even when they are also attorneys or mental health professionals. Legal advice can be offered by an attorney to only one parent, so each parent needs his or her own attorney. Each parent has his or her own separate legal interests, and one attorney cannot counsel a separating or divorcing couple on what is legally best for each parent.

If parents want to know what their legal rights are, they will have to consult with a good self-help law reference, do some legal research in a law library, or pay for a consultation with an attorney. There is also online help that provides basic information on these issues.

Though it often makes sense to get expert information about the legal issues involved in your divorce or parenting disputes, once one person has hired a lawyer, the other person usually has to do so as well. Once two attorneys are involved in the case, the chances that your case will become even more adversarial are higher. Other alternatives to traditional legal representation include hiring a lawyer to handle limited aspects of the case—for example, to prepare and file documents with the court, to research particularly complicated questions, or to represent you at a hearing. Another option is to find lawyers who practice collaborative law. The idea for this type of practice is to ensure both parties get the information they need—without escalating the conflict.

G. Choosing Between Court-Ordered and Private Mediation

Increasingly, parents cannot simply ask the court to resolve their custody or visitation dispute. Instead, courts often order parents to resolve their custody or visitation dispute through mediation. Most states authorize, but don't require, their courts to order mediation. But a few states, including California, require it.

STATES IN WHICH A COURT MAY ORDER MEDIATION

Alabama	Kentucky	North Dakota
Alaska	Louisiana	Ohio
Arizona	Maine	Oklahoma
California	Maryland	Oregon
Colorado	Michigan	Pennsylvania
Connecticut	Minnesota	Rhode Island
Delaware	Mississippi	South Carolina
District of Columbia	Missouri	South Dakota
Florida	Montana	Texas
Georgia	Nevada	Utah
Idaho	New Hampshire	Virginia
Illinois	New Jersey	Washington
Indiana	New Mexico	West Virginia
Iowa	North Carolina	Wisconsin
Kansas		

If you live in a state that authorizes or requires mediation, you have a choice. You can present the dispute to the court and accept the mediation the court orders, or you can hire a private mediator to help you reach agreement and avoid going to court in the first place.

The advantage of court-ordered mediation is that it is likely to be free or nominally priced. Private mediators, on the other hand, will probably charge a significantly higher fee. The advantages of a private mediator, however, are many:

• You can shop for a mediator who suits both parents.
• You will have greater flexibility in scheduling.
• You can take as much time as you need (and can afford).
• You can focus your full attention on the mediation without worrying about what the mediator will recommend to the court. (See Section H, below.)

As a general rule, if you are using mediation as a backup to negotiating your own parenting plan, you will most likely want to use a private mediator. Most court mediation services are designed to settle only the basic custody and visitation questions that arise during a divorce or modification request, not help parents draft a detailed parenting agreement.

If you want to try court-ordered mediation and you live in a state where it is available, you must file the appropriate legal papers setting out your dispute and asking that it be resolved by the court. (See Chapter 17 for how to find an attorney or paralegal to help you do this.) You will then be informed that you are required to participate in mediation, and may even be given a person to contact, or a date and time for your mediation hearing.

Mediators in court-based programs generally have a mental health, social service, or probation department background. They are usually trained in the art and science of facilitating negotiations, and have general knowledge of family law and the principles of child development.

Court-appointed mediators are often limited to spending from one to six hours on any one case, depending on their caseload. Whenever possible, court-appointed mediators try to help parents find areas of agreement, and report that agreement to the court. If the parents are unable to reach an agreement through mediation, however, the court may ask the mediator, or a separate custody evaluator (see Section I, below), to assess the family's situation and make a recommendation about how the custody and visitation issues should be decided. When this happens, the mediator's or evaluator's recommendations are often the most important factor influencing the court's decision.

➡️ For more information about court-ordered mediation and evaluation, read Sections H and I. If you want more information about private mediation, skip ahead to Section J.

H. When the Mediator Makes a Recommendation to the Court

Most states that authorize court-ordered mediation do not ask the mediator to file a recommendation about custody or visitation with the court if the mediation doesn't result in an agreement. Instead, the court will make its own decision, perhaps based on an independent evaluation that the court orders.

Alaska, California, and Delaware are exceptions to this rule. In these states, judges may ask their court-appointed mediators to make a recommendation if the parents fail to reach an agreement. Regardless of your state, if you use court-ordered mediation, ask the mediator whether he or she will make a recommendation to the court if you and the other parent don't reach agreement.

If your mediator will make a recommendation to the court, your strategy and focus during mediation will change. In this situation, you have two audiences: the other parent and the mediator who can influence a later court proceeding. Not only must you try to reach an agreement with the other parent but you must also try to make a favorable impression on the mediator. Many mediators are impressed by parents who demonstrate:

- a primary concern for their children's best interests
- a willingness to consider a variety of settlement options, and
- a desire to facilitate contact between the children and the other parent.

To prepare for mediation that involves the possibility of a recommendation to the court by the mediator, you will want to research the factors your mediator will consider when deciding what to recommend to the court and how the mediator's report will be treated by the court. You can get this information by talking to a person in the mediation program or by asking a knowledgeable attorney. (See Chapter 17.)

I. Custody Evaluations

Many states allow judges to appoint a custody evaluator if the parents cannot reach an agreement on their own or through mediation. You may or may not be charged for this service. The evaluator, generally a mental health professional, spends time with the children and the parents to understand how the family functions, and to gain insights about what future arrangements might be in the children's best interests. Custody evaluations are often ordered when the parents disagree about custody and visitation, and:

- there is a history of domestic violence
- there is a history of child abuse or neglect
- there are allegations of substance abuse, or
- someone other than the biological or adoptive parents should perhaps be granted custody or visitation.

As a general rule, a judge who orders an evaluation is likely to adopt the evaluator's recommendation.

J. Choosing a Mediator

As mentioned, mediators generally fall into two groups: those who are connected to the court and those who are in private practice.

1. Court-Connected Mediators

If your state requires mediation whenever parents dispute custody and visitation issues, the court will have a list of mediators or an in-house mediation program. You will have little, if any, choice over who conducts your mediation. If you need help finding your local family conciliation or mediation court service, you can contact the court, ask an attorney or paralegal, or contact one of the organizations listed in Chapter 17.

2. Private Mediators

If you have a choice of mediators, because the court gives you a choice or because you are doing private mediation, narrow your list of potential mediators to two or three candidates, then have each parent interview them. Ideally, the person you choose is the one most likely to:

- be neutral—he or she has no preconceived ideas about how you should decide custody and visitation issues
- have expertise—he or she has had training and experience in dealing with custody and visitation issues
- focus on children—he or she understands general child development principles and knows how to identify children's interests, and
- have facilitation skills—he or she knows how to structure a mediation session so that each parent is heard and conflict is addressed and diffused, and he or she can assist you in overcoming impasses and planning for the long term.

When interviewing a mediator, you might ask questions such as:

- *What kind of training have you had?*
- *What subjects or skills did your training emphasize?*
- *How much experience have you had in working with individuals or families going through a divorce or separation?*
- *How much do you know about childhood development?*
- *How well versed are you in the effects of divorce and separation on children?*
- *Do you have any biases about how parenting issues should be settled, such as favoring custody with the mother or joint custody?*
- *What is your fee?*
- *How long do you think our mediation will take?*
- *What can I do to make mediation more productive?*

Although you may feel awkward asking these questions, you should be able to get a good sense of whether you can trust the mediator by monitoring your reaction to the mediator's answers. That is, the answers themselves are not as important as how you feel about the mediator.

3. Finding a Private Mediator

If you need help in finding your local family conciliation or mediation court service, you can contact the court, ask an attorney or paralegal, or contact the Association of Family and Conciliation Courts. The AFCC can be reached as follows:

> Association of Family and Conciliation Courts
> 6515 Grand Teton Plaza, #210
> Madison, WI 53719-1048
> Voice: 608-664-3750
> Fax: 608-664-3751
> Web: www.afccnet.org

If you want to find a mediator in private practice, you can check your telephone directory under "Mediation" or "Divorce Assistance," or you can contact:

- a community meditation program
- the court
- a paralegal
- a legal forms preparation service
- a public mental health agency, or
- the local bar association.

If none of these efforts generates a sufficient list of mediators, you can contact one of the following national organizations for a referral in your area:

- Mediate.com publishes a directory of all kinds of ADR (Alternative or Appropriate Dispute Resolution) service providers. They can provide a list of mediators in your area and are available as follows:

> Mediate.com
> P.O. Box 51090
> Eugene, OR 97405
> Voice: 541-354-1629
> email: admin@mediate.com
> Web: www.mediate.com

- The Association for Conflict Resolution is a national organization with databases on mediators, arbitrators, and other alternative dispute resolution professionals. It also provides general information on conflict resolution.

> Association for Conflict Resolution
> 1015 18th Street NW, #1150
> Washington, DC 20036
> Voice: 202-464-9700
> Fax: 202-464-9720
> email: acr@acrnet.org

- The American Arbitration Association has its own panels of mediators. They have local area offices in most states (consult your telephone directory) and will give you local area information about their mediation services, or you can reach the national headquarters as follows:

> American Arbitration Association
> 335 Madison Ave., 10F
> New York, NY 10017-4605
> Voice: 212-716-5800
> Customer Service: 800-778-7879
> Fax: 212-716-5905
> Web: www.adr.org

K. Preparing for Mediation

To prepare for mediation, complete the worksheets in Chapter 3. By doing so, you and the other parent will have written down your individual views on your children and separate parenting, and will have some idea of the issues to be addressed during mediation. These worksheets can provide your mediator with a wealth of information.

Prior to your first mediation session, you should ask your court-appointed or private mediator about the availability of:

- informational brochures explaining the mediation process
- informational classes or videotapes on mediation or custody disputes, or
- materials that might be available in your public library to help you prepare for mediation. (Chapter 17 has titles of books or articles that might be helpful.)

As you prepare for mediation, keep in mind the following five points:

1. **Focus on your children.** The best preparation for mediation is to think about how you can meet your children's needs for high-quality care and meaningful ongoing relationships with both parents. This step is

especially important if your mediation is with a court-appointed mediator who will make a recommendation to the court if you and the other parent can't agree. (See Section H, above.) You will want the mediator to know that your positions reflect your children's needs and interests.

2. **Minimize conflict.** Your ability to work with the other parent with a minimum of conflict is crucial to a successful separate parenting relationship. Ongoing conflict between parents can be one of the most destructive forces in a child's life. In particular, explore ways to reduce the conflict by minimizing the contact you have, while maintaining the best possible relationship with your children. Issues to focus on in Chapters 6 through 9 are:

  • Making Decisions
  • Exchanging Information
  • Where Our Children Will Live
  • Maintaining Contact
  • Special Occasions and Family Events, and
  • Improving Transition Times.

3. **Handle your anger.** Angry feelings and poor communication are common when parents separate or divorce. For some parents, the anger is so intense that they will go to great lengths to avoid reaching any agreement. Others will take great pains to make sure their agreement inflicts humiliation, loss, or significant inconvenience on the other parent. If this situation continues over time, you may need professional help to put your feelings into perspective so that you can focus on making decisions for your children.

   If you and the other parent cannot make these decisions on your own, through mediation, or with the help of a counselor or attorneys, resolution will probably come via a court order. This is likely to cost a considerable amount of time, money, and grief for everyone involved.

4. **Be positive.** Positive thinking reflects confidence in yourself, both in what you want to achieve and in your determination to find an acceptable solution. For some, this attitude comes naturally. For others, it requires a commitment to sort out their own thoughts and feelings so that they are certain of what they want. In either case, take a deep breath, put your "best foot forward," and see what happens!

5. **Be informed.** If you want to know your legal rights and obligations in a separation or divorce, you can consult an attorney or hire one to represent you. (Various attorney-client relationships are described in Section M2, below.)

L. If You Can't Reach an Agreement

If you cannot reach an agreement resolving your parenting issues, you can:
  • continue discussions on your own
  • schedule further mediation sessions
  • seek an independent evaluation and recommendation
  • seek counseling
  • submit the matter to arbitration, or
  • litigate the issues in court.

M. Alternatives to Mediation

Many parents, attorneys, and courts are confused about how mediation differs from counseling, attorney advocacy, or arbitration. As you will see from the following descriptions, counseling, legal advocacy, and arbitration can be complementary to, but are fundamentally different from, mediation.

1. Counseling

The focus in counseling or other forms of therapy is to help one or both parents explore, understand, and resolve the personal and emotional aspects of a situation. Many parents use counseling to reduce or remove the anger, jealousy, bitterness, and other feelings they have about the separation or divorce. This can help improve the working relationship with the other parent. In short, counseling explores "inner" space while mediation helps parents develop detailed plans for how they will parent separately.

Occasionally, a counselor who has worked with one or both parents may then attempt to mediate the parenting disputes. This practice is problematic. During therapy, patients disclose their thoughts, feelings, and motivations to the therapist. Having this information makes it difficult, if not impossible, for the counselor to be a truly neutral facilitator.

2. Attorney Representation

Although many parents think that divorce and attorneys go hand in hand, recent studies show that in nearly one-half of all divorces, at least one party is proceeding without a lawyer. Some do it alone because of the high cost of legal representation. Others choose to represent themselves to retain control over their case. When parents complain about involving attorneys, it is usually because they feel that they have lost too much control over their cases, the decisions, and the costs of finding a resolution.

You can use an attorney in one of two ways. First, an attorney can be a resource for legal information and ideas about how the law might affect your decisions. Attorneys can also negotiate on your behalf, examine your rights, represent your interests, or advocate your position in court or during arbitration. (Arbitration is covered in Section 3, below.)

Lawyers, without representing either party, can serve as mediators. If a lawyer represents either parent, however, the lawyer must advocate for that parent. The lawyer can work to facilitate negotiations between the parents, but the lawyer cannot serve as a neutral mediator.

3. Arbitration

The process and results of arbitration are very similar to a court case, but less formal. You and the other parent (or, more likely, your attorneys) present your positions and requests for particular decisions to the arbitrator, who decides the dispute. Most parents choose to be represented by an attorney during arbitration.

There are two types of arbitration:

- **Binding arbitration** means you cannot appeal the arbitrator's decision to a court, unless you prove that the arbitrator abused the process.

- **Nonbinding arbitration** means that you can appeal the arbitrator's decision to a court but may have to pay the other parent's court costs if you do not get a better result in court than you did in arbitration.

Only a few states specifically offer arbitration as an acceptable dispute resolution method in custody and visitation cases. (Chapter 16, Section C contains a list of states that permit, prohibit, or are silent on the subject of arbitrating custody and visitation disputes.)

a. Choosing an Arbitrator

In almost all cases, parents use a single arbitrator to settle their differences, and the arbitrator is generally an attorney. Occasionally, the arbitrator will be a mental health professional, but generally this happens only when the issues in dispute involve an assessment of the children's mental health. (More information about arbitrators is in Chapter 17.)

b. Arbitration Shouldn't Rise to a Court Trial

One of the dangers of arbitration is that it can turn into a miniature court trial. When this happens, arbitration becomes just as time-consuming and costly as a court trial, and the proceedings become just as adversarial. Discovery, the process by which each side finds out the other's evidence, can be just as extensive for arbitration as for a court trial.

One way to keep arbitration from turning into a court trial is to set limits in advance. For example, the parents can agree to share information rather than conduct extensive discovery. ■

Dealing With Changes in Your Agreement

Change is an almost inevitable part of any separate parenting arrangement. Any number of things might trigger a need for you to initiate, or respond to, requests for changes in your parenting agreement. Because your children keep growing and changing, their needs, interests, and activities will change as well. You and the other parent are both, presumably, moving on with your separate adult lives. New partners, new jobs, or new homes can all mean changes—to a greater or lesser degree—in your existing arrangements.

Change—any change—offers both good news and bad news. The good news is that change provides you and the other parent with an opportunity to modify, or eliminate, things the parents or children don't like in the current arrangement. The bad news is that some of the things you do like may also come up for discussion. All change brings a mixture of good and bad effects, and it takes a while to assimilate those changes—even if the overall effect is for the best. In short, change is difficult, and most people resist it—especially if they did not initiate the process.

A. Why Changes Are Necessary—And How to Handle Them

Children are a study in transformation. Just when you have figured out how to handle one developmental stage, your child is on to the next one. If you are a diligent consumer of child development or parenting skills books, you may suspect that your child gets up in the middle of the night to read ahead and plan especially challenging "curves" to throw your way! As your child enters puberty, you may feel as though the steady rhythm of responding to developmental changes that surface every month or two has been replaced by a roller-coaster ride in which moods, interests, and behavior change almost daily. Though consistency in your basic parenting style and principles is important, it is equally important that you recognize and fine- tune that style to keep pace with your child's changing world.

Just as children change, so do their relationships with their parents. Children reach out to their parents differently throughout their various ages and stages, leaning toward one or the other according to their needs and that parent's availability at a particular time. The routine and structure that your child used to demand from you may, predictably, give rise to a battle cry for "freedom from oppression" as puberty approaches. "Daddy's little girl" may become uncomfortable with his way of doing things as she gets older, and prefer to live with her mother as she becomes a woman. "Mommy's little boy" may not accept her as an authority figure as he grows older, and he may prefer the company of his father as he tries to define himself as a man. Alternatively, mother-daughter and father-son relationships that once worked beautifully may now lead to constant conflict, where the only solution seems to be a change in focus to the other parent.

And children aren't the only ones who change. Parents change, too, especially as they reformulate their lives after a separation or divorce. Changes in marital status often mean changes in employment, friends, activities, and residence—to say nothing of changes in personal values, priorities, and lifestyle. For some, being single again means that all elements of their lives are subject to review and possible change. For others, it means that they are now free to pursue the new life for which they have long planned.

Regardless of your particular circumstances, moving on with your life (whether immediately following the separation or divorce or some years later) can mean physically moving, finding new partners, creating or blending new families, seeking new employment, dealing with new money pressures, and facing new challenges as you try to juggle your own life while continuing to meet your children's needs.

Given these seemingly endless opportunities to confront change, what's a parent to do? How can you balance your needs and desires with those of your children? The other parent? Your extended family? Once again, it pays to go back to the basics. Separation and divorce are solutions to adult problems. Although it is vitally important for children that their parents be happy, financially stable, safe, and secure, it is also important that, to the greatest possible extent, the children have significant and ongoing relationships with both of their parents, have some sense of stability in their living arrangements, school, and social settings, and be relatively free to concentrate on the important tasks of childhood and growing up. As you try to balance all of these needs, wants, and interests, your job is to try to find solutions that put your children's interests in the forefront.

RELEVANT ISSUES

Issue	Number
Making Decisions	8
Resolving Disputes	9
Where Our Children Will Live	1
Maintaining Contact	18
Moving	33
If Our Homes Are Far Apart	37
Holidays	5
Vacations	14
Special Occasions and Family Events	13
Transporting the Children	16
Treating Each Child as an Individual	23
Consistency in Raising Children	4
Undermining the Parent-Child Relationship	30
When Nonrelatives Live in the Home	38
When Parents Have New Partners	36

B. When You Are the One Initiating Change

When you are the one initiating change, you are (for a time at least) in the driver's seat. You are the one who defines the issues, and you have the first opportunity to describe your preferred solutions. This somewhat enviable position, however, is not without its drawbacks. Once you put the subject of change on the table for discussion, you take the risk that you may not be completely satisfied with the final result.

Remember that for most of us, change is scary. Our "knee-jerk" reaction to change is often an emphatic "NO!" The way you present the other parent with your request for changes is one important key to successfully achieving your objectives. The other critical factor is understanding that your wishes are not the only ones to consider. Productive and lasting changes allow everyone to gain at least part of what they want in the final outcome.

Before you make any formal proposal for change, consider the following:

- why the changes are necessary
- what you want to accomplish by making the changes
- who will be affected by these changes
- what objections might be raised, and
- how you can respond to each of those objections.

After you have carefully thought through each of these points, consider how you might best present your requests. For example, if you are the mom and want the children to come and live with you during the school year, you may decide that:

- The change of residence is necessary because the children (ages 10, 12, and 14) say they want it.
- You want to respond to the children's wishes to the greatest possible extent, and to provide more parent involvement and "follow-through" for their school-related activities.
- The change in residence will be a positive change for you (because you will be able to get more involved with each child's classroom), for the children (because they will have the benefit of more parent involvement in school-related activities), for their father (because he will be able to focus on his work without worrying about shortchanging the kids), and for their paternal grandparents (because they will not lose their relationship with the children).
- The father and paternal grandparents are sure to object, because they do not want to lose any of the influence they currently have over the children's daily lives.
- The list of objections would likely include: Dad feels the children are too young to have the deciding vote on this issue, the children are complaining because they dislike the routine in his home and prefer the comparative freedom with you, and there is no compelling reason to initiate a change given that everything seems to be going well so far.
- You will answer these objections by pointing out that: The children should have an increasingly decisive voice in the custody and visitation arrangements, you want a more substantial role in their everyday lives (including the discipline that is part of the bargain), the children have nothing to lose and everything to gain by being raised in both parents' homes, your school system offers more opportunities than the one they are attending now, the children will be able to continue their visits with their paternal grandparents during their traditional one-week vacation together each summer, and the children will gain significant time with their maternal grandparents.

Though this kind of preparation gets you a long way down the road toward an agreement, it doesn't guarantee success. It offers a structure for organizing your thoughts, anticipating conflict, and creating a setting within which the conflicts that do arise can be resolved. (To take this process further, consult Chapter 4, How to Negotiate a Parenting Agreement.)

C. When You Are the One Responding to a Request for Change

For many of us, the maxim "If it ain't broke, don't fix it" works well. Therefore, few of us react well when told that something needs to be fixed when we consider it to be working just fine. For some, change is so scary that it can even feel like a kind of assault when proposed by others. Parents who are notified that the other parent wants to make changes in a parenting arrangement commonly experience disillusionment, frustration, and anger. Requests for changes in a parenting arrangement may even dredge up many of the thoughts, feelings, and animosities associated with the marriage and its demise. This is especially true if the parent who feels that the existing arrangements are working well either did not initiate the divorce, or initiated the divorce after discovering his or her partner's infidelity.

Although you probably won't welcome a request for modification, it does happen, must be dealt with, and may well be successful—even over your objections. The key to success in dealing with this situation is to curb your knee-jerk reactions, consider carefully and objectively what might be motivating the request, and view the request as an opportunity to entertain discussion and accomplish changes that serve your children's best interests even better!

When presented with a request for modification of an existing custody and visitation agreement (or after being served with a court document that communicates this information), you will need to step back, take a deep breath, and develop as objective a perspective as possible on the following issues:

- why the other parent consider these changes necessary
- what the other parent wants to accomplish by making the changes
- who will be affected by these changes
- what objections you have to the proposed changes, and

- how you can respond to the reasoning behind the proposed changes and to the objections the other parent is likely to have to your position.

If we pursue the example cited in section B, above, and you are Dad, your response to Mom's position and proposals may go something like this:

- Certainly the children should have an increasing level of input into the custody and visitation arrangements as they get older, but are 14-year-olds (let alone 12- and 10-year-olds) capable of making this kind of decision?
- You realize that Mom wants more involvement with the children, but that will be difficult given the distance between your homes—unless, of course, Mom wants to increase the number of calls, letters, care packages, and trips to see the kids.
- The ripple effect of a change of this magnitude is significant. You recognize that the children don't like sticking to a routine at your home, but the allure of Mom's home would soon fade once she began imposing order, too. You are more than willing to find ways to include maternal Grandma and Grandpa in the kid's lives at your house.
- You counterpropose that making a change now is premature, especially with the 10-year-old just about to complete elementary school. Perhaps a change of custody in a year, when the 10-year-old would already be switching schools, would be preferable.

Again, this is only the start of a fairly lengthy dialogue, but the approach has the seeds of an agreement. For more ideas about how to take this kind of discussion further, consult Chapter 4, How to Negotiate a Parenting Agreement.

D. When Tensions Are Running High

As with tension under any other circumstances, the first thing to do is to recognize that it often alerts you to a problem. After realizing there is a problem, you can then find ways to diffuse the tension. Perhaps the hardest, but most important, thing you can do is find a way to focus on how this dispute relates to your children's best interests. In some cases, your soul-searching will tell you that you must hold to your original position and your existing agreement "come hell or high water." In other situations, you will discover that at least some of the proposed changes have merit, and that you will have to find a way to accommodate these changes. You will find a detailed discussion on deescalating conflict in Chapter 4.

RELEVANT ISSUES

Issue	Number
Making Decisions	8
Resolving Disputes	9
If Extended Family Members or Close Friends Are Fueling the Dispute	32
Separating Adult and Parenting Issues	24

E. What to Do After You Negotiate the Changes

RECORD THEM, RECORD THEM, RECORD THEM!

At a minimum, you and the other parent should record your new agreements on the parenting agreement form, which you will find in the Appendix of the book. If you have already received a court order confirming your original arrangements, you should seek a modification of the order to reflect whatever changes you have negotiated.

If you do not have a court order that reflects your current agreement, problems will arise when an existing—and outdated—order is enforced in a moment of pique. This kind of conflict will not only wreak havoc on your existing, or future, positive relationship with the other parent, but it can also cause your children untold grief in trying to figure out what is happening to them and why.

RELEVANT ISSUES

Issue	Number
Making Changes	25
Making Substantive Changes to the Agreement	26
Explaining the Agreement to Your Children	27

Understanding Your Children's Needs

Understanding your children's needs following a separation or divorce can be challenging, but it is certainly not impossible. To help you meet the challenge, this chapter includes the following:

- strategies for dealing with children of all ages and both sexes
- strategies for dealing with children at different ages and developmental stages (although your children may react differently at the ages and developmental stages described, the information may still help you to understand your children as time goes along), and
- strategies for dealing with children who have special needs.

A. Strategies for Your Children at Any Age

Children of all ages and both sexes usually share these three reactions to their parents' separation or divorce:

- they maintain a passionate desire to see their parents reunited
- they feel sad and angry, and
- they want their parents to stop fighting.

Therapist-researcher Linda Bird Francke, author of *Growing Up Divorced* (Linden Press/Simon & Schuster, 1983), estimates that children need three years to get used to their parents' separation or divorce, and that the first year is the most difficult for them. During that time, almost all children experience shock, depression, denial, anger, low self-esteem, shame, and (especially among younger children) guilt—they think they caused the divorce.

First and foremost, children need to know that their basic physical needs will be met. Despite the fact that often one parent provides considerably more child care than the other, most children feel cared for by both parents. A separation or divorce brings on feelings of loss and fear that their needs won't be met. It is often hard for children when they realize that they will be cared for by only one parent at a time.

Children want the conflict between their parents to lessen, if not end altogether. However difficult it may seem now, you and the other parent must find ways to work together without having your discussions deteriorate into arguments.

The strategies in this section suggest ways to reassure your children that they will continue to be loved and cared for. Each strategy identifies specific issue/option sets from Chapters 6 through 9.

1. Reduce Conflict Between Parents

Ongoing conflict can be devastating for children of any age. Children burdened by ongoing conflict often have problems performing in school and relating to their friends, parents, and other relatives. You will take an enormous amount of pressure off your children if you can work with the other parent without arguing regularly.

Managing conflict is difficult, but it can be done. Chapter 4 suggests ways to manage conflict during your negotiations with the other parent. Chapter 17 has information on resources beyond the book that can help you understand, manage, and resolve conflict.

RELEVANT ISSUES

Issue	Number
Making Decisions	8
Resolving Disputes	9
Exchanging Information	11
Improving Transition Times	17
When Parenting Styles and Values Differ	34
Disparaging Remarks	3
Undermining the Parent-Child Relationship	30
Denying Access to the Children	31

2. Help Children Maintain Good Relationships With Both Parents

Almost all children whose parents separate or divorce struggle at one time or another with how to be loyal to both parents. Some children have trouble showing that they love each parent equally. Others are pressured by one parent (directly or subtly) to show they love that parent more than the other. Parents who demand this of their children are putting them in an almost impossible situation. Dr. Isolina Ricci (*Mom's House, Dad's House*, Macmillan Publishing, 1980) offers an important insight into the tension that these feelings produce:

If we think of ourselves as part our mother and part our father, it may be easier to see how conflicting and frightening it can be to have one part inside of us hate the other part that is also inside.

To minimize any "loyalty" issues for your children, try to:

- balance the time that your children spend in each home
- be aware of what your children's lives are like in each home
- strengthen your children's relationship with each parent, and
- reduce your children's exposure to the conflict between you and the other parent.

RELEVANT ISSUES

Issue	Number
Exchanging Information	11
Where Our Children Will Live	1
Maintaining Contact	18
Moving	33
If Our Homes Are Far Apart	37
Holidays	5
Vacations	14
Special Occasions and Family Events	13
Disparaging Remarks	3
Undermining the Parent-Child Relationship	30

3. Establish a Sense of Family With Each Parent

It is common for both adults and children to worry about how parents and children will get along after the adults separate or divorce. Whether the parents remain single or have new partners, each parent must develop new ways to establish a family environment for the children. Here are some suggestions that might work for you:

- establish a "normal" schedule with regular routines and special traditions that your children can share
- do not raise false hopes of reconciliation
- find a secure spot for your children to leave their things, and
- explore your new neighborhood with your children if you moved away from the family home.

RELEVANT ISSUES

Issue	Number
Resolving Disputes	9
Maintaining Contact	18
Improving Transition Times	17
When Parenting Styles and Values Differ	34
Consistency in Raising Children	4
When Nonrelatives Live in the Home	38

4. If a Parent Has a New Partner

Managing your life as a single parent will be quite challenging. It will be even more complex if you form a new relationship, especially when your children are living in your home.

Here are some ways to deal with the challenges a new partner might introduce:

Keep the relationship separate from your children until it becomes serious. Your children may develop a close attachment to your new partner and may have difficulty dealing with any breakup. One way to safeguard your children's feelings is to minimize contact between your new partner and your children. When your children and new partner do meet, keep it brief and casual until the relationship becomes serious. When your partner does stay over, be sure your children know there will be a guest at breakfast.

Be honest, but selective, in what you tell your children. Many parents are so pleased to have a new love interest that they are tempted to talk to their children as if they were adults. Though your children may be flattered if you take them into your confidence, information about adult relationships can be overwhelming for children. For these reasons, openly acknowledge your new relationship and feelings when it becomes serious, but keep the details to yourself.

Decide what relationship your new partner will have with your children. If your relationship with a new partner becomes serious, you must consider what role your partner will have with your children. This subject will certainly be of interest to your children, and it may cause some conflict between you and the other parent.

This decision may best be made after everyone involved is consulted. Among the questions you'll want to consider are your partner's role in:

- administering discipline
- providing child care
- sharing in household responsibilities
- participating in family events
- traveling on vacations, and
- making parenting decisions.

RELEVANT ISSUES

Issue	Number
Making Decisions	8
Resolving Disputes	9
Special Occasions and Family Events	13
When Parenting Styles and Values Differ	34
Consistency in Raising Children	4
Disparaging Remarks	3
Undermining the Parent-Child Relationship	30
When Nonrelatives Live in the Home	38

5. Keep Your Children From Growing Up Too Soon

Although everyone must assume new responsibilities after a separation or divorce, you must be careful not to overload your children. Though most children are pleased to help when times get tough, some parents take this too far.

For example, older children are sometimes asked to assume nearly all responsibilities for caring for younger siblings, cooking, and cleaning. Although you may not feel you have many options, your goal is to avoid turning your child into a full-time housekeeper and babysitter.

In addition, many parents experience intense emotional pressures from the changes that come after separation or divorce. The need to make more decisions, respond to your children's questions, and support your children during their own adjustment period can leave you feeling overwhelmed. Although parents and children are natural sources of support for each other, parents should not rely heavily on their children for this support. Taking on the quasi-adult roles of confidante and comforter can cause serious psychological problems for your children later in life. Find another adult to confide in and relieve your own stress so you are ready and able to support your children.

You can address these concerns by including counseling or other emotional support in your parenting agreement, and by sharing more evenly the physical tasks of child rearing.

RELEVANT ISSUES

Issue	Number
Psychiatric and Other Mental Health Care	20
Where Our Children Will Live	1
Undermining the Parent-Child Relationship	30
When a Parent Needs to Develop Parenting Skills	35

6. Help Children Who Are Having Difficulty Adjusting

Separation and divorce present difficulties for all children, but some children have an unusually difficult time adjusting. Boys tend to become more aggressive, and girls often become depressed and withdrawn. No one expects children or parents to be happy with all aspects of a parenting arrangement, but children should be able to develop a generally positive attitude over time. If your children are having problems adjusting, you will need to intervene.

First, you need to know what's "normal" and what's not. Several resources can help you understand how children generally react to separation and divorce and how to recognize the symptoms of a truly troubled child.

Ask your librarian or public mental health department for a list of books, magazines, and videos containing information on these issues. Three excellent books are:

- *Divorce and Your Child*, by Sonja Goldstein and Albert Solnit (Yale University Press, 1984)
- *How It Feels When Parents Divorce*, by Jill Krementz (Alfred A. Knopf, 1984), and
- *Mom's House, Dad's House*, by Isolina Ricci (Macmillan Publishing, 1980).

Chapter 17 and the bibliography include additional resources that might help you assess your children.

RELEVANT ISSUES

Issue	Number
Psychiatric and Other Mental Health Care	20
Religious Training	21
Driving and Owning a Car, Motorcycle, or Off-Road Vehicle	40
Making Decisions	8
Exchanging Information	11
Domestic Violence, Child Abuse, and Child Neglect	28
Alcohol or Drug Abuse	29
Maintaining Contact	18
Reinvolving a Previously Absent Parent	39
Special Occasions and Family Events	13
Grandparents, Relatives, and Important Friends	19
Improving Transition Times	17
When Parenting Styles and Values Differ	34
Consistency in Raising Children	4
Disparaging Remarks	3
Undermining the Parent-Child Relationship	30
Denying Access to the Children	31
When a Parent Needs to Develop Parenting Skills	35
Explaining the Agreement to Your Children	27

7. Be Ready for Change

Parents often forget that their children grow up and change dramatically over the years. When you negotiate your initial parenting agreement, you'll be tempted to assume that it will stand, unchanged, until your children reach adulthood. Though it is possible that your first agreement will be your last, it's highly unlikely.

RELEVANT ISSUES

Issue	Number
Making Changes	25

B. Strategies for Your Children at Different Ages and Developmental Stages

Children seldom develop in the exact age progression that psychiatrists, psychologists, and other counselors describe. Nevertheless, these categories are useful because they describe the sequence of developmental changes most children follow, even if they get there a bit earlier or later than most. Furthermore, boys and girls may grow and develop somewhat differently.

Judith Wallerstein and Joan Kelly were the first researchers to systematically evaluate and document children's responses to divorce by age. Linda Bird Francke reaffirmed this research during interviews with 100 children of different ages. In *Growing Up Divorced* (Linden Press/Simon & Schuster, 1983), she concluded that:

- initially, both boys and girls experience high levels of stress and depression after the actual separation or divorce, and boys typically have more long-term adjustment problems following the separation or divorce
- girls whose fathers leave when they are very young and remain relatively uninvolved with the family are more likely than their counterparts whose fathers remain home to become sexually precocious
- single mothers often have more difficult relationships with their sons than they do with their daughters, and
- children between the ages of 9 and 15 have more difficulty handling a parent's remarriage than children who are either younger or older.

1. Infants and Toddlers

Infants and children under the age of two must rely upon their parents and other care providers for almost all of their needs. Food, clothing, toilet training, entertainment, physical protection, and emotional comfort are the most obvious.

In addition, children this age have fairly limited memory and seldom understand that people and objects exist even though they cannot be seen and touched.

Researchers know that children under two can form a number of relationships (or attachments) to their care providers. They also suffer when there are too many differences in the way they are cared for and in the routines that are followed.

If your children are under two years old when you separate or divorce, consider the bird-nesting option described in Issue 1, Where Our Children Will Live, discussed in Chapter 6. If this isn't feasible, seriously consider designating one parent as the primary caretaker and giving the other parent frequent, if brief, visits.

If neither parent can provide the constant, demanding care required for very young children, you might turn to a relative or close friend to be your child's primary caretaker. This is preferable to your children receiving inconsistent care or being neglected.

2. Preschool Children

Preschoolers can, and do, accomplish some tasks on their own, but they still rely heavily on care providers for most of their necessities. Children this age understand that people continue to exist even when they are not physically present. Because most preschoolers are used to thinking of their parents as a unified team, separation from one often introduces a fear that the child will lose the other parent as well. Children this age can easily persuade themselves that the separation or divorce would not have happened if they had behaved better. You will need to pay attention and reassure them that this is not true.

Boys tend to have more trouble than girls dealing with the realities of a separation or divorce after their parents have parted company. Some speculate that this is because many parents provide their sons with minimal physical and emotional comfort. Parents may also expect their sons to get over their anger or pain—or at least hide those feelings. These responses to sons may help your child handle a situation like a "little man" but are likely to lead to an inability to face and resolve painful emotional issues as he grows up.

Children often formulate their sexual identities and preferences during this stage. For this reason, finding ways in which parents or other adults of both sexes can have a significant and ongoing relationship to your children is especially important.

As you plan for your preschooler's living arrangements, keep in mind the following:

- overnight visits can be started or increased at these ages
- parents should expand communication and cooperation between the households
- children should be encouraged to keep pictures of both parents at both homes
- children should have frequent contact with both parents, and
- parents need to explain their parenting agreement in terms that the children can easily understand.

RELEVANT ISSUES

Issue	Number
Psychiatric and Other Mental Health Care	20
Exchanging Information	11
Where Our Children Will Live	1
Maintaining Contact	18
Reinvolving a Previously Absent Parent	39
Moving	33
If Our Homes Are Far Apart	37
Special Occasions and Family Events	13
Grandparents, Relatives, and Important Friends	19
Treating Each Child as an Individual	23
Undermining the Parent-Child Relationship	30
Denying Access to the Children	31
When a Parent Needs to Develop Parenting Skills	35

3. Early Elementary School Children

Children in the early years of elementary school are transitioning into the larger world of relationships with friends and teachers. As a result, they are better able than preschoolers to handle the changes that come with a separation or divorce. Preschoolers are still closely tied to their parents, and separations from either parent are difficult to handle.

Early elementary school–age children are generally fine with overnights and can tolerate not seeing a parent for somewhat longer periods of time. Children in this age group, however, still have very strong wishes to see their parents get back together, and they spend lots of time worrying that their behavior or misbehavior caused the separation or divorce. Children this age are keenly aware of how their parents are feeling and often want to take care of each parent. For this reason, these children can become very skilled at hiding their worries so that they do not hurt their parents' feelings. Children this age may also be preoccupied with worries that they too will be left or "divorced" and will have no one to take care of them. Professionals suggest that parents support these children by reminding them that separation and divorce is between adults, and that each adult will continue to be a parent. Parents can also:

- create a calendar that allows the child to anticipate when he or she will spend time with each parent
- help children to choose and pack special books, toys, or clothes he or she wants to take to the other parent's house
- establish a clear, frequent, and regular schedule of visits
- set up or allow frequent telephone calls or other contact with an absent parent.

RELEVANT ISSUES

Issue	Number
Psychiatric and Other Mental Health Care	20
Education	6
Religious Training	21
Exchanging Information	11
Where Our Children Will Live	1
Maintaining Contact	18
Reinvolving a Previously Absent Parent	39
Special Occasions and Family Events	13
Improving Transition Times	17
Treating Each Child as an Individual	23
When Parenting Styles and Values Differ	34
Disparaging Remarks	3
Undermining the Parent-Child Relationship	30
Denying Access to the Children	31

4. Older Elementary School Children

Grade schoolers are better able than younger children to deal with most parenting arrangements. They understand and can usually follow schedules in a parenting agreement, although transitions between homes can present a problem. In general, calm children tend to handle the transitions better than irritable children.

Children in these middle years are busy forming their own identities and value systems and lean heavily on their parents for guidance. Children need active participation by both parents in their daily lives, school, and outside activities.

These children are also especially sensitive to both parents' feelings and would do almost anything to avoid hurting either parent. As a result, some children are afraid to let their parents know if they are dissatisfied or angry. You may not know that your children are hurting unless you look hard. Here are some signs:

- inconsolable grief over their parents' breakup
- unhappiness, no matter where they are or what they are doing, and
- behavior that seems to be "too good to be true."

One ten-year-old who didn't want to hurt his parents, but was thoroughly unhappy with the arrangements, summed up all of his frustrations by saying, "I just wish I could grow up faster. It's better than being a kid."

Experts and parents alike recommend that you strive to achieve the following goals for separately parenting your elementary school–age children:

- tailor the schedule to meet your child's personality
- stick to the schedules you establish
- don't put children in the middle by asking them to carry messages to the other parent
- offer counseling or other emotional support, and
- support your children's participation in outside activities.

RELEVANT ISSUES

Issue	Number
Psychiatric and Other Mental Health Care	20
Education	6
Religious Training	21
Exchanging Information	11
Where Our Children Will Live	1
Maintaining Contact	18
Reinvolving a Previously Absent Parent	39
Special Occasions and Family Events	13
Improving Transition Times	17
Treating Each Child as an Individual	23
When Parenting Styles and Values Differ	34
Disparaging Remarks	3
Undermining the Parent-Child Relationship	30
Denying Access to the Children	31

5. Adolescents

Adolescence is a turbulent time for both boys and girls. In addition to the hormonal changes their bodies experience, adolescents become increasingly dependent on their peer groups, have more activities independent of their parents and siblings, and try to distinguish their values and attitudes from those of their parents.

A separation or divorce is difficult for most teens. As one 15-year-old said during mediation, "I wish that they (his parents) would just remember that they aren't the only ones going through this."

A teen's concerns can run the gamut. Some panic at the idea that they have to give their friends two phone numbers to call for social engagements. Others struggle with constant conflict with one parent and little or no contact with the other. The parenting arrangements that once worked may now be unrealistic, given your teen's activities and preferences. Although adolescents are not yet legally capable of making all of their own decisions, parents should allow their teens more and more input into the decisions that shape the parenting agreement.

When you adjust your parenting agreement to meet your teen's interests and needs, consider:

- letting your teen decide where he or she wants to live

- strengthening your teen's relationship with one parent or another important adult if the teen and the other parent fight constantly
- involving your teen in identifying problems and developing solutions
- participating in parent-teen mediation, and
- guarding against forcing your teen(s) to grow up too soon.

RELEVANT ISSUES

Issue	Number
Education	6
Surname	22
Religious Training	21
Driving and Owning a Car, Motorcycle, or Off-Road Vehicle	40
Military Service	42
Allowing Underage Marriage	43
Making Decisions	8
Where Our Children Will Live	1
Maintaining Contact	18
Moving	33
If Our Homes Are Far Apart	37
Holidays	5
Vacations	14
Special Occasions and Family Events	13
Grandparents, Relatives, and Important Friends	19
Treating Each Child as an Individual	23
Disparaging Remarks	3
Making Changes	25

C. Strategies for Children With Special Needs

Children with special educational, physical, or emotional care needs require equally special consideration in your parenting agreement. Your needs for child care, ongoing medical or educational assessment, and support will be substantial. Also, your agreement may have to stay in place longer than for other children. Rather than ending your parenting agreement when your children become adults or graduate from college, you may find that your separate parenting relationship lasts indefinitely.

As you consider each issue/option set in Chapters 6 through 9, you may have to add your own agreements to make sure you are meeting your child's needs. Here are some issue/option sets that may require your special attention, and some suggestions that go beyond what is in those chapters.

Issue 1:   Where Our Children Will Live

Because some special-needs children require intense, long-term care, consider including provisions that give the primary caretaker periodic breaks.

Issue 2:   Medical, Dental, and Vision Care

- Keep the number of health care providers down so there is consistency in your children's care.
- All health care providers should be kept informed of your children's condition and progress.
- Be explicit about the kinds of ongoing assessment, therapy, medications, or other treatment that may be necessary.
- Identify who will meet with doctors, therapists, or other personnel to ensure that your children's ongoing care needs are met.

Issue 4:   Consistency in Raising Children

- Make an effort to keep your expectations and standards for behavior consistent between both parents' homes.
- Make sure that discipline is consistently applied in type and manner in both homes.

Issue 6:   Education

- Be explicit about how any special education needs will be met.
- Identify who will be involved in meetings with teachers, administration, or other school personnel to ensure that your children's ongoing educational needs are met.

Issue 7:   Insurance

- Decide how your child's ongoing needs for health insurance or other kinds of insurance will be met.
- Make sure that you incorporate your decisions into any agreements that provide for your children's financial future, such as a child support agreement.

Issue 8:   Making Decisions

If your special-needs child will not be able to make his or her own decisions upon reaching legal adulthood, you may need to establish an adult guardianship and add language to that effect in the parenting agreement.

Issue 12: Child Care

- Make sure the number of child care providers is kept to a minimum to provide consistency.
- Ensure that any child care providers are capable of caring for your special needs children.

Issue 20: Psychiatric and Other Mental Health Care

- Plan how mental health support or assessment may be offered to your children.
- Plan how mental health or emotional support may be provided to other family members.

Issue 38: When a Parent Needs to Develop Parenting Skills

A parent who is not used to providing full-time care for a special-needs child may need training.

Issue 39: Reinvolving a Previously Absent Parent

A parent who has been uninvolved with a special-needs child because of the cost, time, or special care required may need training, counseling, or other support before providing any care. ■

Multiracial, Multicultural, and International Families

Virtually all parents who separate or divorce experience conflict over some, if not many, child-rearing issues. Parents whose cultural, religious, ethnic, or national identities differ often find that separate parenting presents even greater challenges. For example, you may have been attracted to your partner—at least in part—because of your cultural, religious, ethnic, or national differences. These once-intriguing differences, however, may now be a source of conflict concerning your children.

Fortunately, diversity within a family need not be the source of unresolvable problems. Many parents find that by first acknowledging their different viewpoints on certain issues, they are able to address the following common concerns:

- accommodating differences in child-rearing practices
- encouraging the children to celebrate the traditions of both parents
- sorting out the role of power within the family
- accommodating religious differences
- working within the American legal system, and
- deciding whether another country has authority over parenting (custody) issues.

A. Accommodating Differences in Child-Rearing Practices

In the United States, we have developed increasingly clear standards about how children must be raised and cared for, and the kinds of discipline that are, and are not, acceptable. These standards may conflict with the practices of other cultures or religions and may lead to serious disagreements. Sometimes these other practices are so different from the generally accepted American norm that a parent is accused of child abuse or neglect when following them.

Most frequently, practices that clash with American standards pertain to discipline in general and corporal punishment (such as spanking, caning, or striking with an object) in particular. Some cultures and religions consider corporal punishment essential to properly mold a child's behavior. A nation's legal code or a religious doctrine may spell out the methods for inflicting this kind of punishment.

By contrast, corporal punishment is rarely acceptable in the United States, especially in public schools and other public institutions. In fact, in some states all forms of corporal punishment are illegal. Other states prohibit it after a certain age, such as 12.

RELEVANT ISSUES

Issue	Number
When Parenting Styles and Values Differ	34
Consistency in Raising Children	4
When a Parent Needs to Develop Parenting Skills	35

Another area in which certain cultures or religions don't follow the dominant American norm is medical care. For example, parents of certain cultures or religions will refuse specific kinds of medical intervention on behalf of their children. Other parents distrust or reject Western medicine and instead follow Eastern practices, such as acupuncture. Still other parents prefer holistic healing or other alternative medicines.

RELEVANT ISSUES

Issue	Number
Medical, Dental, and Vision Care	2
Psychiatric and Other Mental Health Care	20

DON'T AGREE TO BREAK THE LAW

If you and the other parent are divorcing or legally separating, a court will probably review your parenting agreement. If any provision violates a state or federal law that governs the treatment of children, the court will reject your proposed parenting plan. It will probably also order a social worker to investigate both parents' homes and submit an evaluation to the court. The court will make whatever orders it deems necessary to protect your children's best interests, which will always be interpreted in accordance with the U.S. legal system.

B. Encouraging Children to Celebrate the Traditions of Both Parents

One way to minimize the child-rearing conflicts you experience because of cultural, religious, ethnic, or national differences is to instill in your children a sense of specialness. Often children feel lost, angry, and rejected after their parents separate or divorce, and the children's low feelings exacerbate the parental conflicts. You can help your children adjust to the separation or divorce, and therefore lessen your conflict with the other parent, by doing any of the following:

- teaching them who they are
- celebrating special traditions, and
- teaching them to respect (and embrace, if relevant) the ceremonies, rituals, and traditions of their other parent.

For some parents, the core of their disagreement is about whose culture or religion is "better" or represents the "truth." You can hold firmly to your beliefs, but always remember that your children have two parents. Rather than trying to prove which culture or religion is better, try to find ways to equip your children to make their own decisions about both. One way to do this is to raise your children in both cultures or religions.

If those cultures or religions differ to the point that you cannot fully integrate your children into both, you can minimize your conflict—and differences—by finding a common principle, such as a commitment to family, and working from there. Perhaps mediators, elders, or leaders within your particular communities can offer suggestions on living together peacefully.

Another suggestion is to teach your children about both cultures or religions but withhold certain ceremonies, rituals, or traditions, such as initiations into a church or congregation, participation in funerals, undergoing religious communion, or administering certain medical care. You might set limits because your children are not considered full members of the culture or group, or because certain functions might frighten or overwhelm your children.

RELEVANT ISSUES

Issue	Number
Religious Training	21
Holidays	5
Vacations	14
Special Occasions and Family Events	13
When Parenting Styles and Values Differ	34

C. Sorting Out the Role of Power Within the Family

One feature of certain cultures, religions, and ethnicities is that near-absolute power is given to men, who make most of the substantive decisions that affect all family members. In this situation, the bargaining power between the parents may be very unequal, and you may have to use certain dispute resolution methods to accommodate the situation. For example, in a culture in which men issue orders, fathers will seldom accept information or direction unless it comes from another male. These parents might choose a male mediator, and the mother might hire a male attorney to negotiate with the father or his attorney.

RELEVANT ISSUES

Issue	Number
Making Decisions	18
Resolving Disputes	9
Disparaging Remarks	3
Undermining the Parent-Child Relationship	30

D. Working Within the American Legal System

The way that a culture describes conflict often indicates how that culture prefers to resolve conflict as well. In American society, conflict usually means there are two or more competing interests—one will win while the other(s) loses. For the most part, divorce or matrimonial litigation in our legal system encourages each parent to confront the other and prove who will uphold the best interests of the children. Although litigation may be appropriate when a parent with a history of abuse, neglect, or serious instability insists on significant unsupervised time with the children, litigation is usually unnecessarily costly and bitter. To parents from outside the United States, American litigation can be bewildering.

Some cultures believe conflict results from inharmonious relationships. Once a relationship becomes inharmonious, they believe it is the community's responsibility to help the individual rediscover and fulfill his or her proper role. In many of these cultures, the best interests of the child are synonymous with the best interests of the group. The role that any one individual is expected to fulfill is generally a function of his or her age, sex, social standing, and economic resources.

Many of these communities are fairly cohesive, and the elders within the community or extended family are well regarded for their wisdom and leadership. When facilitators are needed to resolve conflict, elders are called upon because their status allows them to be persuasive problem solvers. Given this view of conflict and resolution, it is easy to understand why some parents are mystified when they are told that their decisions must hinge on the child's best interests as determined by state legislatures, the mental health profession, and the courts.

Even mediation, which often is a versatile tool for resolving disputes, can be culturally biased. For example, selecting a mediator in the United States typically means finding someone totally neutral and unknown. In many cultures, however, parties are willing to participate in the process and reach agreement because the facilitator is well known to them. Additionally, the predominant mediation model in the United States today presumes that the parties will come to an agreement. In other cultures, mediation is most effective when the facilitator suggests the solution and then persuades the parties to agree.

If you or the other parent come from a background that is substantially different from the dominant Anglo-American culture, you may need to find attorneys, mediators, counselors, or others sensitive to the issues and cultural differences. If you feel at a disadvantage because of language, either because you recently arrived in this country or because you don't understand the American legal system, you need to find knowledgeable support people from your community who have the information you need.

To resolve your conflicts, look for people who can connect the priorities of each culture with the issues of disagreement.

RELEVANT ISSUES

Issue	Number
Psychiatric and Other Mental Health Care	20
Making Decisions	8
Resolving Disputes	9
When Parenting Styles and Values Differ	34

E. Deciding Whether Another Country Has Authority Over Parenting (Custody) Issues

If one or both parents are not U.S. citizens, your separate parenting may involve additional issues related to international borders. You—or the other parent—may justifiably fear that your children will be taken out of the United States without your knowledge or consent. Although protecting your children from a parent who truly wants to kidnap and hide his or her own children can be hard, laws do exist to help. (Chapter 16, Section F has information on laws that can help you if your children are taken out of the country.)

RELEVANT ISSUES

Issue	Number
International Travel and Passports	41
Making Decisions (If there is any question over which country actually has jurisdiction, consider adding specific language.)	8

Although not located on foreign soil, American Indian nations have a special legal standing in the United States. Section 1911(a) of the Indian Child Welfare Act states:

An Indian tribe shall have jurisdiction exclusive as to any state over any child custody proceeding involving an Indian child who resides on or is domiciled within the reservation of such tribe, except where such jurisdiction is otherwise vested in the State by existing Federal law. Where an Indian child is a ward of a tribal court, the Indian tribe shall retain exclusive jurisdiction, notwithstanding the residence or domicile of the child.

This Act covers the termination of parental rights, foster care, and adoptive placements as well as custody proceedings. If you are unsure whether or not you must resolve your differences in a tribal court, see an attorney. ■

CHAPTER

15

Nontraditional Families

The traditional image of a family is a mother, a father, and their children. Millions of American families, however, look very different, and are often referred to as "nontraditional families." Some of these families consist of childless couples—married or unmarried, gay or straight—although many include children. Nontraditional families—as we define them below—make up the substantial majority of U.S. families.

A.   What Are Nontraditional Families?

Nontraditional families fall into one of the following categories:

Stepfamilies. In a stepfamily, a single parent establishes, usually by marriage, a new long-term relationship. The children usually refer to the new partner as a stepmother or stepfather. The partner calls the children his or her stepchildren.

Blended families. A blended family consists of at least two, and as many as four, stepfamilies. At its core, it's a former couple, their children, the new relationships entered into by the members of the former couple, and the children of those new relationships. Dr. Constance Ahrons describes these families as binuclear families in her book *The Good Divorce* (Harper Collins, 1994). Here is an example of a blended or binuclear family: Mark and Evelyn marry and have a daughter, Lisa. They get a divorce, sharing custody of Lisa. Mark marries Shauna, who is also divorced with a child from her previous marriage. Mark and Shauna have a son, Rueben. Evelyn comes out as a lesbian after divorcing Mark and forms a relationship with Cindy. Together they adopt a child.

Single parents. Many people—through circumstance or choice—are single parents. Although many separated or divorced parents may be called "single parents," this category is for those parents who have chosen to bear or adopt a child on their own, without a partner. Obviously, the separate parenting issues in this book are not relevant for these parents unless they have involved another adult in raising the children. For example, a single mother may get help from her own parents or from a close friend in raising her children.

Grandparent-headed families. Some parents go beyond "getting help" from their own parents in raising children. In many families, especially those torn apart by violence or drugs, the grandparents have custody of, or guardianship

over, their grandchildren—either formally (by court order) or informally (by agreement of the parents).

Unmarried couples. Many unmarried heterosexual couples have children together.

Same-sex-parent-headed families. Thousands of lesbians and gay men have children through donor insemination, surrogacy, or adoption. Most of these children are being raised by two mothers or two fathers, though some families are more extended, including donors and their partners.

Open-adoptive families. In general, a legally married husband and wife who adopt a child do not fall into the category of a nontraditional family. This changes, however, if the couple maintains a relationship with the birth mother—meaning the child is raised by the adoptive parents but has a relationship with the birth mother.

B.   The Legal Relationship of a Nontraditional Parent and His or Her Children

Probably the greatest challenge faced by nontraditional families is the lack of societal and legal recognition. Despite the fact that fewer and fewer American families consist of a mother, a father, and their children, the institutions—including the legal system—that deal with families are still geared for the traditional family model. Nontraditional families often feel left out, ignored, and unsupported. These problems are exacerbated when the adults in the family divorce or separate. Sometimes, a person who has spent years raising children now finds himself or herself shut out because he or she is not considered a legal parent.

In a nontraditional family, it is imperative that when the adults raising the children split up, they continue to look out for the best interests of their children. If that means maintaining contact with all the adults involved in raising the children, then the parenting agreement must explicitly provide for this. Don't expect a court to do it—a court will usually order continuing contact only when the adult is a recognized "legal parent." (Some courts will order contact between children and a "psychological" parent, but often only if the legal parent doesn't object.)

Parents generally fall into one of four categories:
- legal parents
- biological, nonlegal parents
- psychological parents, and
- legal guardians.

Depending on the category and the state you live in, a parent may or may not have the legal right to custody or visitation with, or the legal responsibility to care for or support, the children.

As you read about the various categories of legally recognized and unrecognized parents, remember that you are not obligated to follow the strict letter of the law. If it's in the best interests of your children for them to maintain contact with the adults who have been raising them, then by all means continue that contact.

1. Legal (Biological and Adoptive) Parents

Legal parents have both the authority and the obligation to provide basic care and comfort for their children. They are charged with making the decisions that affect their children's health, education, and welfare. They are further charged with providing for their children's financial support.

The legal mother is usually, but not always, the woman who conceives and gives birth to the child (see Section 2, below) or who legally adopts the child.

The legal father is a man who legally adopts a child, was married to the mother when the child was conceived or born, or was declared the father in a paternity action. In addition, a man may be presumed to be the legal father if he:

- attempted to marry the mother (even if the marriage wasn't valid) and the child was conceived or born after the attempt

- married the mother after the birth and agreed either to have his name on the birth certificate or to support the child, or
- welcomed the child into his home and openly held himself out as the father.

A legal parent's obligations and rights end *only* if a court issues an order terminating parental rights. If you are the biological father of a child you have not seen for some time, you are still considered a parent unless a court says otherwise. This means you have the right to seek custody of or visitation with your child, and you can be sued to pay child support.

2. Biological, Nonlegal Parents

In a number of situations, a person is biologically related to a child but nevertheless is not considered the child's legal parent.

a. Birth Mothers

The most common biological, nonlegal parent is a birth mother who gives up her child for adoption. A birth mother traditionally severs all ties with the child (and adoptive parent(s)) following the adoption.

In recent years, however, a number of adoptive parents have chosen to keep an ongoing relationship with their child's birth mother. This arrangement is often called an open adoption. In some families, the relationship is little more than an exchange of holiday and birthday cards. In others, it includes regular visits and attendance at family celebrations.

b. Surrogate Mothers

A surrogate mother is a woman who bears a child for someone else. Some surrogate mothers become pregnant with the semen of a man who wants to be the father. Others have an already-fertilized egg of another woman implanted in their uterus, in which case the surrogate mother is not genetically related to the child. Either way, upon the birth of the child, the surrogate mother relinquishes all rights and responsibilities for the child and turns the child over to the man (in the former situation) or the man and/or woman (in the latter situation).

Surrogate mothers offer infertile and gay male couples a way to become parents. The process is not without risk, however. The surrogate mother might change her mind and refuse to relinquish the child. Some states have passed laws regulating surrogacy contracts. Many states are silent on the issue.

A few highly publicized cases in which the surrogate mother changed her mind have drawn attention to the issue. In general, courts have ruled that a surrogate mother has the rights of a legal parent if she contributed genetic material to the child—that is, she became pregnant with the semen of a man who wanted to become the father. If, however, an already-fertilized egg of another woman is implanted in her uterus, the surrogate generally has no parental rights.

Some parents who obtained their children through a surrogacy arrangement choose to retain an ongoing relationship with the surrogate mother, similar to the open adoption described above.

c.   Semen Donors

Donor insemination is a process in which a woman is inseminated by a means other than sexual intercourse. In most cases, the semen comes from someone other than the woman's husband. This type of artificial insemination offers infertile and lesbian couples a way to become parents. The process is not without risk, because a semen donor who is known to the couple might change his mind and sue for paternity.

If the woman is married when the insemination and birth occur, her husband, not the donor, is considered the legal parent. If the woman is unmarried when the insemination and birth occur, whether the donor is considered the legal father depends on a number of factors, including the procedure and the state. In some states, the woman and the donor may enter an agreement stating their intentions, including that the donor not be considered the legal father. In California, if the insemination is performed by a doctor, the donor is not considered the legal father. If no doctor is used, the donor may be considered the legal father.

As with open adoptions and some surrogacy arrangements, some parents maintain an ongoing relationship between the semen donor and the child.

d.   Ova Donors

In another reproductive technique, a woman donates an egg, which is fertilized in vitro and then implanted in the uterus of a different woman who wishes to become a mother. Usually, the egg is fertilized with the semen of the husband of the woman into whom the egg is implanted.

Because of the lack of uniformity among the states on the legal relationships created in ova donor situations, this kind of arrangement deserves careful research. The ova donor will probably not be considered a legal parent in most cases. The ova donor is similar (legally) to a surrogate mother, even though the ova donor shares genetic material with the child. Second, the ova donor can be equated to a semen donor, who usually is not considered a legal father.

3. Psychological Parents

"Psychological parent" is a general description of an adult who has formed a significant emotional bond with a child by contributing substantially to the child's care and upbringing. These parents are sometimes also called "functional parents." Psychological parents are not legally responsible for the care or support of a child; nor are they automatically entitled to custody of, or visitation with, the child.

In some situations, a court will grant visitation between a child and a psychological parent if the court believes it would be detrimental to the child for the relationship to end.

a. Stepparents

A stepparent is the new spouse of a legal parent. In general, the stepparent and stepchild have no legal relationship. This means that unless the stepparent legally adopts the child, the stepparent is not obligated to care for or support the child and is not entitled to seek custody or visitation. Of course, many stepparents are instrumental in the upbringing and support of their stepchildren.

In a few states, including Michigan and Wisconsin, some stepparents have been granted the status of "equitable" parent. Most often, this occurs when the stepparent and child consider themselves to be parent and child, and when the legal parent has encouraged the relationship. Equitable parents are often granted shared custody of, or visitation with, the children, and can be ordered to pay child support.

b. Co-Parents

A co-parent is the partner of a biological or adoptive parent. The status and rights of a co-parent are very important issues for lesbian and gay couples, in particular, who decide to raise children together. The law in this area is evolving, and the issues surrounding a co-parent's legal rights toward a partner's child remain controversial. It's important that co-parents research ways that both parents can remain in a child's life if they split up. Just as with heterosexual parents, children need to know that they will not lose access to the adults who have been important in their lives—even if those adults are no longer a couple.

CO-PARENTS WHO ARE ALSO LEGAL PARENTS

Until 1985, gay and lesbian couples (and their lawyers) assumed that state laws were written so that adoptions were available only to married couples and single people. If a "single" person—such as the partner of a biological parent—sought to adopt, the biological parents' rights would first have to be terminated—not the result a lesbian or gay couple wanted.

Then the lawyers got smart and began reading the text of the state adoption statutes. Most laws, they realized, authorize adoptions by married couples and single people, but don't expressly exclude unmarried couples. Similarly, the stepparent adoption statutes expressly authorize adoptions by the new spouse of a legal parent if the other legal parent is dead, had his parental rights terminated, abandoned the child, or consented to the adoption, but they don't forbid an unmarried partner from becoming a stepparent.

Many states now allow joint adoptions by gay and lesbian couples, also known as second-parent adoptions. When a court grants a joint or second-parent adoption, both mothers or both fathers are considered legal parents.

---

c. Other Important Adults

Grandparents, aunts and uncles, and adult friends of legal parents often form significant emotional bonds with children. In all states, grandparents (and in some states, aunts and uncles) can ask the court to grant them visitation with these children following a divorce or separation. It's up to the court whether or not to grant the visitation, but many will, recognizing the special relationship children often have with their grandparents.

4. Legal Guardians

A legal guardian is an adult given the legal right—either by the parents or by a court—to care for and control a minor child. Formal legal guardianships (those ordered by a court) tend to be set up for children who lack stable parenting. For instance, grandparents (or aunts and uncles) are often appointed legal guardians of their grandchildren (or nieces and nephews) when the parents are unable to care for the children because of drug abuse, imprisonment, or lack of basic parenting skills. A legal guardian often needs a court order so that schools, hospitals, and other institutions understand that the guardian has the legal right to make decisions about the child.

If the legal guardian has completely taken over the parenting role, a court may grant custody of the children to the guardian. The court may also order the legal guardian to allow the parents to visit with the children. Some legal guardians have a more limited role because they are only asked to care for a child who is away at school. When this happens, the legal guardian is there to make quick decisions in the event of an emergency.

C. Recognizing the Nontraditional Parent's Role

If your children have a close relationship with a biological, nonlegal parent; a psychological parent; or a legal guardian, you will want to provide for the continuation of that relationship in your parenting agreement, unless you believe your children are being harmed.

You have several ways to handle this, depending on your children's relationship with the adult. If your children haven't been living with the adult, as might be the case with a close friend or nearby relative, you can either incorporate a regular visitation schedule in your parenting agreement or allow your children to initiate contact.

If, however, your children have been living with the adult, and for all intents and purposes that adult is another parent to your children, do what you can to minimize the harm to the kids. You may be angry and want that person out of your life. And that person may have no legal standing whatsoever to claim "parenthood." But if your children know that person as a parent, put your anger and the legal labels aside and fill out the parenting agreement in this book as if you were a legally married couple getting a divorce, both entitled to continuing contact with your children.

RELEVANT ISSUES

Issue	Number
Making Decisions	8
Grandparents, Relatives, and Important Friends	19
When Parents Have New Partners	36

D. Resolving Conflict in a Way That Meets Your Family's Needs

Most nontraditional families need to find ways to resolve disputes outside of the courtroom. The court system is geared to working with traditional families. This does not necessarily mean that nontraditional families suffer discrimination within the court system, although lesbian and gay couples often justifiably feel that way.

In most situations, the dynamics of nontraditional families require more effort and understanding than the legal system can give. Court calendars are overcrowded and court personnel are overworked; judges cannot take the time to thoroughly investigate your children's relationship with their stepsiblings, their grandparents, your partner, and all the other important people in their lives.

When adults who have raised (or at least lived together with) children in a nontraditional family decide to live apart, they often find mediation helpful for defining the role the nonlegal parent will have in the children's lives and for developing a plan to carry it out. If mediation isn't an option or doesn't work, consider arbitration—where you can obtain a resolution without having to negotiate with the other person. (Chapter 11, Making Mediation and Arbitration Work for You, has information on how each process works and how to select a mediator or arbitrator.)

No matter which process you use, the facilitator should understand the issues that are important to you and structure the process so that it will meet your needs. You may need to go beyond the suggestions in Chapter 11 to find the right facilitator. For example, if you're a lesbian couple splitting up, consider contacting a gay community center, support group, religious organization, or other gay or lesbian institution for help finding someone to mediate your parenting issues.

E. Creating New Relationships After the Divorce or Separation

You may be reading this chapter because, while your traditional family divorced or separated a while ago, you or your children's other parent have formed a new relationship, creating a nontraditional family. A new relationship can bring joy to the new couple and anguish for the still-single parent. Depending on who is now coupled and who is still single, you or your ex may be jealous or suspicious of the new partner. Or, you or your ex may be scared that your children will want to live in the other household, especially if the new mate has children of similar ages to yours.

Similarly, your children might feel awkward when a parent has a new partner. If you form a new relationship, you must find ways to maintain the existing parent-child relationship while creating and cementing new bonds. One highly effective way to do this is to find times when just you and your children can spend time with each other. Don't use the excuse that "everyone is too busy." If you don't spend quality time with your children, they may begin to feel left out, especially if your new partner has children or you and your new partner have a child together. Occasional lunch dates, trips to the park or video parlor, or other one-on-one activities can make all the difference in the world.

With your new family in place, you often have the perfect excuse to start building some new family traditions that can give your children a sense of belonging in your new family. These rituals can be simple or elaborate, but they must happen consistently to become routine. If your new family has established a family activity night, then setting aside one night a week or month will be a priority. If your new tradition is a holiday (either real or invented), then be sure to celebrate it annually.

Finally, remember that language is powerful and finding names or descriptions for new relatives can be challenging. Some children call a parent's new partner something like Mom or Dad (or Mother or Father); other children use the new partner's first name. Still others invent a name, or use a word from a language other than English. Describing step-siblings can present similar problems and solutions (such as inventing a name or using a non-English word). Other children simply describe the stepsiblings as "new" brothers or sisters in order to avoid a lengthy explanation.

RELEVANT ISSUES

Issue	Number
Maintaining Contact	18
Holidays	5
Special Occasions and Family Events	13
Treating Each Child as an Individual	23
When Parents Have New Partners	36

■

State and Federal Laws Affecting Child Custody

Most custody and visitation laws are enacted by state legislatures, not Congress. Nevertheless, state laws include some basic similarities. For example, every state expresses a preference for ensuring that parents consider what is best for their children when making the decisions that follow from a separation or divorce. In fact, unless a court is convinced that harm will come to the children or to a parent, courts in every state generally:

- prefer that the parents share in parenting their children
- place a value on children maintaining frequent and continuing contact with both parents
- insist that both parents have access to medical, educational, religious, and other relevant information about their children, and
- recommend or order mediation before deciding custody and visitation disputes.

There are some custody and visitation laws that apply in all states. For example, the Uniform Child Custody Jurisdiction Enforcement Act, 28 U.S.C. § 1738A, requires all states to recognize and enforce child custody and visitation orders that have been issued in other states. This Act has been adopted in all states to stop parents from trying to move their cases to another state to try to get the result they want.

The information and charts in this chapter highlight certain legal issues that often come up in child custody and visitation cases. They are not intended to be a treatise on child custody law, or to offer definitive legal advice about how to handle your individual case. Statutes are often repealed or amended, and court cases interpreting statutes can be difficult to understand and track. If you want complete and up-to-date information on a specific law for your state, do your own research or consult an attorney. (See Chapter 17, Help Beyond the Book.)

A. Custody and Visitation

The term *custody* generally refers to:

- the legal authority to make decisions about a child—sometimes called *legal custody*, and
- maintaining physical control over a child—sometimes called *physical custody*.

Visitation describes the time that a noncustodial parent, grandparent, or other important person spends with a child. All states specifically provide grandparents the right to ask for visitation as part of a court order.

DIFFERENTIATE BETWEEN LEGAL AND PHYSICAL CUSTODY

In the states listed below, a court may make different awards for legal custody and for physical custody. In all other states, a custody award encompasses both legal and physical custody.

Alabama	Idaho	New Jersey
Arizona	Indiana	Ohio
California	Iowa	Pennsylvania
Colorado	Massachusetts	Utah
Connecticut	Minnesota	Virginia
District of Columbia	Mississippi	West Virginia
Georgia	Missouri	Wisconsin
Hawaii	New Hampshire	

Many states differentiate between legal and physical custody—that is, the court may make one decision regarding legal custody and another decision regarding physical custody. For example, Lorraine may be awarded primary physical custody, while Lorraine and Justin together are awarded legal custody. In the other states, the court simply makes a custody award that encompasses both legal and physical custody. The trend is toward differentiating between the two.

Depending on the state and the situation, a court can award *sole custody* to just one parent or *joint custody* to both parents. A joint custody award can be for legal and physical custody or for legal custody only. Rarely would a court order joint physical custody but give only one parent legal custody.

Because the general goal is to keep both parents actively involved in raising their children, courts try to award joint legal custody. Joint physical custody is a bit trickier. Though joint physical custody doesn't necessarily mean that the children will spend exactly half of the time with each parent, it does require coordination so that the children spend significant amounts of time with both parents.

Here are the types of questions courts ask when considering a joint custody arrangement:

- Are both parents willing and able to cooperate in advancing their children's welfare?

- Do the children have a close relationship with each parent?
- Can the parents communicate and make joint decisions regarding child care and education, or has child rearing become a battleground?
- Are the parents' homes sufficiently close to each other to accommodate the practical considerations of shared parenting?
- How much time does each parent have for the children?
- Will each parent encourage sharing of love, affection, and time with the other parent?
- Will joint custody promote frequent and continuing contact with both parents?

JOINT CUSTODY

Only Arkansas, New York, North Dakota, and Rhode Island have no statutes relating to joint custody. In these states, joint custody may be allowed under court decisions.

Joint custody required:

Louisiana

Joint custody permitted even if parents don't agree to the arrangement:

Alabama	Indiana	New Hampshire
Alaska	Iowa	New Jersey
Arizona	Kansas	New Mexico
Colorado	Maryland	North Carolina
Delaware	Massachusetts	Ohio
Florida	Michigan	Oklahoma
Georgia	Minnesota	South Dakota
Hawaii	Mississippi	Vermont
Idaho	Missouri	Wisconsin
Illinois	Montana	

Joint custody available only if both parents agree:

Arkansas	Nebraska	Texas
California	Nevada	Utah
Connecticut	Oregon	Virginia
District of Columbia	Pennsylvania	Washington
Kentucky	South Carolina	West Virginia
Maine	Tennessee	Wyoming

Virtually every state has specific statutes allowing judges to order joint custody. In some states, judges can even order joint custody over the objections of the parents. This might happen in cases where, for example, the judge believes that parents seem equally qualified, their homes are not far apart, and they seem capable of resolving their differences outside of court.

Split custody is the unusual situation in which a court grants custody of one or more children to one parent and grants custody of different children to the other parent. Though only a few states have laws expressly discouraging judges from splitting children between their parents' homes, the practice is generally criticized by mental health professionals and child advocates and is rarely ordered by a court.

Most states prevent judges from considering the gender of the parents when awarding custody. These laws are meant to eliminate the automatic preference of awarding custody, especially custody of very young children, to their mother.

GENDER OF PARENT CANNOT BE A FACTOR

Judges are prohibited from favoring a parent based on gender when awarding custody.

Alabama	Indiana	North Dakota
Alaska	Kansas	Oklahoma
Arizona	Kentucky	Oregon
Arkansas	Maine	South Dakota
California	Maryland	Utah
Colorado	Missouri	Vermont
Delaware	Nebraska	Virginia
District of Columbia	Nevada	Washington
Florida	New Hampshire	Wisconsin
Georgia	New Mexico	Wyoming
Hawaii	New York	

B. Best Interests of the Child

The standard used by courts in making custody and visitation rulings is called the *best interests of the child*. Courts typically will place a higher value on protecting a child's best interests than on any other factor when deciding custody and visitation.

Nearly every state has specific statutes listing factors that a court should consider when assessing the best interests of the children. But those lists are not meant to be exhaustive. Judges have the discretion to consider virtually all relevant information when deciding on the best interests of the child.

These are some of the more common examples of what courts can consider.

Parent's ability to meet the child's emotional and financial needs. A judge will consider a parent's ability and willingness to meet each child's need for love, guidance, and education as well as food, clothing, and medical care. The court will consider:

- how much time each parent has available for the child
- the time a parent has spent caring for the child before and during the divorce or separation proceedings, and
- the commitment each parent has to helping the child develop emotionally and physically into a responsible adult.

Example: *Eight-year-old Sara's father arranged his career so that he would be available to care for Sara before and after school, fix dinner, follow an evening routine, and read her a bedtime story. Because of her career, her mother was much less available to provide this kind of daily care. The judge decided that Sara would live primarily with her father during the school year and spend part of her summer living with her mother. The judge reasoned that Sara would experience the fewest possible disruptions by living most of the time with her father.*

Every state allows a judge to order one parent to pay child support to the other parent. The idea behind this policy is to make sure that children are able to have a roughly comparable standard of living at each home. Although it is certainly important for children to have access to some of the stability, security, and advantages that money can buy, poverty or living on welfare is not a sufficient reason to deprive the poorer parent of custody.

Example: *Chris and David are seven- and ten-year-olds whose father has dedicated his life to his career, making quite a substantial salary, and who recently moved out of the family house. Their mother has not worked outside of the home since they were born, but has been a caring and loving full-time mom. The judge awards custody to the mother and orders the father to pay child support.*

"Moral fitness" and conduct of the parents. Some states allow a judge to consider parents' conduct—including lifestyle, living accommodations, and other factors—in deciding their moral fitness. "Moral fitness" is a fairly subjective term and can mean different things to different judges. To many judges, parents are considered morally fit if they are focused on the child; provide a safe, secure, and nurturing environment; and are generally good role models.

Many judges consider a parent to be morally unfit if that parent has a series of short-term, live-in relationships or allows the children to be around a new partner, roommate, or friend who is involved in drugs or illegal activities. For these reasons, it is possible that judges may look beyond one parent's adultery, so long as they seem to be a good, caring parent and the circumstances surrounding the adultery did not appear to have harmed the child. When a parent's misconduct affects a child's health, safety, or welfare, some states require a judge to explain a decision that allows a violent parent to win custody or unsupervised visits.

The sexual habits and living arrangements of a parent may or may not be used to judge moral fitness, depending on the state and circumstances. For instance, in most states, a judge will probably not decide that a parent is unfit if he or she lives, unmarried, with a responsible, long-term partner. A judge will probably not consider poor behavior from many years ago, so long as the parent has shown that he or she is presently a good parent and appears to be capable of continuing that pattern into the future.

SEXUAL ORIENTATION AND CUSTODY

A lesbian or gay parent faces a difficult struggle trying to gain custody in many American courtrooms. This is true even if the parent's gay or lesbian partner has been involved in parenting for much or all of the child's life. Because not all states allow gay or lesbian parents to adopt, it can be difficult to get the same legal rights to custody and visitation as heterosexual parents.

It is fair to say that many, if not most, judges are ignorant about, prejudiced against, or suspicious of gay and lesbian parents. Only a few judges understand that a parent's sexual orientation, alone, does not affect the best interests of the children. But judges often use the best interests standard to deny a gay or lesbian parent custody.

Physical safety of the child. Because the safety of a child is a primary concern of the courts, assuring that a child will not be physically neglected or subject to or exposed to violence or abuse is of utmost importance. Most states allow parents to physically discipline their child within reason. Most states have laws that prevent a parent or potential caretaker with a history of abuse against another parent or a current spouse, cohabitant, or companion from gaining custody of a child. Withholding custody from a parent who has abused his or her spouse is not considered punishment against the parent, but is done in the best interests of the child because of the profound impact that seeing, hearing, or knowing about violence between parents can have on a child.

Quite a few custody cases involve the children's exposure to tobacco smoke. Most states now recognize the virtually undisputed evidence that environmental tobacco smoke is harmful to children. Courts will weigh this factor against all the others in making a decision. For instance, though a court might prefer to grant custody to a nonsmoking parent if a child has respiratory problems, that same court might grant custody to the smoking parent if the nonsmoking parent was found to be violent.

Although a judge cannot weigh the comparative merits of the parents' religions in deciding custody, religious beliefs can be taken into account if they are potentially dangerous to the child's education or general welfare. For instance, if a parent's religious beliefs prevent him or her from giving the child immunizations or blood transfusions, the court may determine that this is potentially harmful and give decision-making authority for these issues to the other parent.

Quality of child's relationships with others. Another factor that courts consider when trying to protect a child's best interests is maintaining that child's relationship with brothers, sisters, grandparents, and the extended community they live in. Deciding the quality of the child's relationships can include how the child gets along with family members, the amount and nature of time spent together, and which parent or caretaker has taken a greater responsibility for meeting the child's emotional and practical needs.

Example: *Tawila is 11 years old. Her father is seeking custody and would be able to provide an emotionally supportive home for her, but Tawila has not been getting along at all with her father's new wife, and her schoolwork has been suffering. In this situation, the judge might order that Tawila live primarily with her mother; recommend or order family counseling between Tawila, her father, and stepmother; allow increasing amounts of time for visits; or change the structure of the living arrangements if Tawila's relationship with her stepmother improves.*

Courts also consider sibling bonds extremely important. Because divorce or separation causes such disruption in a child's life, courts try to keep other relationships in a child's life unchanged, if possible. For that reason, as mentioned earlier, most states will not order split custody—where close siblings are separated—except for compelling reasons. A judge will consider splitting siblings more readily if, for example, there has been violence or other serious problems between the children, or if they are of dramatically different ages or have different parents.

Example: *Lisa, 17, wants to stay with her father so she can finish high school at her current school. Lisa's mother and father agree, however, that Lisa's mother should be the primary caretaker of Lisa's three-year-old twin brothers. In this situation, the court might support splitting the children up for much of the year. But the judge might also order that the children spend significant amounts of time together at each parent's home.*

Continuity and household stability. Courts consider continuity and household stability—staying with the same parent or caretaker and/or living in the same residence—as an important factor in deciding child custody disputes. Stability is important because it means that the child can count on some aspects of his or her life remaining the same after the separation and divorce of his or her parents. Courts prefer, therefore, to allow children to remain in the family home or the same community, as long as there are no safety concerns.

Continuity is also an important factor that judges consider if parents want to change their custody and visitation arrangements after the first custody order is made. In general, unless a parenting plan has been scheduled for review by the court, parents can only file for a change in their custody and visitation order if there has been a significant change in circumstances. But the definition of "significant" is a little vague. For example, a change in one parent's employment may be significant or insignificant, depending on many factors. For example, a change from one 9-to-5 job to another might have little impact on visitation. But if the new job requires lots of travel, it may be hard to maintain the old visitation schedule.

Maintaining continuity if one parent wants to move away. Although the court cannot prevent a parent from moving, a judge can order custody to shift from the moving parent to the remaining parent to preserve a child's contact with the remaining parent, family members, schools, friends, and community. Different states and different judges will balance the needs of children and their parents using different criteria. In some states, courts require the moving parent to show that the move will have a beneficial effect on the child. Other courts shift the responsibility to the remaining parent to show why the move would be against the best interests of the child. Other factors that judges consider when making these decisions include the amount of time the child spends with each parent, the quality of life and relationship the child has with each parent, and the relative advantages and disadvantages of moving or remaining with one or the other parent.

Other life changes may also affect custodial or visitation rights. A judge won't modify an existing custody arrangement, however, unless it is essential and appropriate to the circumstances. If a custodial parent begins abusing drugs or neglecting the child's welfare, for example, the court is likely to remove the child from the situation. Often, however, a judge will consider increasing the amount of time a parent has with his or her child once he or she has proven he or she can remain clean and sober and committed to providing a stable and nurturing environment for the child.

Continuity of residence and caretaking has received great recognition in the courts, especially when a party seeking custody is a nonparent. For instance, when a child has lived with a grandparent for a significant period and is well adjusted and happy, the importance of keeping this stable setup may mean that the child will remain with the grandparent while gradually rebuilding a relationship with his or her birth parent or parents. The process of rebuilding a healthy parenting relationship might include supervised visits, an order that the parent attend one or more parenting classes, or a shared custody arrangement that ensures the child will be able to keep close ties to his or her grandparent.

Child's preference. Most states consider where and with whom an older child would rather live. At most, however, the child's wishes are one factor in deciding custody, and the court can follow or ignore them. In many cases, the child's preference will act as a tiebreaker when both parents or potential custodians are equally fit.

A judge will consider the preference only of a suitably mature child. Usually, the older a child is, the more weight is given to the child's wishes. Though some states require that a child of a certain age—usually 12—be able to state his or her preferences for where he or she will live and how often he or she will spend time with the other parent, the judge still must make sure that choice is in the child's best interests. Often, a judge will either ask the child directly, or will order a child custody investigation or evaluation to understand the reasoning behind the child's preferences and to make a recommendation that would be in the child's best interests. The court will most likely give serious weight to the child's choice if it is based on sound reasoning and achieves the child's long-term best interests. The court will probably ignore the preference if it has been influenced by one of the parents, is based on promises of indulgences, or may lead to only transient happiness or enjoyment.

Example: *Onoke is a 12-year-old boy who wants to stay with his father after his parents divorce so he can stay at a junior high where he has been doing well and has a circle of friends. The judge will give Onoke's choice more weight* *than if he chose to live with his dad because he gets to stay up later and eat fast food more often than at his mom's.*

Friendly parent. Because courts believe that a child needs the love and guidance of both parents if possible, judges will make an effort to preserve the child's relationship with both parents. Thus, judges consider the ability of one parent to foster a positive relationship between the child and the other parent. A parent must demonstrate the ability to encourage his or her children to have a loving relationship and frequent contact with the other parent. Courts take interference with the other parent's visitation rights or attempts to undermine the child's relationship with the other parent very seriously. In short, a judge will consider this fundamental question: In whose custody will the child have a better chance of contact with both parents? For example, a judge may take away custody from a parent who repeatedly cancels scheduled visits for punitive or vindictive reasons.

CAN RACE PLAY A ROLE IN CUSTODY DECISIONS?

In *Palmore v. Sidoti*, 466 U.S. 429 (1984), the U.S. Supreme Court ruled that it was unconstitutional for a court to consider race when a noncustodial parent petitions a court for a change of custody. In the case, a white couple had divorced and the mother had been awarded custody of their son. She married an African-American man and moved to a predominantly African-American neighborhood. The father filed a request for modification of custody based on the changed circumstance that the boy was now living with an African-American man in an African-American neighborhood. A Florida court granted the modification. The U.S. Supreme Court reversed, ruling that societal stigma, especially a racial one, cannot be the basis for a custody decision.

C. Mediation

By now, you should have a good grasp of child custody mediation. Just a reminder—mediation is a nonadversarial process in which a neutral person (called a mediator)

meets with disputing persons to help them settle a dispute. (It is discussed in depth in Chapter 11.)

In nearly every state, parents can be ordered to participate in mediation before bringing a custody or visitation dispute to court. At the same time, however, when domestic violence is an issue, many courts either will not make the victim mediate the dispute, or will allow the parents to meet with the mediator separately and at separate times.

In a few states, the judge can ask a mediator to make a recommendation regarding custody and visitation if the parents cannot settle the issues during the mediation. In more than half the states, mediation is considered confidential—the mediator cannot testify in court about anything said during mediation. If the parents cannot reach agreement in mediation, then the matter will either be referred to a child custody evaluator or investigator, or taken to court for a hearing so that the judge can make the decision.

In some states, child custody mediators must possess certain education, training, and experience to participate in court-sponsored mediation. If you are not required to mediate the custody and visitation issues but choose to anyway, you're free to select whomever you want as the mediator—as long as the other parent agrees.

OTHER TECHNIQUES FOR RESOLVING CUSTODY AND VISITATION DISPUTES

Mediation isn't the only way to resolve custody and visitation disputes beside litigation. In about half the states, a judge has the authority to appoint an investigator—usually a social worker—to look into the homes of both parents, talk to the children and parents,
and make a recommendation about custody and visitation.

A handful of states permit disputing parents to use arbitration to resolve custody and visitation issues. Arbitration is a process similar to court because the parties, or more likely their attorneys, present a "case" and the arbitrator resolves the issues. But it is often quicker and less expensive than a court trial. For more difficult cases, or cases that have been in the court system for a long time, the judge may appoint a special master to review the dispute and make whatever decisions may be necessary to resolve the parents' ongoing disagreements in a way that will implement the court order. (Arbitration is discussed in Chapter 11, and the role of the special master is discussed in Chapter 17.)

PARENTS CAN BE ORDERED TO PARTICIPATE IN MEDIATION BEFORE BRINGING A CUSTODY OR VISITATION DISPUTE TO COURT

Alabama	Kansas	Ohio
Alaska	Louisiana	Oklahoma
Arizona	Maine	Oregon
Arkansas	Maryland	Pennsylvania
California	Minnesota	Rhode Island
Colorado	Mississippi	South Carolina
Connecticut	Missouri	South Dakota
Delaware	Montana	Texas
Florida	Nevada	Utah
Georgia	New Hampshire	Virginia
Idaho	New Jersey	Washington
Illinois	New Mexico	West Virginia
Indiana	North Carolina	Wisconsin
Iowa	North Dakota	

PARENTS CAN BE EXCUSED FROM MEDIATION IF IT IS INAPPROPRIATE BECAUSE OF DOMESTIC VIOLENCE, CHILD ABUSE, OR OTHER REASONS

Alaska	Maryland	North Dakota
Arkansas	Minnesota	Oklahoma
California	Montana	Ohio
Colorado	North Carolina	Oregon
Delaware	North Dakota	Pennsylvania
Florida	Nebraska	Texas
Hawaii	Nevada	Utah
Iowa	New Jersey	Virginia
Indiana	New Hampshire	Washington
Kansas	New Mexico	West Virginia
Louisiana	North Carolina	Wisconsin
Maine		

Most states consider mediation between parents who disagree about child custody and visitation issues to be confidential (meaning what is said in mediation cannot be brought up later in court). Confidential mediation is designed to allow parents to talk freely about how they think child custody and visitation decisions should be made. Often, this is a time when parents can express their worries, float ideas, and consider a range of options for resolving their differences—without worrying that what they say will later be used against them. In mediation, agreements can only be reached when both parents are willing to accept the plan. When parents cannot agree on the most important issues, such as when the children will be with each parent, they must go to court to get a final decision from a judge.

Most judges have had very little training in child development issues. For these reason, courts often look for expert opinions about what the children in a particular family may need. In many states, courts can request, or order, an evaluation of the family. Child custody evaluators are most often mental health professionals but may also be case workers or other investigators who are trained to assess a child's best interests. In some states, such as California, Delaware, and South Dakota, the court might ask the mediator to make a recommendation about how to resolve the remaining issues. In especially difficult or high-conflict cases, the court may also appoint a lawyer who will just represent the children's interests in the lawsuit.

Parents often approach nonconfidential ("recommending") mediation differently than they do a confidential mediation process. When parents cannot agree in recommending mediation, mediators will often add information they gather from other professionals or their own limited investigation (consisting, when budgets allow, of telephone calls, interviews, or home visits) to the impressions they formed during their conversations with the parents to form a recommendation that the judge can use to make a final decision.

Whichever approach to mediation the courts in your state use, it is important to think carefully about how to best raise your concerns, explain your views and preferences, and reflect what you believe to be in your children's best interests *before* your mediation session begins. See Chapter 11 for more information on ways to make mediation work for you.

JUDGES CAN ASK A MEDIATOR FOR A RECOMMENDATION ON CUSTODY AND VISITATION IF THE PARENTS CAN'T SETTLE THE ISSUES DURING MEDIATION

California	Delaware	South Dakota

A COURT CAN ORDER A CUSTODY INVESTIGATION OR EVALUATION TO HELP IT MAKE A DECISION

Arizona	Indiana	New Mexico
California	Kansas	New York
Colorado	Kentucky	North Dakota
Connecticut	Michigan	Ohio
Delaware	Minnesota	South Dakota
Florida	Mississippi	Utah
Georgia	Missouri	Washington
Hawaii	Montana	West Virginia
Idaho	Nevada	Wisconsin
Illinois	New Jersey	

CHILD CUSTODY MEDIATORS MUST POSSESS CERTAIN EDUCATIONAL, TRAINING, AND EXPERIENCE QUALIFICATIONS

Arkansas	Montana	Oregon
California	Nebraska	Pennsylvania
Idaho	Nevada	South Dakota
Indiana	New Hampshire	Texas
Kansas	New Jersey	Utah
Kentucky	North Carolina	Washington
Louisiana	North Dakota	West Virginia
Maryland	Ohio	Wisconsin
Minnesota		

D. Interference With Custody

Custodial interference occurs when a parent or guardian keeps a child away from a person who has a legal right to custody. In most states, it is a crime to take a child from his or her parent or guardian with the intention of depriving that person of custody. In many states, depriving a parent or guardian of custody is a felony if the child is taken out of state. In most states, the parent or guardian deprived of custody may also file a suit for damages against the person who took the child.

Many states recognize good-cause defenses to custodial interference. In most cases, a defense negates the charge; in other situations, it reduces the charge from a felony to a misdemeanor. Commonly accepted defenses include the following:

- taker has or seeks legal custody (accepted in about a dozen states)
- taker is protecting child or self from bodily harm (accepted in about one-half of the states), and
- taker reported taking of the child to police or parent and promptly returned child (accepted in slightly more than a dozen states).

E. Interstate Custody Disputes

All states and the District of Columbia have adopted the Uniform Child Custody Jurisdiction Act, or UCCJA, which sets standards for when a court may make a custody determination and when a court must defer to an existing determination from another state. In general, a state may make a custody decision about a child if one of the following is true. The conditions are stated in order of preference.

1. The state is the child's home state—this means the child has resided in the state for the six previous months, or was residing in the state but is absent because a parent has removed the child or kept the child outside the state.

2. There are significant connections with people—such as teachers, doctors, and grandparents—and substantial evidence in the state concerning the child's care, protection, training, and personal relationships.

3. The child is in the state and either has been abandoned or is in danger of being abused or neglected if sent back to the other state.

4. No other state can meet one of the above three tests, or a state can meet at least one of the tests but has declined to make a custody decision.

If a state cannot meet one of these tests, even if the child is present in the state, the courts of that state cannot make a custody award. Also, a parent who has wrongfully removed or kept a child in order to create a home-state jurisdiction, or significant connections, will often be denied custody. If more than one state meets the above standards, only one state can award custody. Once the first state makes a custody award, another state cannot make another "initial" award or modify the existing order.

Having the same law in all states helps achieve consistency in the treatment of custody decrees. It also helps solve many of the problems created by kidnapping or disagreements over custody between parents living in different states.

Example: *Sam and Diane met and married in Missouri. They moved to Delaware where their child (Sam Jr.) was born. Sam, Diane, and Junior lived in Delaware until Junior was ten. At that time, Sam took Junior to Missouri to divorce Diane and raise Junior himself. When Sam went to court in Missouri and requested custody, his request was denied because Delaware is Junior's home state, the state where he has significant connections, and Sam removed Junior from Delaware in an effort to create home-state jurisdiction in Missouri. (Diane should go to court in Delaware and request custody, even though Junior is living in Missouri.)*

The Uniform Child Custody Jurisdiction and Enforcement Act, or UCCJEA, requires all states to honor and enforce child custody decrees issued anywhere in the country (including in an Indian court), or issued by a foreign country. A law called the Parental Kidnapping Prevention Act, or PKPA (28 U.S.C. §1738A and 42 U.S.C. §§654, 663), is a federal statute that addresses kidnapping by noncustodial parents and deals with inconsistent child custody decisions made by state courts. The law provides penalties for kidnapping and requires states to recognize and enforce the custody decisions of courts in other states, rather than make a second, and possibly inconsistent, decision.

F. International Custody Disputes

"Comity" is a legal doctrine under which countries recognize and enforce the other countries' legal decrees. Under the Uniform Child Custody Jurisdiction Act and the Uniform Child Custody Jurisdiction and Enforcement Act (see Section E, above), courts in the United States must recognize proper custody decrees of other nations. In turn, many other countries recognize U.S. custody orders.

The International Child Abduction Remedies Act (12 U.S.C. §§601 through 610) is a federal U.S. law that enables The Hague Convention on the Civil Aspects of International Child Abduction to be followed in the United States. The Hague Convention is an agreement between the United States and over 60 other nations. Its purpose is to provide the prompt return of children wrongfully removed or retained in any participating country, and to ensure that the rights of custody and access under the law of one country are effectively respected in another. It addresses jurisdictional questions and provides common rules and procedures to determine child custody in a dispute that crosses international borders.

If a child is abducted from the United States to another country or a child is abducted from another country and brought to the United States, you can contact the U.S. State Department Office of Citizen and Counselor Services for help.

Finally, to prevent a child from being taken out of the United States without the custodial parent's consent, that parent can:

- provide the State Department with a copy of a custody order showing who is the custodial parent, and
- request that the State Department withhold a child's passport unless it is requested by the custodial parent.

G. Custody and the IRS

The following tax benefits are available to parents to offset the cost of raising children:

- earned income credit
- child care credit
- medical expense deductions, and
- head of household filing status.

Only a custodial parent is entitled to claim the child care tax credit. In general, employed custodial parents of a dependent child under the age of 13 are eligible for the credit for child care expenses incurred so that the parent can earn an income. As the custodial parent's income increases, however, the credit phases out.

Both parents can claim a deduction for medical expenses actually paid, but only if those medical expenses exceed 7.5% of their adjusted gross income. If your total medical expenses are high enough, you may want to allocate them to the lower wage earner so that parent can take the deduction.

Only a parent with physical custody (meaning custody more than half of the time) can file as head of household. If the parents have joint legal and physical custody (and physical custody is divided 50-50), neither can file as head of household, because the dependent child resides with neither parent for more than 50% of the year. If you have more than one minor child and share physical custody, you can specify your arrangement as 51% for one child with one parent and 51% for the other child with the other parent. Because each parent has a dependent child in the home more than 50% of the year, each parent can file as head of household. ■

CHAPTER

17

Help Beyond the Book

Understanding and resolving child custody and parenting issues can be a challenge. By reading this book and completing the various worksheets, you and the other parent have gone a long way toward building a successful separate parenting relationship. You now have more information, problem-solving skills, and insights than most parents who separate or divorce—and your children are the lucky beneficiaries of your efforts!

Many parents find that child custody and separate parenting issues are too difficult, emotional, or technical to handle completely on their own. If this is true for you, consider taking any of the following courses of action:

- do some legal research
- research nonlegal issues, or
- work with any number of professionals, including mediators, counselors, attorneys, arbitrators, paralegals, or child custody evaluators.

A. Researching Legal Issues

This brief discussion tells you how to use a reference from this book to look up a state or federal statute or court decision.

1. Finding a Law Library

To look up state or federal statutes or court decisions, go to your county law library (usually in the county courthouse) or the library of a law school that is open to the public. (Most law school libraries open to the public are ones at state universities. A private university law library must let members of the public in, too, if that library is a "federal depository." This means that it houses federal government documents.) Some, but not all, large public libraries also have collections of state or federal statutes; call before you go.

2. Finding Background Materials

Before turning to statutes and cases to answer a legal question on child custody, it is often helpful to use a background resource. This will not only help you narrow your question but will also, more often than not, get you to the right statute and case as well.

Three excellent books for researching state laws on child custody and visitation are:

- *Handling Child Custody, Abuse, and Adoption Cases,* by Ann M. Haralambie (Shepard's/McGraw-Hill)

- *Child Custody and Visitation Law and Practice* (Matthew Bender)
- *Joint Custody and Shared Parenting,* edited by Jay Folberg (Guildford Press).

3. Finding Statutes

When you look up a statute, try to use what is called an "annotated" version of the statutes. Annotated statutes include not only the texts of the statutes but also brief summaries of court cases and legal articles that have discussed each statute. After you look up a statute, you may want to read the cases listed to see how courts have construed the language of the statute.

Federal statutes. Federal statutes are organized by subject in a set of books called the *United States Code* (U.S.C.), which is available in almost every law library. Libraries often have one or both annotated versions of the U.S.C.— either *United States Code Service* (U.S.C.S.) or *United States Code Annotated* (U.S.C.A.). If you know the statute's common name or its citation, you should be able to find it easily.

> EXAMPLE: *You want to read some of the provisions of the International Child Abduction Remedies Act, 12 U.S.C. §601 and following. You would look in Title 12 of the U.S.C., U.S.C.S., or U.S.C.A. (the numbers are on the spine of the book) and find section 601. The statute begins with section 601 and includes many sections.*

State statutes. State statutes, which fill many volumes, are often organized into "codes." Each code covers a separate area of law, such as Marriage and Divorce, Family Law, or Husbands and Wives. Although you probably won't have a citation from this book, you can look up the subject of the law you want to read in the index to the code or statutes.

4. Making Sure You Have the Most Recent Version of the Statute

Each year, state legislatures and Congress pass hundreds of new laws and change (amend) lots of existing ones. When you look up a statute, it's crucial that you get the most recent version.

To do that, always look for a pamphlet that is inserted in the back of the hardcover volume of statutes. It's called a pocket part, and it contains any changes made to the statute in the hardcover book since the hardcover was printed. Pocket parts are updated and replaced every year—it's

The name of the case includes the name of the plaintiff (Palmore) followed by a v. (meaning versus), followed by the defendant's name (Sidoti). 466 is the volume number where the case is found in the series called *United States Reports* (abbreviated by U.S.) at page 429. The case was decided in 1984.

Only cases decided by the U.S. Supreme Court are published in the *United States Reports*. (They are also published in the *Supreme Court Reports*.) Most of the cases you'll want to read will have been decided by courts within your state, and they are published in volumes entitled something like *[name of your state] Reports* or *[name of your state] Appellate Reports,* or possibly in a reporter for a region of the United States, such as the *Atlantic Reporter*. A law librarian can help you figure out exactly which series of reports contains the case you are looking for.

6. Making Sure the Case Is Still Good Law

Judges don't go back and change the words of earlier decisions, as legislatures amend old statutes, but cases can still be profoundly affected by later court decisions. For example, any state's highest court, usually called the Supreme Court, has the power to overrule a decision of a trial court or an appellate court. If it does, the trial court's or an appellate court's written decision no longer has any legal effect.

There are several ways to check to make sure a case you're relying on still represents valid law. The most common is to use a collection of books called *Shepard's*, which lets you compile a list of all later cases that mention the case you're interested in. Unfortunately, the *Shepard's* system is too complicated to explain here. If it's important to you, consult one of the legal research tools mentioned below.

7. More Legal Research

Legal research is a subject that can (and does) easily fill a whole book of its own. Here are some good resources if you want to delve further into the subject:

- For a thorough, how-to approach to finding answers to your legal questions, see *Legal Research: How to Find & Understand the Law*, by Stephen Elias & Susan Levinkind (Nolo).
- For an entertaining and informative video presentation of the basics of legal research, take a look at *Legal Research Made Easy: A Roadmap Through the Law Library*, by Professor Robert Berring of the University of California-Berkeley (Nolo/LegalStar).

much cheaper than producing a whole new hardcover volume every year.

Look up the statute again in the pocket part. If there's no entry, that means the statute hasn't been changed as of the date the pocket part was printed. If there is an entry, it will tell you what has changed in the statute.

5. Finding Cases

If you want to look up a case (court decision) and you have the citation, all you need to do is decipher those strange numbers and abbreviations.

Here's an example. The proper citation for the case holding that it is unconstitutional for a court to consider race in a custody dispute is *Palmore v. Sidoti*, 466 U.S. 429 (1984).

B. Researching Nonlegal Issues

The bibliography at the end of this chapter (Section F) lists a wide range of books and articles that discuss both the legal and nonlegal aspects of separate parenting. What follows is a list of books and articles that are particularly strong in certain areas. To find additional titles, browse in your public library or local bookstore.

1. Children and Divorce

- *Boys and Girls' Book About Divorce*, by Richard A. Gardner, M.D. (Jason Aronson, Inc.)
- *Divorce and Your Child: Practical Suggestions for Parents*, by Sonja Goldstein, LL.B. & Albert Solnit, M.D. (Yale University Press)
- *Growing Up Divorced*, by Linda Bird Francke (Linden Press/Simon & Schuster)
- *How It Feels When Parents Divorce*, by Jill Krementz (Alfred A. Knopf)
- *Mediation and the Special-Child Family*, by Jeff Davidson (Jossey-Bass), particularly pages 79–83.
- *My Parents Are Divorced Too*, by Bonnie Robson, M.D. (Everest House)
- *When Children Grieve*, by John W. James and Russell Friedman (HarperCollins)

2. Conflict Resolution

- *Using Divorce Mediation: Save Your Money and Your Sanity*, by Katherine E. Stoner (Nolo)
- *Fighting Fair*, by Robert Coulson (The Free Press)
- *Getting to Yes: Negotiating Agreement Without Giving In*, by Roger Fisher & William Ury (Harvard Negotiation Project/Penguin Books)
- *A Guide to Divorce Mediation*, by Gary Friedman, J.D. (Workman Publishing)

3. Shared Custody

- *The Joint Custody Handbook: Creating Arrangements That Work*, by Miriam Galper Cohen (Running Press)
- *Mom's House, Dad's House: Making Shared Custody Work*, by Isolina Ricci, Ph.D. (Macmillan Publishing Co.)

4. Parenting Skills

- *Divorce and Your Child: Practical Suggestions for Parents*, by Sonja Goldstein, LL.B. & Albert Solnit, M.D. (Yale University Press)
- *Mom's House, Dad's House: Making Shared Custody Work*, by Isolina Ricci, Ph.D. (Macmillan Publishing Co.)

5. General Information About Divorce and Related Topics

- *Divorce and Child Custody*, by Deanna Peters & Richard L. Strohm (Layman's Law Guides)
- *Divorce and Decision Making: A Woman's Guide*, by Christina Robertson (Follett Publishing Company)
- *Nolo's Pocket Guide to Family Law*, by Robin Leonard & Stephen Elias (Nolo)
- *Uncoupling: Turning Points in Intimate Relationships*, by Diane Vaughan (Oxford University Press)
- *How to Avoid the Divorce From Hell (and Dance Together at Your Daughter's Wedding)*, by M. Sue Talia (Nexus Publishing Co.)
- *Divorce & Money: How to Make the Best Financial Decisions During Divorce*, by Violet Woodhouse, with Dale Fetherling (Nolo)

C. Research on the World Wide Web

The following websites may have material that will be useful or help answer any questions you have.

Child Support Resources
U.S. Office of Child Support Enforcement www.acf.dhhs.gov/ACFPrograms/CSE/index.html
Association for Children for Enforcement of Support (ACES) www.childsupport-aces.org

General Divorce and Custody Resources
Divorce Links www.divorcelinks.com
Stepfamily Association of America www.stepfam.org
Clearinghouse on Child Abuse and Neglect www.calib.com/nccanch
International Academy of Collaborative Professionals www.collabgroup.com
State-by-State information and resources www.custodysource.com/state.htm
Divorce Cycle www.divorcecycle.com

Mental Health Resources
American Academy of Child and Adolescent Psychiatry www.aacap.org
American Association for Marriage and Family Therapy www.aamft.org/index_nm.asp
American Psychiatric Press, Inc. www.appi.org
Mental Health Net www.mentalhelp.net
National Association of Social Workers www.naswdc.org

Legal Information and Research
American Bar Associaiton Consumer's Guide to Legal Help on the Internet www.abanet.org/legalservices/findlegalhelp/home.html
Nolo.com Self Help Law Center www.nolo.com
Findlaw www.findlaw.com
Reference Desk www.refdesk.com/factlaw.html
LawHelp.org www.lawhelp.org
National Center for State Courts Pro Se Litigation: State Links www.ncsconline.org/wc/Publications/KIS_ProSestlinks.pdf

For Dads
Fathers' Rights and Equality Exchange http://themenscenter.com

For Moms
Women's Resources www.womansdivorce.com

General Parenting Support
Parent Soup www.parentsoup.com/experts/step
The National Parenting Center www.tnpc.com

D. Finding Professionals Who Can Help

Often, talking to a professional can be a great help if you hit a roadblock in negotiating or carrying out your parenting arrangements. Below are some suggestions on how to find people who can help, and what to expect of them. Because your relationship with any professional will be a personal one, whenever possible, meet with two or three different people to see whose education, experience, and style best match your needs.

Each section below includes a few questions you might use to structure your initial meeting with a professional. Use these questions as only one tool when you make a decision. In making your decision, you should also rely on your instinct, the professional's answers, and any personal referrals you've received. The key is that you feel comfortable working with the person. This means that you want someone who can:

- understand your general situation
- learn about your particular circumstances, and
- communicate effectively so you can make appropriate decisions.

1. Mediators

Mediators can help parents resolve separate parenting issues. The goal of mediation is for you and the other parent to develop an agreement that protects your children's best interests and is acceptable to both of you. Parents can use mediation to resolve some or all of their parenting issues or as a tool for reopening lines of communication and improving information exchanges. (Detailed discussion on mediation and mediators is in Chapter 11.)

When interviewing a mediator, you might ask questions such as:

- What kind of training have you had?
- What subjects do you usually help parents with in handling parenting disputes?

- How much experience have you had working with parents who are separating, divorcing, or renegotiating an existing parenting plan?
- Are there any issues that might come up that you do not deal with (such as money or property issues)?
- How do you approach mediation?
- Will you make a recommendation regarding how we should resolve a problem if we cannot resolve it on our own?
- Will everything we discuss in mediation be confidential?
- Do you have any preferences for ways that parents should structure their parenting plans (such as having joint custody)?
- What are your fees?
- How long should this process take?

2. Counselors, Therapists, and Other Mental Health Professionals

Counseling, therapy, or other mental health assistance can be an important part of dealing with separation, divorce, and separate parenting issues—for both parents and children. For example, if parents find that they cannot discuss any issue without arguing, they may need to deal with underlying feelings about themselves, each other, or the end of the relationship. (Information about the role of counseling is in Chapter 11.)

Mental health professionals are fairly easy to find. You may be able to get referrals from friends or relatives, the local mental health department, a battered women's shelter, a school counselor, your religious advisor, or your family physician. If none of those lead to possible candidates, you can look in your yellow pages directory under:

- Counseling
- Mental Health
- Psychiatrists
- Psychologists
- Psychotherapists, or
- Social Workers.

When interviewing a mental health professional, you might ask questions such as:

- What kind of training have you had?
- What subjects or skills did your training emphasize?
- How much experience have you had in working with individuals or families going through divorce or separation?

- How much do you know about childhood development?
- How well-versed are you in the effects of divorce and separation on children?
- Do you have any biases about how parenting issues should be settled, such as favoring custody with the mother or joint custody?
- What is your fee?
- How long do you think I will need to spend with you to resolve the issues we've talked about?

3. Collaborative Law

This relatively new type of law practice is designed to help parents work through their divorce outside of court, with the help of professionals, in as nonadversarial a way as possible. In this model, a combination of practitioners—usually lawyers, mental health professionals, and financial experts—work together to resolve the issues in the divorce. In general, each parent has access to their own lawyer (either in the form of a "divorce coach" or other family lawyer), and there are mental health professionals available to help parents work through the difficult feelings and understand and meet their children's needs. If financial issues are involved, the parents receive information from designated financial experts (and advice from their lawyers about what options might best meet their needs). At the core of this process is the agreement among all concerned that they will not take their differences to court but instead will find ways within the network of available professionals to reach an agreement that they can live with. These services are available in most states.

4. Child Custody Evaluators

Most child custody evaluators are mental health professionals but may not advertise these evaluation services. To get a list of potential evaluators, you can contact your court, a court-connected mediation program, a local mental health department, a family law or matrimonial law attorney, or the local bar association.

When interviewing a child custody evaluator, you might ask all but the last question listed in Section 2, above, for counselors, therapists, and other mental health professionals, as well as the following:

- How long does a child custody evaluation take?
- What kinds of information will you be looking for from me, the other parent, and our children?

- How can I help make the evaluation process go smoothly?

5. Professionals With Training in Domestic Violence

Not every mental health professional or health care worker has the training and experience to understand and effectively deal with domestic violence issues. To find someone who does, be specific about what you are looking for. Many public mental health departments and all battered women's shelters have access to volunteer or paid staff members who know how to recognize and respond to families who have experienced domestic violence. Additional resources may be available through local police departments, hospitals, and schools (especially in larger cities and metropolitan areas).

When interviewing a domestic violence support professional, you might ask questions such as:

- What kind of training have you had?
- What are the different ways you could help me?
- Do you have experience in working with children?
- Have you ever accompanied someone to mediation?
- Have you ever accompanied someone to a court hearing?
- Who else do you work with to support victims of domestic violence?

6. Professionals With Expertise in Dealing With Child Abuse

Assessing the nature and extent of child abuse or neglect often requires special training and expertise. For example, doctors can help detect physical assaults, and psychologists or pediatric psychiatrists can help recognize and document emotional, sexual, or other forms of abuse.

To find a professional with training in these areas, contact:

- the child protection division of your local welfare department
- your local police department
- your doctor
- a hospital
- your religious advisor
- the school your children attend, or
- a battered women's shelter.

When interviewing a professional who will be helping your child deal with issues associated with child abuse, you might ask questions such as:

- What kind of training have you had?
- What subjects or skills did your training emphasize?
- How much experience have you had in working with children whose parents are separated or divorced?
- How do you work with children my child's age?
- Who else do you work with once you have a clearer picture of what happened and how it has affected my child?

7. Attorneys

If you choose to work with an attorney after reading this book, you will probably want someone who is willing to work with you rather than take over your case. More and more family and matrimonial law attorneys offer their clients a role in shaping their own cases. Nevertheless, choosing the right attorney for your particular case is critically important.

Traditional lawyering tends to be highly adversarial. But only a handful of cases merit this approach. Most separate parenting issues would be more easily resolved by a cooperative problem-solving approach rather than a contest to assign blame or guilt and declare who is a "better" parent.

If you decide that you need an attorney's advice, you should first decide exactly what kind of help you need. For example, you may want:

- general information on certain issues of law
- information on how courts in your area tend to decide certain questions, or
- an analysis of what might happen if you took your case to trial.

Attorneys are very easy to find. You may be able to get referrals from friends or relatives, a battered women's shelter, or a paralegal. If you are gay or lesbian, are from another country, are a member of a religious or ethnic minority, have a physical disability, or are in some other way considered a minority, you might want to find a lawyer particularly sensitive to your needs. Try contacting a local support group or legal organization in your community for names of possible attorneys. If none of those lead to candidates, you can contact your local bar association or look in your yellow pages directory.

What is most important is that you find an attorney whose skills and experience are adequate, whose style is compatible with the job you want performed, and who will let you keep control over your case. Finding someone with a lot of family or matrimonial law experience is a plus, but keep looking if that person opposes mediation (and you want it) or wants to take over your case entirely.

To find the right attorney for your situation, make a list of exactly what kind of help you want from an attorney, figure out how much you can afford, and then interview two or three possible candidates. Start your initial meeting by explaining your needs and asking the following questions:

- Do you have any specialized training other than your legal education? (Some attorneys have advanced legal degrees, such as in tax law, which can be helpful if you are going through a divorce; other attorneys are considered specialists in particular fields; still others have mediation training.)
- How many custody cases have you handled?
- How much do you know about childhood development?
- How well-versed are you in the effects of divorce and separation on children?
- Do you have any biases about how parenting issues should be settled, such as favoring custody with the mother or joint custody?
- What legal issues do you anticipate will need resolving?
- How do you feel about resolving parenting disputes outside of court, such as through mediation or arbitration?
- How long do you think it will take to settle the issues we've discussed?
- What is your fee?

Each question defines a slightly different role for your attorney. Shopping for legal assistance in this way can be discouraging, because many attorneys hesitate to give any advice without full authority over the case. If you persevere, however, you'll find an attorney willing to work with you in the way that will be best for you.

8. Legal Typing Services (Independent Paralegals)

Thirty years ago, people who didn't want to hire a lawyer to help with a legal problem had two choices: handle the problem themselves or not have it handled at all. Now, busi-nesses known as "typing services" or "independent parale-gals" exist in many places to assist people in filling out the forms necessary to complete their own legal work. Independent paralegals often can help in routine family law matters, including the preparation and filing of a separate parenting agreement in the appropriate court on the appropriate form.

Independent paralegals are different from lawyers. They cannot give legal advice or represent you in court—by law, only lawyers can do those things. When you consult an independent paralegal, it will still be up to you to decide what steps to take in your case, and to gather the information needed to complete necessary court forms. Independent paralegals can, however:

- steer you to the written instructions and legal information you need to do your own legal work
- provide the appropriate court forms, and
- type your papers in a format acceptable to a court.

The following statement, posted in Divorce Centers of California, a prominent typing service near San Francisco, summarizes its services well:

WE ARE NOT ATTORNEYS

We are pro per assistants. Attorneys represent people. We assist people to represent themselves. If you want someone to represent you, you will need to hire an attorney. If you want to "do it yourself," we can help. We believe that representing yourself is the only way to gain, and keep, control over your own life and your own legal problems. You don't need legal training to use the courts or manage your own legal affairs. You have a constitutional right to represent yourself without an attorney. Let us assist you!

A recommendation from someone who has used an independent paralegal is the best way to find a reputable one in your area. Failing that, services often advertise in classified sections of newspapers under Referral Services, usually immediately following attorneys. Also check the yellow pages under Divorce Assistance or Legal Help. A local legal aid office may provide a reference, as will the occasional court clerk. Also, many offices advertise in local free papers.

When interviewing a typing service or independent paralegal, you might ask questions such as:

- What kind of training have you had?

- Do you have experience filing forms in the court I will be using?
- Do you have experience filing all the forms I will be using in my case?
- Who can answer your legal questions about filling out the forms I will be submitting?
- What happens if the court sends a form back saying it is not filled out properly, or that I need more forms prepared?

9. Arbitrators

Arbitration is fairly uncommon in custody and visitation cases, but it might be considered to obtain access to specialized expertise. For example, parents with a special-needs child might ask a specialist to evaluate and decide (which is what an arbitrator does) a particularly difficult legal custody or physical custody issue. (Arbitration is discussed in Chapter 11.)

E. Additional Resources

Bill of Rights for Children of Divorce, by Vance Packard, 87 Mill Road, New Canaan, CT 06840. Vance Packard is a severe critic of the effects of divorce on children and a staunch advocate of a child's right to remain whole in spite of his or her parents' divorce. His views are contained in his "Bill of Rights for Children of Divorce," which is printed below. Mr. Packard has given permission for parents to tear this out and keep it for their own use.

BILL OF RIGHTS FOR CHILDREN OF DIVORCE

1. Children of divorce are entitled to parents who set aside at least 20 minutes every month to discuss, in person or on the phone, the progress and problems of the children—and only the children. There should be no recriminations about any other topic, such as money. The children's schoolwork, health, mental state, activities and apparent reaction to the divorce should be the focus of such talks.

2. Children of divorce are entitled to parents who go out to dinner together with them, if desired by the child, on their birthdays or other important holidays. The parents should also both go to school events important to the children.

3. Children are entitled to have separated parents who do not belittle the other parent in front of the children.

4. Children of divorce are entitled to have parents who refrain from any action that would seem to force the children to take sides.

5. Children of divorce are entitled to be free from any sense of pressure from either parent to serve as informants about the ex-partner's spending, dating or other activities. If children freely choose to chat about the other parent, that is another matter.

6. Children of divorce are entitled to have complete freedom to phone either parent. If distances are involved, the calls will be collect. The children's parents will also agree that it is permissible for the noncustodial parent to call his or her children at least once a week.

7. Children of divorce are entitled to have parents who agree to notify each other in all emergencies or important events involving the children.

8. Children of divorce are entitled to have parents who by agreement are civil and avoid recriminations when they are in the presence of the child.

1. National Support Organizations

Step Family Foundation
(Assists stepfamilies)
333 West End Ave.
New York, NY 10023
Voice: 212-877-3244
Fax: 212-362-7030
Website: www.stepfamily.org

ABA Center on Children and the Law
(Studies how courts deal with children and children's issues)
750 15th St. NW
Washington, DC 20005
Voice: 202-662-1720
Fax: 202-662-1755
Website: www.abanet.org

National Center for Youth Law
(Studies how courts and legislatures deal with children's issues)
114 Sansome St., Suite #900
San Francisco, CA 94104
Voice: 415-543-3307
Fax: 415-956-9024
Website: www.youthlaw.org

Joint Custody Association
(Advocacy for joint custody arrangements and assistance to joint custodial parents)
10606 Wilkins Ave.
Los Angeles, CA 90024
Voice: 310-475-5352
Website: www.jointcustody.org

Kayama
(Assistance with obtaining a Jewish divorce)
1202 Avenue J
Brooklyn, NY 11230
Voice: 800-932-8589
Fax: 718-692-2044
Website: www.kayama.org

Childfind of America
(Assistance for parents who have taken or are considering taking their child in violation of existing court orders)
P.O. Box 277
New Paltz, NY 12561
Voice: 800-AWAYOUT
Fax: 914-255-5706
Website: www.childfindofamerica.org

Lambda Legal Defense and Education Fund
(Legal information and referral for gay and lesbian parents)
Lambda GLBT Community Services
P.O. Box 31321
El Paso, TX 79931-0321
Website: www.lambda.org

Gay & Lesbian Advocates & Defenders
(Legal information and referral for gay and lesbian parents)
P.O. Box 218
Boston, MA 02112
Voice: 617-426-1350
Website: www.glad.org

Lesbian Mothers' National Defense Fund
(Fundraising and advocacy for lesbian mothers)
P.O. Box 21567
Seattle, WA 98111
Voice: 206-325-2643

National Center for Lesbian Rights
(Legal informational and referral for gay and lesbian parents)
870 Market St., Suite 570
San Francisco, CA 94102
Voice: 415-392-6257
Website: www.nclrights.org
and
462 Broadway, Suite 500A
New York, NY 10013
Voice: 212-343-9589

2. Mediation Resources

Association for Conflict Resolution
1015 18th Street, NW, Suite 1150
Washington, DC 20036
Voice: 202-464-9700
Fax: 202-464-9720
Email: acr@ACRnet.org
Website: www.acrnet.org

3. Arbitration Resources

American Arbitration Association
335 Madison Avenue, Floor 10
New York, NY 10017-4605
Voice: 212-716-5800
Fax: 212-716-5905
Email: websitemail@adr.org
Website: www.adr.org

4.   Domestic Violence Resources

Domestic violence tends to carry forward from one generation to the next. Do yourselves and your children a favor—get help now and try to break the cycle.

You can get a referral to professionals with experience in domestic violence from many sources, including the following:

- battered women's shelters
- local mental health departments
- hospitals
- doctors
- school counselors
- religious institutions
- police departments
- social service agencies
- women's groups, and
- community organizations.

Many books and videos provide real and practical insights into managing anger and frustration more productively. A librarian, local mental health department, or private practice counselor, psychologist, or psychiatrist may be able to suggest materials or offer information about how to help your children deal with the issues.

5.   Alcohol or Drug Abuse Organizations

Perhaps the best-known programs for alcohol and drug abuse are Alcoholics Anonymous, Al-Anon, and Narcotics Anonymous. To find a local group, contact one of the national organizations as follows:

Alcoholics Anonymous
475 Riverside Dr.
New York, NY 10015
Voice: 212-870-3400
Fax: 212-870-3003
Website: www.alcoholics-anonymous.org

Al-Anon Family Groups
(For friends and families of alcoholics)
1372 Broadway
New York, NY 10018
Voice: 888-425-2666
Fax: 212-869-3757

Narcotics Anonymous
16155 Wyandotte St.
Van Nuys, CA 91406
Voice: 818-359-0084
Fax: 818-785-0123
Website: www.na.org

Other ways to find alcohol or drug treatment programs or support groups include contacting your local mental health department, police department, hospital, family physician, library or consulting your yellow pages directory under the following headings:

- Alcoholism Information and Treatment, or
- Drug Abuse and Addiction.

F.   Bibliography

- Ahrons, Constance R., Ph.D., *The Good Divorce*, Harper Collins Publishers, 1994.
- Brown, Neil D., Samis, Michelle D.C., "The Application of Structural Family Therapy in Developing the Binuclear Family," *Mediation Quarterly*, 1987, pp. 51–69.
- Bryant, Suzanne, "Mediation for Lesbian and Gay Families," *Mediation Quarterly*, 1992, pp. 391–395.
- Burbano, Maria Elena; Cordona, Ray, "Cross-cultural Issues In Mediation," *Mediation Quarterly*, 1992.
- Campbell, Linda E.G.; Johnston, Janet R., "Multifamily Mediation: The Use of Groups to Resolve Child Custody Disputes," *Mediation Quarterly*, 1987, pp. 137–162.
- Charlesworth, Stephanie, "The Acceptance of Family Mediation in Australia," *Mediation Quarterly*, 1991.
- Cloke, Kenneth, "Shared Custody: A Case Study in Mediation," *Mediation Quarterly*, 1988, pp. 31–35.
- Cohen, Miriam Galper, *The Joint Custody Handbook: Creating Arrangements That Work*, Running Press, 1991.
- Corcoran, Kathleen O'Connell; Melamed, James C., "From Coercion to Empowerment: Spousal Abuse and Mediation," *Mediation Quarterly*, 1990, pp. 303–316.
- Coulson, Robert, *Fighting Fair*, The Free Press, 1983.
- Davidson, Jeff, "Mediation and the Special-Child Family," *Mediation Quarterly*, 1987, pp. 79–83.
- Davis, Albie M.; Salem, Richard A., "Dealing With Power Imbalances in the Mediation of Interpersonal Disputes," *Mediation Quarterly*, 1984, pp. 17–26.

- Edelman, Joel; Crain, Mary Beth, *The Tao of Negotiation*, Harper Business Press, 1993.
- Emery, Robert E.; Jackson, Joanne A., "The Charlottesville Mediation Project: Mediated and Litigated Child Custody Disputes," *Mediation Quarterly*, 1989, pp. 3–18.
- Erickson, Stephen K.; McKnight, Marilyn S., "Dan and Linda: A Typical Divorce Mediation Case," *Mediation Quarterly*, 1988, pp. 3–21.
- Fisher, Roger; Ury, William, *Getting to Yes: Negotiating Agreement Without Giving In*, Harvard Negotiation Project, Penguin Books, 1981.
- Francke, Linda Bird, *Growing Up Divorced*, Linden Press/ Simon & Schuster, 1983.
- Friedman, Gary J., J.D., *A Guide to Divorce Mediation*, Workman Publishing, 1993.
- Gadlin, Howard; Ouellette, Patricia A., "Mediation Milanese: An Application of Systemic Family Therapy Approach to Family Mediation," *Mediation Quarterly*, 1987, pp. 101–118.
- Gardner, Richard A., M.D., *Boys and Girls' Book About Divorce*, Jason Aronson, Inc., 1983.
- Garwood, Fiona, "Divorce and Conciliation in Sweden and Scotland," *Mediation Quarterly*, 1991, pp. 293–301.
- Goldstein, Sonja, LL.B.; Solnit, Albert, M.D., *Divorce and Your Child: Practical Suggestions for Parents*, Yale University Press, 1984.
- Haynes, John M., "John and Mary: Sharing Parenting After Divorce," *Mediation Quarterly*, 1988, pp. 23–29.
- Haynes, John M., "The Process of Negotiations," *Mediation Quarterly*, 1983, pp. 75–92.
- Heitler, Susan M., Ph.D., *From Conflict to Resolution: Strategies for Diagnosis and Treatment of Distressed Individuals, Couples and Families*, W.W. Norton & Co., 1990.
- Hurt, Barbara J., "Gentle Jeopardy: The Further Endangerment of Battered Women and Children in Custody Mediation," *Mediation Quarterly*, 1990, pp. 317–330.
- Ihara, Toni; Warner, Ralph, *The Living Together Kit*, Nolo Press, 1990.
- Kaplan, Nancy M., "The Development and Operation of the Northwest Mediation Service," *Mediation Quarterly*, 1984, pp. 47–58.
- Kelly, Joan B., "Mediation and Psychotherapy: Distinguishing the Differences," *Mediation Quarterly*, 1983, pp. 33–44.
- Kirkpatrick, Gary, "The Good, The Bad, The Indifferent," *Mediation Quarterly*, 1988, pp. 37–45.
- Kirkpatrick, Martha, M.D.; Smith, Catherine; Roy, Ron, M.D., *Lesbian Mothers and Their Children: A Comparative Survey*, American Orthopsychiatric Association, Inc., 1981.
- Krementz, Jill, *How It Feels When Parents Divorce*, Alfred A. Knopf, 1984.
- Leitch, M. Laurie, "The Politics of Compromise: A Feminist Perspective on Mediation," *Mediation Quarterly*, 1987, pp. 163–175.
- Lemmon, John Allen, Ed.D., "Dimensions and Practice of Divorce Mediation," *Mediation Quarterly*, 1983.
- Leonard, Robin; Elias, Stephen, *Nolo's Pocket Guide to Family Law*, Nolo Press, 1994.
- LeResche, Diane, "Comparison of the American Mediation Process With a Korean-American Harmony Restoration Process," *Mediation Quarterly*, 1992, pp. 323–339.
- Levy, Bert, *Trust—The Main Ingredient for a Successful Mediation*, Bancroft Whitney, 1993.
- Lutker, Eric R., Ph.D.; Wand, Carl F., Esq., *Do It Yourself Divorce*, The Forms Man, 1992.
- Maccoby, Eleanor E.; Mnookin, Robert H., *Dividing the Child: Social and Legal Dilemmas of Custody*, Harvard Press, 1992.
- Maxwell, David, "Gender Differences in Mediation Style and Their Impact on Mediator Effectiveness," *Mediation Quarterly*, 1992, pp. 353–364.
- Mayer, Bernard, "Mediation in Child Protection Cases: The Impact of Third-Party Intervention on Parental Compliance Attitudes," *Mediation Quarterly*, 1989, pp. 89–106.
- McIsaac, Hugh, "Toward a Classification of Child Custody Disputes: An Application of Family Systems Theory," *Mediation Quarterly*, 1987, pp. 39–50.
- Mehren, Elizabeth, "Lesbian Mothers: Two New Studies Shatter Stereotypes," *Los Angeles Times*, June 1, 1983.
- Melton, Gary, *Families and the Courts in the Twenty-First Century*, University of Nebraska, 1992.
- Millen, Richard H., *You and Divorce Mediation*, Richard H. Millen, 1991.
- Miller, Brian, "Gay Fathers and Their Children," *The Family Coordinator*, 1979.
- National Center for State Courts, *National Symposium on Court-Connected Dispute Resolution Research*, State Justice Institute, 1994.

- Oshiro, Donna A.; O'Donnell, Clifford R., *A Culturally Competent Legal System: Cultural Factors in Family Court Cases in Hawaii*, University of Hawaii, 1992.
- O'Toole, Kathleen, "Joint Custody Can Work," *Academy of Family Mediation News* #10.4, 1992.
- Pagelow, Mildred Daley, "Effects of Domestic Violence on Children and Their Consequences for Custody and Visitation Agreements," *Mediation Quarterly*, 1990, pp. 347–363.
- Peters, Deanna; Strohm, Richard L., *Divorce and Child Custody*, Layman's Law Guides, 1993.
- Plesent, Emanuel, "Mediation for Reconciliation," *Mediation Quarterly*, 1988, pp. 47–50.
- Ricci, Isolina, Ph.D., *Mom's House, Dad's House: Making Shared Custody Work*, Macmillan Publishing Co., 1998.
- Robertson, Christina, *Divorce and Decision Making: A Woman's Guide*, Follett Publishing Company, 1980.
- Robson, Bonnie, M.D., *My Parents Are Divorced Too*, Everest House, 1980.
- Rogers, Susan J., "The Dynamics of Conflict Behavior in a Mediated Dispute," *Mediation Quarterly*, 1987, pp. 61–71.
- Samis, Michelle D.C.; Saposnek, Donald T., "Parent-Child Relationships in Family Mediation: A Synthesis of Views," *Mediation Quarterly*, 1987.
- Saposnek, Donald T., "Aikido: A Systems Model for Maneuvering in Mediation," *Mediation Quarterly*, 1987, pp. 119–136.
- Saposnek, Donald T., "Strategies in Child Custody Mediation: A Family Systems Approach," *Mediation Quarterly*, 1983, pp. 29–54.
- Saposnek, Donald T., "The Value of Children in Mediation: A Cross-Cultural Perspective," *Mediation Quarterly*, 1991, pp. 325–342.
- Sargent, George; Moss, Bleema, "Eriksonian Approaches in Family Therapy and Mediation," *Mediation Quarterly*, 1987, pp. 87–100.
- Sherman, Ed, *Practical Divorce Solutions*, Nolo Press Occidental, 1994.
- Stern, Marilyn; Van Slyck, Michael R.; Newland, Lori M., "Adolescent Development and Family Dynamics: Delineating a Knowledge Base for Family Mediation," *Mediation Quarterly*, pp. 307–322.
- Stuart, Richard B.; Jacobson, Barbara, "Principles of Divorce Mediation: A Social Learning Theory Approach," *Mediation Quarterly*, 1987.
- Vaughan, Diane, *Uncoupling: Turning Points in Intimate Relationships*, Oxford University Press, 1986.
- Walker, Janet A., "Family Mediation in England: Strategies for Gaining Acceptance," *Mediation Quarterly*, 1991.
- Wallerstein, Judith S., Ph.D., "Children and Divorce," *Pediatrics in Review*, 1980.
- Wallerstein, Judith S., Ph.D., "Psychodynamic Perspectives on Family Mediation," *Mediation Quarterly*, 1987, pp. 7–21.
- Wallerstein, Judith S., Ph.D., "The Impact of Divorce on Children," *Psychiatric Clinics of North America*, 1980.
- Wallerstein, Judith S., Ph.D.; Kelly, Joan B., Ph.D., "Effects of Divorce on the Visiting Father-Child Relationship," *American Journal of Psychiatry*, 1980.
- Weeks, Dudley, Ph.D., *The Eight Essential Steps to Conflict Resolution*, Jeremy Tarcher, Inc., 1992.
- Yahm, Howard, "Divorce Mediation: A Psychoanalytic Perspective," *Mediation Quarterly*, 1984, pp. 59–63.
- Zaidel, Susan, "Challenges Facing the Development of Family Mediation in Israel," *Mediation Quarterly*, 1991, pp. 281–292. ▪

Appendix: Tear-Out Forms

WORKSHEET 1: DESCRIBE YOUR CHILD

Child's name: _____

1. How would you describe each child?

   _____

   _____

2. What makes each child special?

   _____

   _____

3. How does each child like the current living and parenting arrangements?

   _____

   _____

   _____

   _____

4. Have there been any changes in behavior since the separation or divorce?

   _____

   _____

   _____

   _____

5. Have the children expressed preferences for the future?

   _____

   _____

   _____

6. How does each child react to change?

   _____

   _____

7. What strategies help each child to handle change?

   _____

   _____

8. Who else is important in your children's lives?

   _____

   _____

WORKSHEET 2: DESCRIBE YOUR RELATIONSHIP WITH YOUR CHILD

Child's name: _____

1. What do you and your children like to do together?

   _____
   _____
   _____

2. What are your plans and wishes for your children?

   _____
   _____
   _____

3. How do you and your children handle and resolve conflict? Discipline?

   _____
   _____
   _____

4. How did you share parenting responsibilities and time when you and the other parent were living together?

   _____
   _____
   _____

5. How do you and the other parent share parenting responsibilities and time with your children now?

   _____
   _____
   _____
   _____

6. Are you happy with the current arrangements? (Please explain)

   _____
   _____
   _____
   _____

7. Are your children happy with the current arrangements? (Please explain)

   _____
   _____
   _____

8. If changes are in order, what would you suggest?

_____

_____

_____

_____

_____

_____

WORKSHEET 3: ADDING THE DETAILS

1. List court documents, orders, or agreements that affect your family. (Note that the terms listed here might be different in your state. See Chapter 16 for the terms used in your state.)

   _____

   _____

   _____

   _____

2. Each parent's work schedule:

   _____

   _____

3. Children's schedules of activities, special needs, and interests (such as school, religious training, and after-school activities):

   _____

   _____

   _____

   _____

4. Does either parent have plans to move?

   _____

   _____

   _____

5. Does either parent have a new relationship or plan to remarry?

   _____

   _____

6. Are there any adult relatives or friends with whom the children should or should not have close contact?

   _____

   _____

7. Is counseling needed for the children, parents, or the family?

   _____

   _____

   _____

8. Are there any special medical needs of the children, parents, or the family?

   _____

   _____

9. Do you want your parenting agreement to address domestic violence issues? (Please explain)

   _____

   _____

   _____

10. Do you want your parenting agreement to address the use of drugs or alcohol? (Please explain)

_____

_____

_____

11. Do you have any special concerns about your relationship with the other parent that should be addressed in your agreement? (Please explain)

_____

_____

_____

WORKSHEET 4: CHECKLIST OF ISSUES FOR YOUR PARENTING AGREEMENT

1. Existing court documents, orders, or agreements that must be reconsidered or changed to accommodate your new parenting agreement:

   _____

   _____

   _____

   _____

2. Steps you will have to take to resolve legal or religious issues such as divorce, legal separation, etc.:

   _____

   _____

3. Any concerns or recommendations made by a counselor, school teacher, therapist, or other interested adult regarding your children's emotional, spiritual, or physical well-being:

   _____

   _____

   _____

   _____

4. Ways each of you can support your children's relationship with the other parent:

   _____

   _____

   _____

   _____

   _____

   _____

   _____

   _____

5. Ways each parent can help the children address their feelings, reactions, or concerns about the separation or divorce:

   _____

   _____

   _____

   _____

   _____

   _____

   _____

6. Medical issues that need to be addressed:

_____

_____

_____

_____

_____

_____

7. Ways to reduce conflict between the parents when negotiating agreements, exchanging the children, and addressing the children's needs, interests, and activities:

_____

_____

_____

_____

_____

_____

8. Times when both parents are available to care for children:

_____

_____

_____

_____

9. Times when only _____ can care for children: _____

10. Times when only _____ can care for children: _____

11. Time with other family or friends that should be addressed in the parenting agreement:

_____

_____

12. Family or friends the children should not spend time (or be alone) with:

_____

_____

13. Ways domestic violence issues will be addressed:

_____

_____

_____

_____

_____

_____

_____

14. Ways alcohol or other substance-abuse issues will be addressed:

_____

_____

_____

_____

_____

_____

15. Other provisions:

_____

_____

_____

_____

_____

_____

_____

_____

_____

_____

PARENTING AGREEMENT

A. Parties. The following is a mutually acceptable agreement between _____

_____ and _____

_____ regarding how we will share parenting responsibilities for our children [list names]:

_____   _____

_____   _____

_____   _____

_____   _____

B. How Long This Agreement Lasts. The term of this agreement is _____ [period of time].

If this is a temporary agreement, we will negotiate a new agreement on or before _____ [date].

C. Terms of the Agreement.

#_____   Where Our Children Will Live

_____ Our children will alternate living in each parent's home as follows:

___ They will live primarily with _____ and with _____ on:

___ Alternating weekends from _____ to _____ (give days and times if possible)

___ During the week on _____ (day(s) of the week) from _____ to _____

_____ Overnight

___ They will live primarily with _____ during the school year and with _____ during the summer months.

During the time they are living primarily with one parent, they will live with the other parent on:

___ Alternating weekends from _____ to _____ (give days and times if possible)

___ During the week on _____ (day(s) of the week) from _____ to _____

___ Overnight

_____ The children will live in each parent's home for approximately the same amount of time, and will change homes:

___ Every ___ days

___ Every ___ weeks

___ Every ___ months

___ Other _____

_____ Our children will not live primarily with either parent, but with _____ instead.

Our children will spend time with _____ (parent's name) as follows:

___ Alternating weekends from _____ to _____ (give days and times if possible)

___ During the week on _____ (day(s) of the week) from _____ to _____

___ Overnight

And with _____ (parent's name) as follows:

___ Alternating weekends from _____ to _____ (give days and times if possible)

___ During the week on _____ (day(s) of the week) from _____ to _____

___ Overnight

_____ Our children will live in one home, and each parent will take turns living there:

    ____ Every ____ days

    ____ Every ____ weeks

    ____ Every ____ months

    ____ Other _____

_____ Our children will live at _____ school

and spend time with each of us as follows [specify; include days and times of exchanges]:

_____

_____

_____

_____ We further agree that [specify]:

_____

_____

_____

_____

#_____ Medical, Dental, and Vision Care

_____ Our children's medical, dental, and vision care providers will be [choose one]:

    _____ We will use only the following health care providers:

        _____ [medical]

        _____ [dental]

        _____ [vision]

    _____ We will each choose health care providers. We will exchange names, addresses, phone numbers, and releases so that our providers can share records and information.

_____ _____ [parent] will see to it that our children receive their routine care.

_____ Our children's special health care needs will be met as follows [specify]:

_____

_____

_____

_____ In a medical emergency [choose one]:

    _____ Either parent may seek medical treatment and must inform the other parent as soon as possible thereafter.

    _____ Either parent may seek medical treatment, except for the following procedures or interventions:

    _____

    _____

    _____ _____ [parent] is the only person who may seek medical treatment.

_____ If our children develop an ongoing medical condition or have other special health care concerns, we will assure consistency in their care as follows [choose all that apply]:

    _____ We will share all medical records.

    _____ We will include the medications with our children as they travel between our homes.

    _____ We will each fill all prescriptions and dispense the medications when caring for our children.

    _____ We will exchange written instructions on needed care.

    _____ We will each keep whatever physical supports or enhancements our children need in our home.

_____ Our children will receive the following dental care [specify]:

_____

_____

_____

_____ Our children will receive the following vision care [specify]:

_____

_____ We further agree that [specify]:

_____
_____
_____
_____

#_____ **Disparaging Remarks**

_____ We will refrain from making disparaging remarks about the other parent, his/her partner, and his/her chosen life directly to our children or within our children's hearing.

_____ We further agree that [specify]:

_____
_____
_____

#_____ **Consistency in Raising Children**

_____ The standards for discipline in each of our homes will be as follows [choose all that apply]:

_____ We will abide by the same discipline standards.

_____ The following behavior rules will apply in both homes:

_____
_____
_____

_____ If either of us has a discipline issue with our children, that parent will explain the issue and response to the other so we can be consistent in our discipline.

_____ If our children complain about discipline in the other parent's home, we will encourage them to talk about it with the other parent.

_____ If we cannot agree on discipline standards that will apply in both homes, we will make an effort to understand and respect the other's right to establish behavior rules for our children.

_____ We further agree that [specify]:

_____
_____
_____

#_____ **Holidays**

_____ This agreement covers the following holidays:

_____   _____
_____   _____
_____   _____

_____ Holiday visits will begin at _____ [time] and will end at _____ [time].

_____ We will adopt an odd year/even year plan, as follows:

_____ In odd years, our children will be with _____ [parent] for these holidays:

_____   _____
_____   _____

and with _____ [parent] for these holidays:

_____   _____
_____   _____

In even years, the reverse will be true.

_____ The children will spend one-half of each holiday with each parent as follows:

_____   _____
_____   _____
_____   _____

_____ We will both celebrate the following holidays with our children:

_____   _____

Each parent will celebrate as follows:

_____   _____

_____   _____

_____ We will divide holiday vacation periods as follows:

_____

_____

_____

_____ Our children will always spend the following holidays with _____ [parent]:

_____   _____

_____   _____

and will always spend the following holidays with _____ [other parent]:

_____   _____

_____   _____

_____ We will plan for holidays as they come up. We will decide where the children will spend their holidays at least

_____ [specify time, such as two weeks or one month] in advance.

_____ We further agree that [specify]:

_____

_____

_____

#_____ **Education**

_____ Our children will attend [choose one]:

_____ public school

_____ private school

_____ home school

_____ We will pay for any private or home school as follows [specify]:

_____

_____

_____

_____ Any decision to change schools will be made as follows [choose all that apply]:

_____ If we agree.

_____ After consulting our children.

_____ After consulting with _____ [parent].

_____ Only _____ [parent] may change our
children's enrollment in a particular school.

_____ Any decisions to support our children's special educational needs or talents will be made as follows [choose all
that apply]:

_____ If we agree.

_____ After consulting our children.

_____ After consulting with _____ [parent].

_____ Only _____ [parent] may decide
how to support our children's special educational needs.

_____ We will participate in parent associations as follows [choose one]:

_____ Either parent may participate.

_____ Only one parent may participate at a time.

_____ _____ [parent] will participate.

_____ We will participate in the classroom as follows [choose one]:

    _____ Either parent may participate.

    _____ Only one parent may participate at a time.

    _____ _____ [parent] will participate.

_____ We will participate in parent-chaperoned events as follows [choose one]:

    _____ Either parent may participate.

    _____ Only one parent may participate at a time.

    _____ _____ [parent] will participate.

_____ We will attend parent-teacher or other school conferences as follows [choose one]:

    _____ Both will attend.

    _____ Each will schedule a meeting with the teacher or other school official.

    _____ _____ [parent] will attend and will inform the other of the matters discussed.

    _____ _____ [parent] will attend and will not inform the other of the matters discussed.

_____ Any emergency contact information needed by a school will be completed as follows [choose one]:

    _____ We both will be listed in the following order:

    _____

    _____

    _____ Only _____ [parent] will be listed.

    _____ Others to be listed will be [list names]:

    _____

    _____

    _____

_____ Good school performance means:

_____

We will encourage good school performance as follows [choose all that apply]:

    _____ After discussion and agreement.

    _____ After consultation with our children.

    _____ With the following rewards:

    _____

    _____

_____ Poor school performance means:

_____

We will discourage poor school performance by [specify]:

_____

_____

_____

_____ Our children [check one] ☐ may ☐ may not attend sex education classes at school.

    _____ [parent] will notify the school of this decision.

_____ Our children's post-secondary education will be paid for as follows [specify]:

_____

_____

_____ Any decisions regarding our children's options for post-secondary education will be made as follows [choose all that apply]:

    _____ by agreement between parents and children

    _____ based on the children's interest and ability to be accepted at a particular school

    _____ based on what we can afford

_____ other [specify]:

_____

_____

_____

_____ We further agree that [specify]:

_____

_____

#_____ **Insurance**

_____ Our children's medical insurance will be provided as follows [choose all that apply]:

    _____ We both will obtain coverage if it is available through an employer at low or no cost.

    _____ We will share the costs of any uncovered expenses as follows [specify]:

    _____

    _____

    _____ _____ [parent]

    will obtain coverage up to $ _____ under the following conditions [choose all that apply]:

    _____ Type of coverage: _____

    _____ Named beneficiaries: _____

        _____

    _____ Insurance claims submitted by: _____ [parent]

_____ Our children's dental insurance will be provided as follows [choose all that apply]:

    _____ We both will obtain coverage if it is available through an employer at low or no cost.

    _____ We will share the costs of any uncovered expenses as follows [specify]:

    _____

    _____

    _____ _____ [parent]

    will obtain coverage up to $ _____ under the following conditions [choose all that apply]:

    _____ Type of coverage: _____

    _____ Named beneficiaries: _____

        _____

    _____ Insurance claims submitted by: _____ [parent]

_____ Our children's vision care will be provided as follows [choose all that apply]:

    _____ We both will obtain coverage if it is available through an employer at low or no cost.

    _____ _____ [parent]

    will obtain coverage up to $ _____ under the following conditions [choose all that apply]:

    _____ Type of coverage: _____

    _____ Named beneficiaries: _____

        _____

_____ We will obtain life insurance coverage as follows [choose all that apply]:

    _____ We both will obtain coverage if it is available through an employer at low or no cost.

    _____ _____ [parent]

    will obtain coverage up to $ _____ under the following conditions [choose all that apply]:

    _____ Type of coverage: _____

    _____ Named beneficiaries: _____

        _____

_____ We will obtain _____ insurance as follows [choose all that apply]:

_____ We both will obtain coverage if it is available through an employer at low or no cost.

_____ We will share the costs of any uncovered expenses as follows [specify]:

_____

_____

_____ [parent]

will obtain coverage up to $ _____ under the following conditions [choose all that apply]:

_____ Type of coverage: _____

_____ Named beneficiaries: _____

_____

_____ Insurance claims submitted by: _____ [parent]

#_____ **Making Decisions**

_____ Choose all that apply:

_____ Whenever possible, we will discuss the issues and attempt to reach an agreement.

_____ We both will make an effort to remain aware of our children's interests, activities, school performance, and overall health.

_____ _____ [parent] will make an effort to keep

_____ [other parent] aware of our

children's interests, activities, school performance, and overall health.

_____ _____ [parent], as the primary

caretaker, will be responsible to make [most/all] of the decisions on behalf of our children and will inform

_____ [other parent] as soon as possible thereafter.

_____ _____ [parent], as the primary

caretaker, will be responsible to make all of the decisions on behalf of our children and need not inform

_____ [other parent] of these decisions.

_____ _____ [other adult/guardian]

will be given authority to make decisions on behalf of our children.

_____ We further agree that [specify]:

_____

_____

_____

#_____ **Resolving Disputes When Making Decisions Together**

_____ If disagreements arise regarding this Parenting Agreement or our general parenting arrangements, we agree as follows [choose all that apply]:

_____ _____ [parent] has authority to make final decisions when we can't agree.

_____ Before this parent makes a final decision that resolves a disagreement, he/she will consult with

_____ [other adult] for advice.

_____ _____ [parent] has authority to make final decisions regarding

_____ [specify] and _____ [other parent]

has authority to make final decisions regarding _____ [specify].

_____ We will participate in the following, at either parent's request [choose all that apply]:

_____ counseling

_____ mediation

_____ arbitration

_____ meeting with attorney[s]

_____ other: _____ [specify]

_____ We further agree that [specify]:

_____
_____
_____

#_____ **Labeling the Custody Arrangement**

_____ The custody of our children will be as follows [choose one]: *(Note: Read Chapter 16 before completing this option.*
Your state may require you to differentiate between legal and physical custody.)

    _____ sole custody
        _____ legal
        _____ physical
    _____ joint custody
        _____ legal
        _____ physical
    _____ joint custody, to mean that we will make decisions and share time with our children as follows [specify]:

    _____
    _____

    _____ split custody
    _____ _____ [parent] will have custody of
                       _____ [children's names].
    _____ _____ [other parent] will have custody of
                       _____ [children's names].
    _____ _____ [other adult] will have custody of our children.

_____ We further agree that [specify]:

_____
_____
_____
_____

#_____ **Exchanging Information**

_____ We will not ask our children to carry messages between us.

_____ We will share information about the children [choose all that apply]:
    _____ at least every _____ [specify interval of time]
    _____ with each exchange of our children
    _____ the day or evening before an exchange
    _____ as needed

_____ [Parent/We] will assume the responsibility to establish contact with the appropriate sources of information
regarding our children's [choose all that apply]:
    _____ health care
    _____ school
    _____ sports
    _____ other: _____ [specify]

_____ We will communicate with each other [choose all that apply]:
    _____ in person
    _____ by telephone
    _____ by letter
    _____ by email
    _____ other: _____ [specify]

_____ We further agree that [specify]:

_____

_____

#_____ **Child Care**

_____ In securing child care, we will proceed as follows [choose all that apply]:

    _____ Any child care provider will [choose all that apply]:

        _____ be a licensed child care provider

        _____ be over the age of _____

        _____ be a relative or close friend

        _____ not care for more than _____ children at any time when our children are there

        _____ come into the home

        _____ other: _____ [specify]

_____ Each parent has the discretion to select the child care provider, but may not use [list names or traits unacceptable]:

_____

_____ Each parent will call the other first to care for the children in that parent's absence.

_____ We will try to share child care responsibilities with neighbors and friends.

_____ Our children can care for themselves, but _____ [other adult]
will check in with them.

_____ Our children can care for themselves as long as they follow these rules:

_____

_____

_____

_____ We further agree that [specify]:

_____

_____

_____

#_____ **Special Occasions and Family Events**

_____ Special occasions and family events are defined as follows:

_____

_____

_____

_____ We will attend special occasions and family events together whenever possible.

_____ We will attend special occasions and family events as our children wish.

_____ We will attend special occasions and family events as we decide.

_____ _____ [parent] will attend the following special occasions and family events:

_____

_____

_____ _____ [parent] will attend the following special occasions and family events:

_____

_____

_____

_____ We further agree that [specify]:

_____

_____

_____

#_____ **Vacations**

_____ We will inform each other at least _____ [period of time] in advance of any planned vacation.

_____ We will provide each other with an itinerary of any trip, and contact information.

_____ Our children may accompany one of us on a vacation under the following conditions:

_____ Any time missed from a regularly scheduled visit with the other parent will be made up as follows:

_____

_____

_____ Travel will be restricted to:

_____ local area

_____ in state

_____ in the United States

_____ the following countries: _____

_____ Activities will be limited to _____.

_____ Activities will not include _____.

_____ Our children will not be away for longer than _____.

_____ We further agree that [specify]:

_____

_____

#_____ **Outside Activities**

_____ Our children may participate in [list all appropriate activities]:

_____

_____

_____

_____ Our children may _not_ participate in [list all appropriate activities]:

_____

_____

_____

_____ We will make decisions about which activities our children may participate in as follows:

_____ By consensus agreement.

_____ _____ [parent's name] may make decisions about

[fill in the blank] _____ activities.

_____ _____ [parent's name] may make decisions about

[fill in the blank] _____ activities.

_____ We will use the decision-making process outlined in issue #_____ [fill in the right number from your completed

agreement. This section refers to Issue Number 8 in Chapter 6 called "Making Decisions"].

_____ We further agree that [specify]: _____

_____

#_____ **Transporting the Children**

_____ Transporting our children between our homes will be as follows [choose all that apply]:

    _____ We will meet for exchanges at _____ [specify time and location].

    _____ We will alternate transporting our children back and forth.

        _____ [parent] will actually transport our children

        and _____ [other parent] will share in costs as follows:

        _____

        _____

    _____ _____ [parent] will travel to our children for visits.

    _____ _____ [parent] will bring our children for visits to the other parent.

    _____ Our children may travel on their own by train, bus, or airplane when they reach age _____.

_____ We further agree that [specify]:

_____

_____

_____

#_____ **Improving Transition Times**

_____ We will make the transitions between our homes easier for our children by doing as follows [choose all that apply]:

    _____ Our children will start visits with _____ [parent]

    at _____ [specify time or event, such as after school or after

    work]. The visits will end at _____ [specify time or event].

    _____ When our children are changing homes, we will minimize the contact between us.

    _____ We will exchange information regarding our children the night before they change homes.

    _____ When our children are changing homes, the parent starting the visit will take time to give each child some undivided attention.

    _____ The parent starting a visit will let our children have some quiet time before any scheduled activities or trips.

    _____ _____ [parent] will try to establish and maintain a simple ritual to start and end his/her visits with our children.

    _____ We will try to be patient regarding any questions that the children wish to ask about the custody and visitation arrangements.

_____ We further agree that [specify]:

_____

_____

_____

#_____ **Maintaining Contact When the Children Are With the Other Parent**

_____ Our children and _____ [parent] will make an effort to talk at least every _____ [specify frequency] as follows:

    _____ _____ [parent or children] will initiate each call.

    _____ Calls will be made between _____ and _____.

    _____ If either _____ [parent] or children will be unavailable at the usual time, the unavailable person will arrange a new time by:

        _____ calling the other parent

        _____ sending a note

        _____ email message

        _____ other: _____ [specify]

_____ Our children and _____ [parent] will not call back and forth more than every
_____ [specify] unless something unusual happens or it is a special occasion.

_____ Our children will be given their own telephone line.

_____ _____ [parent] will be responsible to teach telephone rules.

_____ _____ [parent or children] will be responsible for telephone bills.

_____ _____ [parent] and the children can also communicate by:

    _____ letter

    _____ audio- or videotapes

    _____ email or electronic conferencing

    _____ other: _____ [specify]

_____ Visits with _____ [parent] will include
a midweek dinner on _____ [day of week] as follows [specify time for exchange]:

_____

_____

_____

_____ We will arrange for our children to communicate with _____ [parent]
while our children are away on vacation.

_____ We further agree that [specify]:

_____

_____

_____

#_____ **Grandparents, Relatives, and Important Friends**

_____ Our children will maintain their relationships with grandparents, other relatives, and important friends as follows:

_____

_____

_____

#_____ **Psychiatric and Other Mental Health Care**

_____ Our children may undergo psychiatric or other mental health care as follows [choose all that apply]:

    _____ if either parent feels it is necessary

    _____ if it is recommended by a school counselor or other health care provider

    _____ only if we agree

    _____ only if it is made available through the school

    _____ only if it is available at low or no cost to us

_____ Either of us may undergo psychiatric or other mental health care as follows [choose all that apply]:

    _____ if either parent feels it is necessary

    _____ if it is recommended by a school counselor or other health care provider

    _____ only if we agree

    _____ only if it is made available through the school

    _____ only if it is available at low or no cost to us

_____ Our children's other mental health issues, such as _____ [specify],
will be addressed as follows [specify]:

_____

_____

_____

#_____ **Religious Training**

_____ Our children's religious training will be as follows [choose all that apply]:

_____ Our children will be raised _____ [specify].

_____ Our children will be taught about both of our religions: _____

and _____ .

_____ Our children may choose their religious training as long as it generally conforms to the principles of the

_____ religion.

_____ Our children may choose their religious training. _____ [parent]

will supervise such training.

_____ We further agree that [specify]:

_____

_____

_____

#_____ **Surname**

_____ Our children's surname is _____ .

Any decision to change that surname will be made as follows [choose all that apply]:

_____ Our children will keep this surname until they become legal adults.

_____ Our children may choose their surname.

_____ Our children may choose their surname after age _____ .

_____ We will discuss and agree on any change of surname.

_____ _____ [parent] has the authority to change our children's surname.

_____ We further agree that [specify]:

_____

_____

_____

#_____ **Treating Each Child as an Individual**

_____ Each of our children will sometimes need separate or special time with each of us. Therefore, we will set up short

separate visits as follows [specify]:

_____

_____

_____

_____ Each of our children will sometimes need separate or special time with each of us. Therefore, we will set up

separate time for each child while visiting together as follows [specify]:

_____

_____

_____

_____ Each of our children will sometimes need separate or special time with each of us. Therefore, we further agree that

[specify]:

_____

_____

_____

#_____ **Separating Adult Relationship Issues From Parenting Issues**

_____ We agree that we will separate our adult relationship issues from the parenting issues as follows

[choose all that apply]:

_____ agree to resolve all parenting decisions first

_____ schedule separate telephone calls

_____ arrange to discuss adult relationship issues when away from our children

_____ discuss adult relationship issues during joint counseling sessions

_____ We further agree that [specify]:

_____

_____

_____

#_____ Making Changes

_____ We will regularly review this agreement as follows: _____ [list dates or frequency, as appropriate]

_____ We will review this agreement when problems arise.

_____ Reviews will be:

_____ by telephone

_____ in person

_____ through:

_____ counseling

_____ mediation

_____ arbitration

_____ other: _____ [specify]

_____ Our children may participate in the discussions.

_____ Our children may participate in the decisions.

#_____ Making Substantive Changes to This Agreement

_____ If we negotiate a substantive modification of this agreement, _____ [parent]
will prepare (or make sure that someone else prepares) a summary of the agreement so that we may obtain a court
order incorporating our changes. Each parent will be responsible to review the agreement prior to its submission to
the court, and to seek independent advice on the agreement to ensure that it says what we intend it to say,
accomplishes our objectives, and is within the general parameters of what a court is likely to approve.

_____ We further agree that [specify]:

_____

_____

_____

#_____ Explaining the Agreement to Our Children

_____ _____ [parent] will explain this agreement to our children.

_____ [other parent] will be available to answer
any questions the children might have.

_____ We further agree that [specify]:

_____

_____

_____

#_____ Domestic Violence, Child Abuse, and Child Neglect

_____ If events such as _____ [specify] occur,

_____ [parent] may seek a restraining order from the court that will [specify]:

_____

_____

_____

_____ Anyone providing care for our children other than a parent will be told about any existing restraining orders.

_____ _____ [parent] will seek counseling from _____

_____ [provider] regarding _____

_____ [specify]; also [choose all that apply]:

    _____ Parent and provider will be permitted to determine when the need for counseling has concluded.

    _____ At the conclusion of parent's counseling, provider will send a letter to _____

    [other parent] indicating that counseling has concluded to the parent and provider's satisfaction.

_____ We will offer counseling and emotional support to our children as indicated in Issue # _____ [Psychiatric and Other Mental Health Care].

_____ If our children are exposed to a violent or otherwise dangerous situation, the parent in whose care they are will remove them from the situation and, if necessary, find another adult to provide care for them.

_____ Our children may call _____ [adult's name] if they fear for their safety while in _____ 's [parent] care. This adult will care for the children until he/she receives different instructions from the other parent.

_____ We will seek an independent evaluation regarding _____

_____ [specify] for help in how we might best address this situation.

_____ The time the children are with _____ [parent] will be supervised by

_____ [other adult] to ensure the children's safety and well-being. The supervised visits will continue until [choose all that apply]:

    _____ Our children feel ready to spend time alone with _____.

    _____ A counselor indicates that the supervision is unnecessary.

    _____ Other:_____ [specify]

_____ From _____ until _____ ,

_____ [parent] will not spend time with our children.

    _____ During that time, _____ [parent] will maintain contact with our children via [choose all that apply]:

        _____ phone

        _____ letter

        _____ email

        _____ other: _____ [specify]

_____ We further agree that [specify]:

_____

_____

_____

_____ **Alcohol or Drug Abuse**

_____ _____ [parent] will attend a 12-step or similar program.

_____ _____ [parent] will seek counseling from _____

_____ [provider] to deal with the substance abuse; also [choose all that apply]:

    _____ Parent and provider will be permitted to determine when the need for counseling has concluded.

    _____ At the conclusion of parent's counseling, provider will send a letter to _____

    [other parent] indicating that counseling has concluded to the parent and provider's satisfaction.

_____ _____ [parent] will modify his/her behavior around our children so that he/she is "sober" as follows [choose all that apply]:

    _____ Will not operate a motor vehicle within _____ hours of consuming drugs or alcohol.

    _____ Will not consume drugs or alcohol for at least _____ hours before visits with the children.

_____ Will submit to a drug and alcohol screening test performed by _____
_____ [name of organization].
_____ The time the children are with _____ [parent] will be supervised
by _____ [other adult] to ensure
the children's safety and well-being. The supervised visits will continue until [choose all that apply]:
    _____ Our children feel ready to spend time alone with _____ .
    _____ A counselor indicates that the supervision is unnecessary.
    _____ Other: _____ [specify]
_____ [parent] will prevent others
from consuming drugs or alcohol while our children are in [his/her] care.
_____ During that time, _____ [parent]
will maintain contact with our children via [choose all that apply]:
    _____ phone
    _____ letter
    _____ email
    _____ other: _____ [specify]
_____ We further agree that [specify]:
_____
_____
_____

#_____ **Undermining the Parent-Child Relationship**

_____ We will encourage and support our children in maintaining a good relationship with the other parent. If either of us feels that the other is undermining our relationship with our children, we will proceed as follows [choose all that apply]:
    _____ We will discuss the matter and try to reach an agreement.
    _____ We will resolve the dispute through:
        _____ counseling
        _____ mediation
        _____ arbitration
        _____ other: _____ [specify]
_____ We further agree that [specify]:
_____
_____
_____

#_____ **Denying Access to the Children**

_____ If either of us is denied physical access to our children, contact with them, or information about them, we will proceed as follows [choose all that apply]:
    _____ We will discuss the matter and try to reach an agreement that will involve reinstating a visitation schedule.
    _____ We will resolve the dispute through:
        _____ counseling
        _____ mediation
        _____ arbitration
        _____ other: _____ [specify]
_____ We further agree that [specify]:
_____
_____
_____

#_____ **If Extended Family Members or Close Friends Are Fueling the Dispute**

_____ We will encourage our children to have ongoing relationships with members of our extended family and with our close friends as long as those relationships are healthy and do not make disputes we have over parenting or adult relationship issues worse.

_____ If a family member or close friend is fueling our disputes over parenting or adult relationship issues, we agree that, as appropriate, either the parent who has the most frequent contact with this person, or both parents will:

_____ limit the information shared with this person

_____ schedule a "family meeting" to discuss the matter, and identify ways it can be addressed and resolved

_____ ask an attorney to explain the matter to the family member or friend, and ask him or her to stop whatever behaviors are fueling the dispute

_____ schedule a mediation session with the family member or friend to discuss the matter and find ways it can be addressed and resolved

_____ create a talking circle among the extended family or among close friends to discuss the matter and find ways it can be addressed and resolved

_____ get a court order to have the family member or friend stop the behavior that is fueling the dispute

_____ We further agree that [specify]:

_____
_____
_____

#_____ **Moving**

_____ We agree that in the event either parent plans to relocate from _____ _____ [describe community, county, state], that parent will provide the other parent with at least _____ days' notice in order to allow us to assess the impact that this move will have on our current parenting arrangements, and to renegotiate or modify the agreement accordingly.

_____ We agree that neither parent plans to relocate now, but in the event either parent wishes to relocate in the future, we will consider the following [choose all that apply]:

_____ having both parents relocate

_____ changing physical custody of the children to the remaining parent

_____ allowing a move as long as our children are under age _____ / over age _____

_____ time a move with a change in schools

_____ allowing our children to chose whether they will move after age _____

_____ allowing the parent to relocate as planned

_____ finding new ways to meet both parents' needs and goals so that both parents can remain in the area

_____ We agree that _____ [parent] will move to _____ [specify] on or after _____ [date], and after that time, our parenting agreement will be as follows:

_____ It will remain as currently drafted.

_____ It will change as follows [specify]:

_____
_____
_____

_____ We further agree that [specify]:

_____
_____
_____

#_____ **When Parenting Styles and Values Are Very Different**

_____ Although our parenting styles are very different, we agree to try the following strategies to minimize the effect of those differences on our children [choose all that apply]:

_____ We will focus our attention and conversations on our children, rather than on each other.

_____ We will encourage our children to explore the following aspects of each of our cultural heritages [specify]:

_____

_____

_____

_____

_____ We respect the other's right to establish an independent life with our children, as long as it is not detrimental to our children.

_____ If our living arrangement exacerbates the problems our children experience because of our different styles and values, we will consider modifying that arrangement.

_____ We further agree that [specify]:

_____

_____

_____

#_____ **When a Parent Needs to Develop Parenting Skills**

_____ _____ [parent] will work on improving his/her parenting skills as follows [choose all that apply]:

_____ will attend parenting classes through _____.

_____ will review written materials on parenting

_____ will attend counseling with _____ to deal with and resolve these issues.

_____ We further agree that [specify]:

_____

_____

_____

#_____ **When Parents Have New Partners**

_____ We will resolve issues surrounding a parent's new partner as follows [choose all that apply]:

_____ Our children will always know that we are their parents, regardless of their attachment to a parent's new partner.

_____ Our children will refer to new partners as _____.

_____ The adults and the children will have separate sleeping quarters.

_____ Any new partner will participate in decisions regarding the children as follows [specify]:

_____

_____

_____ We further agree that [specify]:

_____

_____

_____

#_____ **If Our Homes Are Far Apart**

_____ If there is a considerable distance between our homes, we agree as follows [choose all that apply]:

_____ The children will spend the school year with _____ [parent] and the summers with _____ [other parent].

_____ The children will live with _____ [parent]
for _____ [specify grade or school level] and with _____
_____ [other parent] for _____ [specify grade or school level].

_____ The children will reside at _____ [name of school] and will visit with
each parent as follows [specify; be consistent with the options you choose under holidays and vacations]:

_____
_____
_____

_____ We further agree that [specify]:

_____
_____
_____

#_____ **When Nonrelatives Live in the Home**

_____ If either of us lives with nonrelatives, our children will have separate sleeping quarters from the adults.

_____ _____ [parent] will be responsible to make sure that no
one in the house consumes nonprescription drugs or becomes a danger to our children because of intoxication.

_____ _____ [parent] will be responsible
to make sure the number of other visitors is kept reasonable.

_____ A nonrelative may not care for our children in the parent's absence.

_____ A nonrelative may not discipline our children in the parent's absence.

_____ We further agree that [specify]:

_____
_____
_____

#_____ **Reinvolving a Previously Absent Parent**

_____ _____ [parent] has been absent
from our children's life for _____ [period of time], and now wishes to become
reinvolved. To make this transition easier for all of us, we agree as follows [choose all that apply]:

_____ We will both seek counseling.

_____ Our children will receive counseling.

_____ We will focus our attention and conversations on our children.

_____ We will build up the amount of time _____ [parent]
spends with our children as follows:

_____
_____

_____ _____ [parent] will retain the support systems and schedules
he/she established while _____ [parent] was absent, as follows:

_____
_____

_____ To make sure that _____ 's [parent] reentry into
our children's lives is for the long term, we will make necessary modifications to this agreement on or
before _____ [specify date].

_____ We further agree that [specify]:

_____
_____
_____

#_____ **Driving and Owning a Car, Motorcycle, or Off-Road Vehicle**

_____ We will permit our children to own a car.

_____ We will not permit our children to own a car.

_____ We will permit our children to drive a car under the following conditions [choose all that apply]:

  _____ After completing a certified training course.

  _____ With the consent of _____ [one or both parents].

  _____ With adult supervision.

  _____ Driving only on unpaved roads.

  _____ Using a family car.

  _____ After buying a car.

  _____ After being given a car.

  _____ After paying their own car insurance.

  _____ They must pay for any tickets received while operating the car.

_____ We will permit our children to own a motorcycle.

_____ We will not permit our children to own a motorcycle under any circumstances.

_____ We will permit our children to drive a motorcycle under the following conditions [choose all that apply]:

  _____ After completing a certified training course.

  _____ With the consent of _____ [one or both parents].

  _____ With adult supervision.

  _____ Driving only on unpaved roads.

  _____ Using a family motorcycle.

  _____ After buying a motorcycle.

  _____ After being given a motorcycle.

  _____ After paying their own motorcycle insurance.

  _____ They must pay for any tickets received while operating the motorcycle.

_____ We will permit our children to own an off-road vehicle.

_____ We will not permit our children to own an off-road vehicle under any circumstances.

_____ We will permit our children to drive an off-road vehicle under the following conditions [choose all that apply]:

  _____ After completing a certified training course.

  _____ With the consent of _____ [one or both parents].

  _____ With adult supervision.

  _____ Driving only on unpaved roads.

  _____ Using a family off-road vehicle.

  _____ After buying an off-road vehicle.

  _____ After being given an off-road vehicle.

  _____ After paying their own off-road vehicle insurance.

  _____ They must pay for any tickets received while operating the off-road vehicle.

_____ We further agree that [specify]:

_____

_____

_____

#_____ **International Travel and Passports**

_____ Our children may obtain a passport under the following conditions [choose one]:

  _____ Either parent may obtain a passport if it is necessary for travel.

  _____ Either parent may obtain a passport, but our children may travel out of the country only if the other parent approves of the itinerary and the dates of the trip.

  _____ Either parent may obtain a passport, but our children may not travel out of the country unless _____ [adult's name] travels with them.

_____ A passport may not be issued to our children under any circumstances.

Only _____

_____ may obtain a passport for the children.

_____ We further agree that [specify]:

_____
_____
_____

#_____ **Military Service**

_____ Our children may enter military service if they are under the legal age as follows [choose all that apply]:

_____ if they so choose

_____ in the event of a war

_____ if they are at least age _____

_____ if we both agree

_____ if _____ [parent] consents

_____ never

_____ We further agree that [specify]:

_____
_____
_____

#_____ **Allowing Underage Marriage**

_____ Our children may marry if they are under the legal age as follows [choose all that apply]:

_____ if they so choose

_____ in the event of a pregnancy

_____ if they are at least age _____

_____ if we both agree

_____ if _____ [parent] consents

_____ never

_____ We further agree that [specify]:

_____
_____

D. Responsibility to Prepare a Final Draft of this Agreement. _____ [parent]
will prepare a final draft of this agreement. Both parents will be responsible to review the agreement for completeness and accuracy.
By _____ [date], both parents will have made any necessary changes and
_____ [parent] will conform this agreement to the specifications of the
_____ court for inclusion in an order of the court.

_____   _____
Signature   Date

_____   _____
Signature   Date

Index